ROBERT BADENBERG

'JUST TO BE' IS SIMPLY 'NOT TO BE AT ALL'

FORSCHUNGEN ZU SPRACHEN UND KULTUREN AFRIKAS
RESEARCH ON AFRICAN LANGUAGES AND CULTURES
RECHERCHES SUR LES LANGUES ET CULTURES AFRICAINES

BAND/VOLUME 17

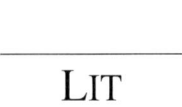

'JUST TO BE' IS SIMPLY 'NOT TO BE AT ALL'

AN ETHNO-LINGUISTIC INVESTIGATION INTO BEMBA WORLDVIEW AND PERSONHOOD

BY ROBERT BADENBERG

LIT

Cover image: Robert Badenberg

This book is printed on acid-free paper.

Bibliographic information published by the Deutsche Nationalbibliothek
The Deutsche Nationalbibliothek lists this publication in the Deutsche Nationalbibliografie; detailed bibliographic data are available in the Internet at http://dnb.dnb.de.

ISBN 978-3-643-91366-1 (pb)
ISBN 978-3-643-96366-6 (PDF)

A catalogue record for this book is available from the British Library.

© LIT VERLAG GmbH & Co. KG Wien,
Zweigniederlassung Zürich 2021
Flössergasse 10
CH-8001 Zürich
Tel. +41 (0) 76-632 84 35
E-Mail: zuerich@lit-verlag.ch   http://www.lit-verlag.ch
Distribution:
In the UK: Global Book Marketing, e-mail: mo@centralbooks.com
In North America: Independent Publishers Group, e-mail: orders@ipgbook.com
In Germany: LIT Verlag Fresnostr. 2, D-48159 Münster
Tel. +49 (0) 2 51-620 32 22, Fax +49 (0) 2 51-922 60 99, e-mail: vertrieb@lit-verlag.de

For Rita

Frank
Ralph & Christina
and
David Ben
– whom I was granted to get to know –

Contents

Tables vii
Preface ix
Foreword xiii
Introduction 1
The Bemba – Travellers and Conquerors 7
Travellers in Time 8
   Bemba History: Chronological Gaps 8
   Bemba History: Language and Ritual 9
Conquerors of Space 10
   Hypothesis: The *'Shimwalule'* Compromise 11
   Hypothesis: The *'Mwine wa Mushi'* Compromise 12
      Transcendence and Immanence: Cultural Ambivalence 12
      Ritual in Word and Deed: Conquering Transcendental Space 13
Political Structure 13
Conclusion 14
Umuntu – More than 'Existing' 19
Man in the Universe 20
   'Being/Becoming' 21
   'Belonging' 23
   'Related to' 25
   'Broken Relations' 26
Excursus: The Verb *uku-ba (-li)* 28
Conclusion 31
Umubili – More than 'Flesh and Bone' 33
Man – Biological and Social Realities 33
Human Body 36
   The Head: *Umutwe* 39
      Short Excursus on Hair 41
      The Sense Organs 42
      The Eye: *Ilinso* 42
      Sense of Vision: The Verb *ukumona* 43
      The Mouth: *Akanwa* 44

- The Teeth: *Ameno* ... 45
- The Tongue: *Ululimi* ... 46
- Senses of Hearing, Feeling and Tasting: The Verb *ukuumfwa* ... 47
- Sense of Smell: The Verb *ukununsha* ... 47
- The External and Internal Chest Region: *Pa Cifuba* and *Mu Cifuba* ... 48
- The Lungs: *BaPwapwa* ... 48
- The Stomach: *Icifu* ... 49
- The Heart: *Umutima* ... 49
  - Linguistic Evidence Emphasizing Anatomical Aspects of *Umutima* ... 50
- Excursus: *Ukucite cupo* - The Most Prominent Act ... 51
  - 'Hot' and 'Cold': Euphemisms for Sexuality and "Access to the Divine" 53
  - Other Euphemisms in Relation to Reproductive Biology ... 55

Social Body ... 57
- *Ubutuuntulu* ... 58
- Excursus: *Ukuumfwa* – A Most Prominent Virtue ... 60
- Conclusion ... 62

Umutima – More than 'Heart' ... 65
Umutima – Most Prominent Organ ... 65
- Three Important Prepositions: *pa*, *ku* and *mu* ... 65
- *Umutima* as 'Psyche' – A Preliminary Definition ... 66

Umutima – Most Prominent Anthropological Term ... 74
- *Umutima* as 'SEIC' – A Comprehensive Definition ... 74
- *Inyumfwikile/ Imyumfwile* – Feelings ... 75
  - The Term *Mu Cifuba* ... 76
  - The Term *Mu nda* ... 76
  - *Mu Mutima* vs. *Mu nda* ... 78
- *Imibeele* – Character Attributes ... 81
  - Perceptions of *Imibeele:* Language Expressions ... 81

Umutima – 'Key term' in Bemba Psychology ... 86
- Introductory Description of *Umutima* as SEIC ... 87
  - Permanent Positive Psychic Dispositions *(imibeele iisuma)* ... 87
  - Permanent Negative Psychic Dispositions *(imibeele iibi)* ... 88
  - Dispositions of the SEIC which are Cognitive (Intellectual) Activities ... 89
  - Temporary Pleasant Psychic Dispositions *(inyumfwikile ya mutima iisuma)* ... 91
  - Temporary Unpleasant Psychic Dispositions *(inyumfwikile ya mutima iibi)* ... 92

Umutima – Vibrant Chamber 93
Comprehensive Description of *Umutima* as SEIC: Psychic Dispositions in Metaphorical Categories 93
Permanent Psychic Dispositions (*imibeele iisuma* and *imibeele iibi*) 94
  1. Metaphors of Form 94
  2. Metaphors of Quality 96
  3. Metaphors of Rest 100
  4. Metaphors of Motion 101
  5. Metaphors of the Human Body 105
  6. Metaphor of a Different Kind 109
  7. Metaphors of War or War Activities 109
  8. Metaphors of Permanent Psychic Dispositions which match Western Categories 113
  9. Metaphors of Psychic Disposition which match Western Categories to a lesser Degree 114
Permanent and Temporary Metaphorically and Non-metaphorically Designated Mental Dispositions: Intellectual Processes 115
Temporary Psychic Dispositions (*imyumfwikile ya mutima – iisuma* and *iibi*) 119
  1. Metaphors of Form 119
  2. Metaphors of Quality 121
  3. Metaphors of Rest 123
  4. Metaphors of Motion 124
  5. Metaphors of the Human Body 127
  6. Metaphors of War or War Activities 131
Psychic Dispositions: Metaphors of Unusual Kind 137

Umutima – Judicial Chamber 139
Umutima – 'Seat of Judgment' 139
  Linguistic Evidence – *Umutima* as 'Conscience' 140
'Conscience' – An Anthropological Theory 141
  Enculturation and Language Acquisition 141
  Enculturation and Socialisation 142
  Right and Wrong 144
  Culture and Conscience Orientation 149
  An Anthropological Theory of Conscience According to Käser ... 160
'Conscience' – 'Vox Dei'? 161
  Differing Perspectives 161
  Paul's Unique Usage of *Syneidesis* 162
  Important Conclusions 163

- *Syneidesis* – A Definition 164
- 'Conscience' – Requisite for Humanizing Humans 165
  - "The Ox-Bow Incident" 165
  - "Interpreting Life" 166
- *Umutima* – From *akatuutu* to *umuntu utuuntulu* 166
  - The Formation of SEIC 166
    - *Kwinika ishina* – Naming Ceremony 167
    - Aided Education – Human Effort and Transcendental Cooperation 169
    - Ideal vs. Reality – When Life Goes Wrong 170
    - Excursus: Issues Pertaining to Name-giving 172
  - The Goal of 'SEIC-Formation' 175
    - Evidence of 'SEIC-Formation' 176
    - When Life Goes Well 177
    - Whole and Complete – *Umuntu Utuuntulu* 177
- Conclusion 178

Umupashi – More than 'Spirit', more than 'Soul' 181

- *Umupashi* – Definitions in the Relevant Literature 182
- *Umupashi* – A Semantic Approach 183
  - 'Iso-gloss' Argument 183
  - Verb Stem Argument 184
  - Noun Class Argument 184
  - Twin-gender and Genderless 185
  - Concluding Argument 186
- *Umupashi* – 'Spirit Double' of a Living Person 187
  - The Concept of 'Spirit Double' 187
  - *Umupashi*: 'Spirit Double' with two Prominent Characteristics 188
    - Resemblance 188
    - Ideal, Genius SEIC 188
    - Non-applicable *umupashi* SEIC Designations 189
  - Excursus: The Concept of 'Spirit Double' - African Cultures and Elsewhere 191
    - The Yoruba and Igbo – West Africa 191
    - The Lugbara (Uganda) and Nyakyusa (Tanzania) – East Africa 192
    - The Chin Peoples – Myanmar 193
    - The Benuaq of East-Kalimantan – Indonesia 194
    - The Israelites – Ancient Near East 195
  - *Umupashi* – 'Spirit Double' with Two Prominent Tasks: Protector and Guardian 197

Protecting the Body 197
    Beneficent Spirit Action – *Umupashi* the Body-protector 197
Safeguarding the SEIC 198
    Fatal Human Action – The Possibility of Destroying *Umupashi* 198
    Self-induced Destruction 198
    Foreign-induced Destruction 199
    Excursus: 'Improving' one's own *Umupashi*.....................................202
Sickness – Body and Spirit.. 202
    Diseases Caused by Violation of Traditional Laws:
    Amalwele ya Makowesha..203
    Diseases Caused by Witchcraft (*Ubuloshi*):
    Amalwele ya Kulowekwa 204
    Diseases Caused by Spirit Beings: *Amalwele ya Mipashi* 206
    "Spirit Sickness": *Ubulwele bwa Ngulu* 207
    Sickness Attributed to one's own *Umupashi* 207

Umupashi – 'Spirit Double' as 'Dream Ego' 208
  Dreams and Dreams 209
  'Double' Episodes 209
  Messaging Episodes.. 210
  Dream of Dreams 211
Umupashi – The 'Being that Survives the Death of the Body'.211
Conclusion...212

Mfwa – More than 'Giving up the Ghost' 219
Death: 'Gateway' to Perpetuity –
  Umweo Wamuyayaya...219
A Bemba Myth 219
    'Gone' – But only 'Gone Away'..220
    Aging is Natural – Death is Not...220
    One Death – But Many Different Kinds 220
    Taking Care of the Dying Body – *ukonga* 221
    Taking Care of a Dead Body – *ukushika* 222
Death of People in Authority... 223
    Pre-independence Days 223
    Post-independence Days: Death of a Chief's son 224
    The Death of Chitimukulu – 'Keeping the King Divine' 225
Death of Common or Ordinary People (*Ababapi*) 232
    Dreaded Death – It is Bad for Widowers..232
    Dreaded Death – It is Worse for Widows...233
Ubupyani – Succession and Inheritance..233

    Ukupyana – Ritualised Removal of Death (*kutamfye mfwa*) 234
    Ukupyana – Ritualized Succession and Inheritance......................236
    Ukupyana – Ritualized Liberation from the Deceased
        (*ukupokela umupashi*)..242
  'Taking care' of *Umupashi* 244
    Liminal Phase – Deceased, Widow and Relatives 244
    Liminal Phase – *Umupashi* too!...245
    Liminal Phase – '*Umupashi* Perspective' 245
  Destiny: Becoming an Honoured Ancestor –
    Mupashi Mukankala 247
  Clothed in Ritual and Closed by Ritual.. 247
  One Needs Means to Reach 249
  'Rich and Generous' 250
  'Reincarnation?' 250
    Umuntu-Umupashi 'Linear Life Companionship'.....................252
    Umupashi 'Life-Cycle' 253
  Conclusion..254

Appendix 1: Bemba Main Chiefs & their Chiefdoms . 261
Appendix 2: The Nine Noun Classes........................... 262
Appendix 3: SEIC and Spirit Double –
        A little Excursion 263
Bibliography... 273
Name Index.. 287

Tables

Figure 1: *Umubili* Taxonomy of Human Being... 38
Figure 2: Noun Class Two (*umu-* sg.) - Body Parts 49
Figure 3: Bemba Traditional Teaching... 52
Figure 4: 'Anatomy' of *Umutima* as SEIC 75
Figure 5: *Imyumfwile/ Imyumfwikile*: Body Sensations and
        Psychic Dispositions 75
Figure 6: *Imyumfwikile ya Mubili* and *Imyumfwikile ya Mutima* 80
Figure 7: *Imibeele* – Language Expressions.. 85
Figure 8: Non-applicable *Imibeele* Designations................................... 86
Figure 9: The Structure of Bemba Terminology of Dispositions
        of the SEIC.. 87
Figure 10: Permanent Positive Psychic Dispositions................................ 88
Figure 11: Permanent Negative Psychic Dispositions 89
Figure 12: Dispositions of the SEIC - Cognitive (Intellectual)
        Activities 90
Figure 13: Temporary Pleasant Psychic Dispositions 91
Figure 14: Temporary Unpleasant Psychic Dispositions......................... 92
Figure 15: Twofold Way Reason Works for Human Beings................... 145
Figure 16: Two Operational Modes of Reason 146
Figure 17: Reason – One-way Operational Mode Only......................... 147
Figure 18: Reason in the Service of Desires 147
Figure 19: Middle-class American Child-rearing Techniques 153
Figure 20: Cross-cultural Differences of Shame 156
Figure 21: Local vs. Global focus.. 157
Figure 22: Motivation to Amending vs. Hiding Behaviour 158
Figure 23: Defensive vs. Non-defensive Response 158
Figure 24: An Anthropological Theory of Conscience According
        to Käser 161
Figure 25: Abridged Table of Noun Class Two (*umu-* sg.) –
        Body Parts 185
Figure 26: Non-applicable *Umupashi* SEIC Designations..................... 190
Figure 27: *Umuntu-Umupashi*' Linear Life Companionship'.............. 252
Figure 28: *Umupashi* 'Life-Cycle' 253

Apatebeta Lesa tapafuka cushi
Where God prepares food there is no smoke
(God provides when we least expect it)

Preface

As the Philosopher said: "Life is neither a feast, nor a spectacle - but a predicament."

My predicament was to connect with the past. Over the last two decades I have written about my anthropological research findings, which culminated in academic degrees and various publications. Some three years back I was under the impression I should bring together material that was scattered here and there in monographs, articles and teaching material, and embark on gathering together the pieces and produce a 'one-piece' product. The idea did not seem to be so difficult to see fruition, after all I could fall back on published material. So, I started. However, I was wrong.

As piecing together commenced and structuring of the material progressed, I got convinced that I had to go back to the bulk of notes and files, revisiting original research material hitherto practically untouched and include important pieces, for instance, most of chapter four, significant parts of chapters five and six. Without it, the 'one-piece' project was in danger of being jeopardized. Chapter two emerged from reading L. Oger, whereas chapters one and three draw in part from an earlier publication (Badenberg 2008) while initial material in chapter five was gleaned from a first attempt to tackle Bemba body, soul and spirit concepts (Badenberg 2002).

What seemed in the beginning to be a relatively fast-forward track enterprise, turned out to be an imagination of the mind driven more by wishes than by realistic estimates. I had to back-track, sift, read, write and re-write, consult important publications on the subject which had meanwhile appeared, and maintain a level of enthusiasm to uphold prospects of successfully finishing my endeavours. There were times when not a single word was written for weeks or months, and times when energetic flushes furthered the project, injecting new vigour into my efforts. Fortunately, there are spells spiced with special moments, when things begin to make sense and things fall into place, urging the labourer onto to the next page and onto the following chapter.

No writing project is ever finished by one's own efforts. There are others who are in their own way and capacity part of this work. Naturally, I had teachers who furthered my thinking and shaped my inquiries. One of them is Prof. Lothar Käser who, from an initial unsuspecting letter exchange twenty-five years ago, challenged me not to be too easily satisfied with what I understood about living in a foreign cultural environment. His instructive correspondence over the years and his Anthropology Course, while studying for a master's degree, taught me, among other things, the ropes of ethnolinguistic research. Being a prolific writer and researcher, the bars were set very high to engage in academic inquiry and field research.

Prof. Ernst R. Wendland is one of those persons who has acquired a wealth of knowledge, experience, and expertise in Bantu languages and their cultural universes as he can draw from five decades of living and working in southern Africa. A renowned, well-respected writer and scholar as well as tireless academic, I sincerely thank him for engaging me while I lived in Zambia and since then for responding to unscheduled correspondence, for his open-mindedness and clarity in his responses. Both graciously agreed to write the foreword. A kindness for which I am appreciative.

I should also want to make mention of my students engaging in discussions and questioning at times the 'fancy' ideas I presented to them in Ethnology or Inter-cultural Communication courses. They undoubtedly helped to clarify my thinking and improve didactics. Among the teaching places I found Holzhausen to extend a particularly welcoming spirit. For many years I was the only male lecturer in the etp (now ssk) team and always felt privileged to work with highly skilled professionals, and I thank them for journeying together, braving the responses of unsuspecting course participants when they were challenged to step outside their cultural comfort zones physically, emotionally, and mentally. Colleagues following my research interest boosted my morale and I thank Dr. Dr. Hannes Wiher, Prof. Manuel Rauchholz, Dr. Oliver Venz, Dr. David Greenlee, and Prof. Klaus W. Müller.

Then, I think of Chewe, a friend and companion for many years who opened many doors for me to his Bemba cultural world. Without him, his interest and openness, his friendship above all, I could not have delved into a world in many ways so much different from the world in which I was brought up. With great dedication, patience and expertise, he addressed the myriads of questions, consulted with others, as I unleashed my inquisitiveness on him (and others) lasting over a decade, only stopped abruptly by his untimely (my point of view!) death in July 2000.

I would like to express my profound gratitude to Derek Cheeseman who, within a twinkling of an eye, responded to my call when asked to read through drafts of chapters and pointedly critiqued as well as expertly edited what a non-native English speaker spilled over the pages of manuscript papers. The conclusions, however, remain the sole responsibility of the author.

I have benefitted and drawn encouragement from other well-wishers, but Rita is champion of them all. Although I resided in Africa when writing commenced and the work progressed until a first draft saw its compilation, I was far away from the original area of research and quite cut-off from active personal engagement with academia, when she engaged with insight as I bounced off my ideas on her. Not to speak of the time when I had to seek medical attention and was de-railed for many months, and not knowing if healing would be within reach. True companionship I say. A heart of love I know.

Foreword

For a long time, European and Western anthropologists have researched foreign social worlds with the unquestioned conviction that their view is *a priori* objective. Clearly, this objectivity does not exist, and cannot exist at all, for a simple reason: The researcher's language significantly influences research and the presentation of research. The Sapir-Whorf Thesis proves that the role of language has a fundamental effect on the perception and recognition of reality. Foreign social and mental realities can never be fully understood by presenting them in one of the common scientific languages with an Indo-European basic structure.

This is also the case with ethnology, which is concerned with the description of foreign social realities within their culturally embedded setting. Much of what is important for people in such societies has been and still is simply overlooked, because important areas of a differently organized conceptual world must remain blind spots for scientists who speak Indo-European languages. Their explorations and descriptions of foreign cultures, gained exclusively from the perspective of a Western mind, remain limited, imperfect, and often inaccurate. Missing is the view members of foreign cultures have of their own culture. Without this, objectivity in the description of their very differently organized world of thought cannot be achieved.

It is, however, clearly evident that objectivity in a perfect sense cannot be achieved by including this view either, but at most a greater proximity to it. One of the basic prerequisites for this approach is that the researcher must speak the language of the society he or she is investigating and describe its semantic relations as far as possible to the exclusion of Euro-American concepts.

This demand is particularly important where language is the only access to foreign realities, because these are not accessible to direct observation but rather hidden in people's minds. One of these realities is the concept of the world and the concept of man of a human people group. Not without reason ethnologists consider this topic to be among the most difficult relevant research projects. Without knowledge of the language in question and without a long-term stay in the habitat of its speakers the research is impossible.

The author of this description of the concept of the world and a theory of personhood of the Bemba, an ethnic group in Zambia, meets this requirement. The few studies published on this topic so far show that both conceptual areas are inseparably linked and that worldviews can only be interpreted correctly if one knows that at their centre lies a highly differentiated view of man. The findings presented here systematically – a "thick description" in the sense of Clifford Geertz – also show in an impressive way that body and soul conceptions can be structured and thought of in a largely different way than speakers of an Indo-European language do. For example, the expression of emotions (joy, fear, etc.), in the Bemba language comprises not only a wealth of vocabulary, but also a surprising wealth of metaphorical formulas. Through years of work, the author has collected and transcribed them meticulously.

His presentation offers a format for future research on this topic.

Lothar Käser
Institut für Ethnologie, Albert-Ludwigs-Universität Freiburg
Schallstadt, Germany

***

'Just to be' is simply 'not to be at all' – The somewhat cryptic, proverbial title of this informative monograph rather covertly introduces us to its fascinating content, namely, a detailed, wide-ranging investigation into the language and associated worldview of the Bemba people of Zambia. Thus, in order to comprehend this title, one must not only know how ordinary folk speak, but more importantly perhaps, how they traditionally conceptualize life and contextualize themselves within their total environment. The latter occurs, we learn, as the individual members of society continually interrelate with one another in an ever-revolving, communally-oriented circle of existence that encompasses past, present, and future throughout the generations of familial ancestors, persons living now, as well as the yet unborn.

Based on his many years of living among and dialoguing with people from all walks of life, Robert Badenberg, in six well-conceived chapters, progressively unpacks for eager readers the central interconnected aspects of this composite conception of Bemba reality. This is crystalised in the crucial concepts of human presence, which is only imperfectly expressed in English by the key terms "personhood" (*umuntu*), "body" (*umubili*), "heart" (*umutima*), "spirit" (*umupashi*), and "death" (*mfwa*). The mention of English here is intentional because, as the author clearly points out and exemplifies in the discerning linguistic aspect of his study, even the use of an Indo-European language as the means of communication can be quite misleading, that is, if readers do not make a serious effort to try and re-think the substance, or essence, of the vital life-related concepts being described from a Bemba thought-world perspective.

This becomes especially important when topics completely absent from, or foreign to a western worldview are discussed, such as the ever-present reciprocal relationship between the spirit world and the cycle of human experience, which does not involve a disjunction between these modes of being, as in western belief, but rather a constant, almost dualistic, cooperative reality. This strongly anthropocentric outlook on life, on death, and the realm beyond is permeated by a transcendental spiritual dimension that both determines the distinctive Bemba construction of personhood and also constantly influences an individual's relationship with the surrounding society, which embraces beings both seen and unseen, perceptibly close as well as those relatively remote.

The author adapts diverse anthropological models in order to reveal the salient aspects of this intricate, multifaceted psychophysical Bemba concept of being, for example, the fundamental set or anatomy of **SEIC** (**S**eat of **E**motions, **I**ntellect, **C**haracter) attributes, which delineate the notion of *umutima* ("heart") as the essential core that defines, motivates, and animates one's personality. And a "person," we must always remember, should never be viewed in isolation, either physically (socially) or metaphysically (spiritually). This is because a living being is always and inevitably accompanied by a personal *umupashi*, as Badenberg denotes and defines it — not "spirit", "shade" or "soul," but more — namely, one's "transcendental human companion," or "spirit double." The author's detailed discussion of this Bemba concept thus serves to support as well as refine an indigenous psychological perception that is common among many non-western societies, but which frequently goes undetected and undescribed since foreign researchers do not recognize its prevailing presence. Throughout his thorough analysis, the author not only teaches and describes his multidimensional theme, but he also models for us an excellent method of analytical and empirical research that might well be applied also in other traditional societies of the world, whether in Africa or elsewhere.

In short, I found Badenberg's book to be a splendid, highly captivating piece of ethnographic and linguistic scholarship, one that uncovers layer upon layer of insight regarding the Bemba people—their culture, language, life-view, and lifestyle. I do not recall a work quite as comprehensive (or well done) in anything else that I have read in this field over the half-century that I have been engaged with Africa. Although being a very scholarly study, the text is also exceptionally accessible; thus, the style of writing is clear and easy to follow in spite of the relative complexity of the subject matter being dealt with. The arrangement of materials both globally and within each chapter is logical and conceptually coherent throughout, while the main text is framed by a helpful historical introduction to the Bemba people and supplemented by several informative appendices plus the requisite indices. Most noticeably, the author's use of varied formats and typestyles make for engaging and appealing pages of print, which are in turn significantly enriched by many instructive summary display-graphs and first-rate descriptive illustrations.

The many keen insights that this attractive volume contains will admirably serve to interest as well as inform a wide variety of local and international readers, from academic scholars and researchers to students on the advanced secondary school level and above. Cross-cultural missionaries, ministers, and communicators in particular would undoubtedly benefit from an initial read-through, followed by a more careful examination of the book's multi-layered content. I am no expert in the discipline, but I would venture to suggest that this text will one day be recognized as a "classic" of anthropological scholarship, ranking right up there with some of the older cited works produced by the studious Catholic White Fathers, who laboured among the illustrious Bemba people during the last century.

Ernst R. Wendland
Stellenbosch University & Lusaka Lutheran Seminary
Lusaka, Zambia

Ukulebulile cilu e ku mwinshi
where there is no pole, there the doorway shall be
(once you start on something, you must see it through)

Introduction

Worldview as a way to understand cultures and their "competing accounts of reality (Sire 1997, 2004), … focuses on cognitive, rational structures of meaning" (Burlington 2008:1). Of course, the cognitive, rational emphasis on viewing and understanding the world is only part of what we know about the world, and includes "how we evaluate it emotionally, and how we respond to it volitionally" (Makkreel 1999:237).

Hiebert (1998) thus speaks of the three **dimensions** of worldview, the cognitive or existential, the affective, and the evaluative assumptions of people groups about the nature of reality, and stresses that they use them for guidance in their lives.

There is no shortage of **definitions** of worldview and emphasis may be placed on existential, cultural, or academic levels (Sire 1997, 2004). For James Sire worldview is a

> commitment, a fundamental orientation of the heart, that can be expressed as a story or in a set of propositions (assumptions which may be true, partially true or entirely false) which we hold (consciously or subconsciously, consistently or inconsistently) about the basic constitution of reality, and that provides the foundation on which we live and move and have our being (2004:122).

Mary Clark is rather concise and defines worldviews as "beliefs and assumptions by which an individual makes sense of experiences that are hidden deep within the language and traditions of the surrounding society" (2002:5). Suffice it to say at this point that Clark's poignant reference to 'language and traditions' brings into focus the stated interest, as the subtitle suggests, in developing the themes of worldview and personhood in this monograph.

Another way of dealing with worldview is to approach it from the angle of its *functions*. Hiebert identifies four fundamental functions (1998:48) adding a fifth from Kraft (1979:56). Our worldview: (1) provides us with cognitive foundations; (2) gives us emotional security; (3) validates our deepest cultural norms; (4) integrates our culture, and (5) monitors culture change.

Worldviews try to sustain a conservative twist by preserving old ways (traditions) but also provide stability over long periods of time against internal or external influences, and in doing so, are (relatively) resistant to change (Hiebert 1998:49).

Worldviews are concepts. David Naugle, for purposes of explaining this concept, provides illustrations of what a worldview *is* and what a worldview *does*. He speaks of a worldview being like lenses "through which we look at the world," or like "a pair of sunglasses or shades. They color everything we see." And to add a third one, a worldview is like contact lenses: "They affect everything you see, but you don't notice them!"

Elaborating on what a worldview does, Naugle uses two other illustrations:

> a. Map and compass: a wv [worldview] guides, directs, orients; where we are, where we are going, and how to get there, personally, culturally.
>
> b. Filter and framework: a wv [worldview] sifts and sorts, accepts and rejects, and gives context to life; it interprets, explains and imparts meaning to things — God, universe, our world, ourselves. It enlightens our minds about the world and our place within it (Naugle n.d.:4-5)

Worldviews operate at the centre of every culture. Obviously, there are elements of culture which immediately meet the five senses ('surface level'), and there are those elements which are hidden, present and operative in the minds of people ('deep structure level'). On the 'surface level' are 'things' (e.g. material culture, human bodies, language, symbols, arts, or music), 'human behaviour' (e.g. conventions on space and time, structure of social relationships, or ethics), and 'human perception' or 'sensory system' (e.g. what can be perceived by the basic human senses of taste, smell, vision, hearing and touch.) Behind the mental curtain, on the 'deep structure level', operate 'ideas' (e.g. notions of human body, notions of spirit beings, beliefs, truth claims, values and norms, assumptions, or commitments/allegiances) and have their moorings.

Apart from succinct definitions or highlighting its functions, some scholars apply a more ***descriptive approach*** to worldview like Moyo (2007) in his attempt to furnish an African worldview. Moyo asserts for African worldviews an absence of the dichotomy between the secular and the religious where effects, like death, sickness, or calamity, have their causes in the spiritual realm, and answers to life's questions are tied into the spirit world rather than the physical world.

Since in this work focus is on a specific ethnic group, the Bemba of northern Zambia, a decidedly African worldview is being investigated. Adeyemo expresses what I am interested in when he refers to worldview as a "complex of a people's beliefs and attitude concerning the origins, nature, and structure of the universe and the interaction of its beings with particular reference to man" (1983:151ff). Two salient points in Adeyemo's definition are crucial for the Bemba worldview with reference to the structure of the universe: (1) the interactions of its beings with (2) particular reference to man. Not unique but important to the Bemba structure of the universe, as Moyo and others point out, is the fact that there is no divide between the immanent and the transcendent realms and the interaction of its beings comprise human beings and spirit beings. As will be demonstrated, the Bemba worldview is anthropocentric to the core; *umuntu* human person) takes central place in the cultural universe where man is called not only to exist but to occupy a regulative place from where to act. But *umuntu* is not the only being occupying a regulative place. At his side are spirit beings, of which *umupashi* is a prominent one, the 'transcendental human companion' (Badenberg 2002) – 'spirit double' to be precise, quite ready to act – interact – with a world full of other beings: human or non-human (no-longer-human) alike.

It is my contention that ***at the centre of any worldview*** there is a concept of man (*Menschenbild*) operating, a ***theory of personhood***. In its broadest definition, personhood refers to

> ...the condition or state of being a person, as it is understood in any specific context. Persons are constituted, de-constituted, maintained and altered in social practices through life and after death. This process can be described as the ongoing attainment of personhood. Personhood is frequently understood as a condition that involves constant change, and key transformations to

> the person occur throughout life and death. People may pass from one state or stage of personhood to another. Personhood is attained and maintained through relationships not only with other human beings but with things, places, animals and the spiritual features of the cosmos. Some of these may also emerge as persons through this engagement. People's own social interpretations of personhood and of the social practices through which personhood is realized shape their interactions in a reflexive way, but personhood remains a mutually constituted condition (Fowler 2004:4).

As Fowler deduces, personhood is 'a condition that involves constant change, and key transformations to the person occur throughout life and death.' This is exactly what happens in the Bemba context and becomes tangible through language. For example, the birth-event merely ushers a new-born family member into the physical world with a physical body. Until the reception of a name, the new-born baby is *akatuutu* – a tiny (little), pure, transparent (empty) 'thing', whose status is changed in the name-giving ceremony when *akatuutu* becomes *umuntu* (human person)! This transformation requires interaction between the human world and the spirit world, between human beings and spirit beings and turns into a (ideally) lifelong cooperation between the new *umuntu* and his or her personal *umupashi*. There are other transformations occurring to persons in the process of life where this 'union' is stressed and which are captured in language, but they are always infused with content from their ancient moorings on 'deep-structure' level and marked with interaction between the human world and the spirit world.

Earlier I mentioned Mary Clark saying that she provided a lead with her definition of worldview, because she explicitly anchors beliefs and assumptions by which an individual, or a people group, makes sense of experiences to be "hidden deep within the language and traditions of the surrounding society." In this book I approach worldview and personhood from a distinct angle, which is an ***ethno-linguistic perspective***.

This perspective stresses the need to be cognisant of what is hidden in language. That is where the existential, the affective, and the evaluative assumptions of a people group about the nature of reality are tangible. By means of an ethno-linguistic study on body and body part terms, coupled with psychophysical associations of a specific body part, in this case (*umutima* – 'heart'), important cultural assumptions about being *umuntu* will be deduced. However, to be clear, a linguistically driven theory of worldview and personhood requires a detailed analysis of six areas: (1) notions of the body, (2) the seat of the emotions, (3) the intellect, (4) character attributes or personal behaviour patterns (traits), and (5) notions of the existence of the person after the death of the body, and not to forget and relevant for many ethnic groups around the globe, (6) notions of a personal spirit being (spirit double) closely associated *with* the *person*, but *not* part of the *body* (Badenberg 2014).

The structure of the contents of this monograph is therefore arranged accordingly, preceded by a brief account of Bemba history. Without detailed written accounts produced by successive indigenous writers who were located well within the circle of events ever since Chiti, the pioneer leader, who led his followers out into to hopeful east, seeking a new future for his group eventually settling in what is today the northern part of Zambia, events were recorded in spoken language and stored in the minds of people. Naturally, gaps would occur in the telling of what unrolled in the passing of time as not all minds could, would (or wanted to?) contribute to a unified story to be preserved for future generations. Nevertheless, core events seem sufficiently clear and there is definitely a story to tell. Chapters two to six pursue the focus on language with particular interest in the Bemba terms *umuntu, umubili, umutima, umupashi,* and *mfwa* respectively, illuminating the anthropocentric core of the Bemba worldview also highlighting a transcendental, highly influential dimension in the construction of personhood. I know of no other publication which unifies major themes of Bemba anthropology, investigating them from an ethno-linguistic perspective in the manner presented here.

In a brief postscript, attention is drawn to the fact that while there is meanwhile an abundance of literature about worldview, but remarkably little is written on how they are actually developed or created.

I pursue two other intentions with this publication. First, I advocate for better and more suitable terminology to illuminate specific characteristics of indigenous terms and concepts, as Venz, too, (2012) has forcefully emphasised, to be employed by academia in order to speak a 'common language' pertaining to phenomena such as 'psyche', 'soul', 'dream-soul', 'body-soul', 'spirit', 'shade', and the like, and hence be in a better position to compare research findings of ethnic concepts of this nature with one another. Second, the methodology employed in this ethno-linguistic investigation is only a novum as it pertains to Bemba anthropological research, but it is not a novum in the sense that it could claim originality. In his

Chuukese Theory of Personhood (2016), Lothar Käser put forward a methodology guiding me, and an appeal "to get to work" calling for parallel studies "leading to new and important knowledge" (2016:14) that inspired me.

I now pass the baton to others to further promote a field of research so rich with knowledge systems. Although they might exist in worlds apart in terms of distance, they are not so far apart in terms of close affinity of certain elements so essential to ideas on worldview and personhood.

Icalo Lifupa
the world is a bone
(history is an unfinished affair – a continual 'gnawing')

Chapter One

The Bemba – Travellers and Conquerors

The Bemba people occupy an area of approximately 20,000 square miles on the North Eastern plateau, between the latitudes 9°-12° south and longitudes 29°-32° east, in the Northern Province of Zambia (see Appendix 1). This vast surface area, Whitely writes, "includes virtually the whole of Kasama administrative district and much of Mpika, Chinsali, Luwingu and Mporokoso" (1950:1). How the Bemba came to settle in this vast expanse of the northern plateau is part of their own tribal history as well as part of the larger migratory movements of the Central Bantu tribes in general.

Maxwell, in his literature review on the Bemba, asserts that they were first mentioned by Lacerda, a Portuguese explorer, in 1798 (Burton 1873:50-164 in Maxwell 1983:vii). Following his countryman, Gamitto made contact with Bemba chiefs some three decades later, making vague statements on their warring lifestyle and claiming they were a people without '"any religion" or "superstitious practices"', statements he later revised admitting he had made them in passing and had no accurate information on these issues (Gamitto 1960, vol. 2:195 in Maxwell 1983:vii).

Carey's (1986) overview of the historical literature on the Bemba encompasses scholars from various fields. He acknowledges the works and writings by missionaries, (Garrec, 1917; Labrecque, 1931; Etienne, 1948; Tanguy, 1954 (1983); Oger, 1972b); colonial administrators (Gouldsbury and Sheane, 1911; Brelsford, 1942; 1944); an anthropologist (Richards, 1939; 1940; 1951; 1970; 1982); and a professional historian (Roberts, 1970; 1973). The works of two linguists (Guthrie, 1962; Werner, 1971; 1979/1999) and the books of two educationists (Snelson, 1974 and Ipenburg, 1992) as well as by Bemba writers (e.g. Ng'andu, 1922) and a teacher, politician, Church minister and Bemba historian (Mushindo, 1977) complement the list of scholars as presented by Carey. Hence, there is no genuine need to undertake a comprehensive study of Bemba history, considering the bulk of the readily available data. I will therefore limit the scope of focus to two features of Bemba history and Bemba culture: time and space.

Travellers in Time

The Bemba belong to the large group of Bantu tribes that migrated into North Eastern Zambia from the Lunda-Luba empires between the Lualaba and Kasai rivers in the present-day Shaba province of the Democratic Republic of Congo (Carey 1986:31; Mushindo 1977:xv). Some traditions state that the place was called Kola (African Elders 1949:1) and the first groups leaving Kola were of Luba stock, speaking the Luba language (Mushindo 1977:xv). In light of the available data, it appears that the Bemba did not emigrate (known as the "Luba-Lunda dispersion") (1986:31) from their place of origin as a whole tribe at one particular time, but were rather organized in the form of clans (Roberts 1973:67-85) who moved out of their original habitat in successive waves of emigration. Robert's reconstruction of oral and written accounts of the Bemba royal Chitimukulu dynasty proposes a "*terminus ante quem* for the settlement of the Bemba royals in Bembaland" c. 1700 (1970:232. See also Tanguy 1996:9).

Bemba History: Chronological Gaps

This chronology leaves approximately two hundred years of immigration, settlement and establishment of harsh and powerful Bemba rule (Hinfelaar 1994:21) and domination of the northern plateau before they themselves had to submit to the colonial powers in 1899 (see Meebelo 1971:34-78). Even their own people had to feel the harsh hand of the ruling royal clan, the *Beena Ng'andu*. Bemba women speak of the Bemba chiefs of former times as "the *Bashamfumu ba ku lubemba* (the Paramounts from Bembaland) … [to have] been *Nkakashi* (mean) and *Bakali* (cruel)" (Hinfelaar 1994:21). "The legendary Bemba were fierce warriors 'who cultivated with their spears rather than with their hoes'" (Oger n.d.:8). The span of approximately two centuries of Bemba reign is preserved in oral tradition, albeit interspersed with gaps and inconclusive data, as Snelson remarks: "there are many gaps in the recorded history of Zambia" (1990:v).

Missionaries and colonial personnel were the first persons to compile written records of Bemba history, extracted from and constructed of Bemba oral accounts beginning at the turn of the twentieth century. The few written documents by early travellers and explorers,[1] the absence of more accurate written information prior to the colonial and missionary era, and the disparity of oral data pose problems for the science of history[2] in which historical events are presented in linear time sequences. However precarious the historical data may be, there is a history to tell, history that is grounded in language, a history that receives validity in real life events within the oral community. As Ki-Zerbo observes, for African societies "history is seen less as a science and more as a form of wisdom, as an art of living given substance through speech" (1990:89). A Bemba proverb aptly attests to that: *umweo wa muntu waba mu kutwi,* "the life of someone is in the ear." Obviously, the proverb does not speak about biological life and its origin in the ear. The proverb reiterates that life, and, more precisely, wisdom to act, emanates from speech and its content of past events preserved in language (e.g. historical records, proverbs, riddles, parables etc.) rather than the facts preserved in the impersonal medium of paper and ink.[3]

Bemba History: Language and Ritual

"Language as a system and tool of communication is a historical phenomenon" because "history is a product of language on two counts: as discourse and as historical evidence" (Ki-Zerbo 1990:89). It is the sound of words conveyed from the mouth of the speaker to the ear of the listener that creates a bond—and thus life—between the two in space and time.[4]

The travelling episodes of the bands of Bemba clusters from the forfeited West to the hopeful East over periods of migratory movements into North Eastern Zambia are deeply engrained within the worldview of the Bemba. For example, during the initiation rite of Bemba girls (*Cisungu*), the east-west axis is a central theme for the initiates, says Hinfelaar, an acknowledged Catholic scholar[5] (1994:3-6). The West signifies not only the place of origin but also the place of turmoil, darkness, night and death.[6] In sharp contrast, the East represents "the future, hope and expectation, light and happiness."[7] Even after the settling of the earliest immigrants from the East had taken place in the land, perpetual travelling did not cease. The first settlers had to give way to subsequent waves of "conquistadors" pressing in from the West. Moreover, the country was infested with the tsetse fly, and the poor fertility of the soil kept people on the move to even greener pastures (Hinfelaar 1994:2). This historical experience made a deep imprint on people's lives. Thus, their past experiences of perpetual travelling permeates the Bemba worldview.

Conquerors of Space

The vast expanse of the northern plateau was not devoid of people groups when the Bemba migratory groups first pressed into their territories. Geographical space was a pertinent issue that had to be settled with the earlier, original inhabitants and earlier immigrants. The immigrating Bemba used predominantly force but were also 'forced' to switch to necessary negotiation and diplomacy to decide the matter of establishing themselves as the dominant power in the vast region. Their immigration was a successive wave of conquest and subjugation of previous immigrants such as the Lungu, Tabwa, and the Fiba (O'Shea 1986:25-26), and the original inhabitants.[8] At the peak of their quest for land, they had penetrated deep into the territories of the Shila, Tabwa, Lungu, Bisa,[9] and Lala and, through the incessant wars with these peoples, had established firm control over them. The original inhabitants, the *Bashimatongwa*[10] and their presence in this part of Central Africa have become history.[11] They were either completely absorbed by intermarriage with the Bemba Bantu people, or driven out and forced to migrate to the south, or even both.

But the matter of claiming and controlling physical space was but one side of the ambitious and cruel war episodes of the marauding Bemba. Such successes of conquest could never have rested on the bravery of the Bemba warriors. Nor can it be ascribed to the shrewd tactics of their commanders alone. Conquered space was more than vast expanses of soil and terrain. It was land that was richly endowed with rivers, trees, mountains, waterfalls, caves, and water-sources – in short, habitats of spiritual powers. Also, the remnants of abandoned villages were strong reminders of forces that could not easily be subdued by bravery and tactics alone (Maxwell 1983:83). All these geographical features and places once filled with human activities were "sacralised by the spirits of former chiefs and fixed in memory by the stories told about them" (:83). Thus, the other side of the Bemba conquest is an episode of geographical space versus transcendental territory. The invasion by Bemba forces into occupied geographical space was simultaneously an invasion into the realm of the spirits of the land. While the matter of geographical space was confronted forcefully, the issue of conquering transcendental space had to be settled with an attitude of compromise.

Hypothesis: The 'Shimwalule' Compromise

Van Binsbergen (1979/1999) hypothesizes that the Bemba *Beena Ng'andu* royal clan immigrants had little interest in strengthening their relationship with earlier Luba immigrants and making them priest-councillors. There was minimal to nil benefit from this union. The *Beena Ng'andu* interest lay clearly in the control over land to which the pre-Luba priests "possessed the key to ultimate legitimacy: ritual control over extended land areas" (Van Binsbergen 1999:70). A compromise was therefore not an option but an act of forced necessity. One way to achieve full control over the land was to absorb the pre-Luba territorial priests into the *Beena Ng'andu* system. Van Binsbergen further suggests, though admittedly hypothetically, that the *Beena Ng'andu*, for example, moved swiftly and made *Shimwalule*, a local original priest, "the most senior non-royal Bemba authority" (1999:71) who, by virtue of his office, also functions as the royal Undertaker (Maxwell (1983:44). Subsequent *Shimwalule* attained authority to oversee the burial of the Chitimukulu, the Bemba Paramount chief "who has important 'ecological' functions" (1999:71).

The hierarchical leadership style of the *Beena Ng'andu* achieved dominance by holding political power in a twofold manner: by commanding service (compare Richards 1970:269) and by controlling resources. Conquests of earlier inhabitants and their territories was established by enforcing a tributary system upon the conquered peoples. Thus, they were effectively at the service of their overlords. The latter came about by integrating the earlier territorial priests into the *Beena Ng'andu* system (as was probably the case with *Shimwalule*). In doing so, they kept a firm hand on the control of ecological power and natural resources. In effect, they consequently became the owners of the land. A successful political system, as exercised by the Bemba, is highly dependent on at least these two factors: defining and controlling the power structure and maintaining control over all available ecological resources.

A third prong of power the *Beena Ng'andu* wielded over the land as they established themselves came through Chitimukulu, the paramount chief, the acknowledged ritual head of the people and chieftainship. As the guardian of the sacred relics and "charged with preserving the memories of dead rulers", Chitimukulu also presided over "the everyday practices of agricultural production and village maintenance" ... "through a system of complex rites connected with fertility," thus exercising "his 'supernatural power'" (Kalusa and Vaughan 2013:50).

Hypothesis: The 'Mwine wa Mushi' Compromise

Hinfelaar (1994) points out that the *Beena Ng'andu*, for example, resorted to yet another compromise, though it was compromise exclusively from the Bemba point of view, but certainly not one for the original inhabitants. Before the Bemba conquest, villages had a *Mwine Mushi*, a local priest, "often the son of a secondary wife and regarded as a *mwine calo* (owner of the land)" (Hinfelaar 1994:21). After the conquest, the villages and their *Mwine Mushi* were complemented by the appointment of the *Mwine wa Mushi* (Headman).[12] His installation was decreed by central appointment (chiefs and/or Paramount chief Chitimukulu) and his function was political rather than spiritual. His function was that of a governor answerable to the chief and responsible to see to it "that royal ritual was observed" (1994:21). The Bemba were resourceful enough to seek a best possible solution to the problem of placating the spirit guardians of the land for themselves. They were in dire need of the blessings of the *mwine calo*, the "owners of the land." A total abolition of the original guardians of geographical space (*mwine mushi*) and their mediating role as guardians of transcendental space would have resulted in a cosmic catastrophe with serious repercussions for the intruders as well as the whole country. This was prevented by the cunning move of incorporating the existing *Mwine Mushi* and introducing the alternative under the guise of the *Mwine wa Mushi*. In terms of language, the adaptation was minimal, but in terms of societal impact, it carried maximum effect. An effective substitution might eventually come to mean an effective abolition of previous archaic structures.

Transcendence and Immanence: Cultural Ambivalence

As far as the Bemba are concerned, their cosmic view of the transcendent reaching out into the immanent constitutes cultural ambivalence. People must find ways and means of coping with the two. Acts committed against *imipashi* (familial ancestral spirits), such as negligence, attract their vengeance. Sickness and other calamities might befall the family or village community. In times of drought, famine or other disasters of magnitude, man and society are compelled to seek and obtain 'mercy' from *imipashi*. But the critical point is that this situation is not without remedy. It is not a cultural one-way street with a dead end. Long-established rituals handed down over generations not only help in approaching *imipashi*, but also in achieving their compliance with human requests.

Ritual in Word and Deed: Conquering Transcendental Space

The correct or appropriate ritual in *word* and *deed* compels the spirits to render their services to the receptive earthly community. Witchcraft basically works that way. Observing to the detail the right order of 'doing things' and 'saying things', (ritual practice), obliges the spirit world to comply, thus effectively achieving the intended purpose. Prayer can also be understood in the same way. In Christian circles it is sometimes understood that the louder and faster you offer the prayer, the more effective it is, or even the more one can be assured of being granted the desired result. I vividly remember participating in a church service held at Itinti (about 15 km east of Kasama) in September 2000, where the service leader, Mr. A., closed the worship time in prayer. He was not 'speaking in tongues', but with such incredible speed, intensity and decibel volume that I got "lost" – a grand performance act. I could not but be under the impression that here is no 'prayer dialogue' going on but 'prayer conquest' in action (Badenberg 2008:202).

Political Structure

Bemba authority is vested in a hereditary Paramount chief called Chitimukulu (from their first leader ChitiMukulu, meaning, Chiti the Great). The *Abeena Ng'andu* – the Crocodile Clan – have dominated the Paramount chief's office since the eighteenth century (Richards 1951 in Chileshe 2005:105). Only male persons descended from Chitimukulu lineage and members of the royal clan are eligible for office. All Bembaland is held [hence he is also referred to as Mwinelubemba Chitimukulu] by the Paramount chief Chitimukulu as he exercises supreme customary judicial powers (Chileshe 2005:105).

Because of their matrilineal social structure, succession of Chiefs is via the female line. A non-negotiable requirement for office for all senior chiefs is matrilineal descent, that is, they "must be sons of the mother or sister (*namfumu*) of the late Chitimukulu" of which there are "three in number, Chitimukulu, Mwamba and Mukuka-Mfumu" (Tanguy 1983:4-5). Territorial chiefs succeed by inheritance but require clearance and recognition by the Chitimukulu.

The political structure centres around Chitimukulu, the senior and territorial chiefs, and a council comprising 40 officials (*bakabilo*) whose main function is advising the Chitimukulu on tribal matters. The other chiefs have their own councillors called *bacilolo* "who have legal executive authority" (1983:5). At village level, authority lies with the headmen (*bamwine mushi*).

Conclusion

Bemba groups migrated to Northern Zambia over a prolonged period of time. Their arrival is a history of successive waves of immigrants from the west conquering, subjugating and establishing supremacy over already settled people groups occupying the vast expanses of the northern plateau. As much as aggressive display of military might have helped them to gain supremacy and setting themselves up as the dominant und ruling people over the land, military power proved insufficient to effectively rule. Cunning diplomacy, and in cooperation with previous transcendental 'power brokers', such as the pre-Luba territorial priests, or the local village priest *mwine calo* as owners of the land, and possibly *Shimwalule*, who now was <u>the</u> *Shimwalule* (royal Undertaker), aided their purposes. The experience of travel and conquest is deeply ingrained in the Bemba worldview, transcending time and space and extending into the transcendental realm. The hierarchical structures centring around Chitimukulu as the guardian of the sacred relics – and the guardian of fertility for land and people – in addition to the many other rituals performed in word and deed - function as anchors or pillars upholding the cultural universe.

The Bemba 'conqueror mentality' has survived defeat and surrender to British might, decades of colonialism, two world wars, independence upheavals, transition from one-party system to multi-party system, and has seen the dawn of a new millennium. Henry Kanyanta Sosala wrote in 2016 as the official ascendant to "the most senior traditional seat of Bemba power" (Paramount chief Chitimukulu):

> The Bemba saw European intrusion in general as a threat to their way of life, which was largely based on conquest and plunder, (to which some anthropologists referred to as "cultivation by spear"). The Law of Generation states:
>
> "We are all linked to previous generations behind us. Our ancestors are in our genes, in our bones, in our marrow, in our physiological and emotion-make-up. We, in turn, will be written into the children who come after us."
>
> This means, "who we are, is who we were." The Bemba are from the warrior stock. The shaping power of that heritage has

continually been working upon us all and that heritage has been influencing us in certain values, behavior patterns etc. For example, in the life of a genuine Bemba (umu Bemba inkonko), reckless daring is held to be royal courage; prudent delay is the excuse of a coward; moderation is the disguise of unmanly weakness; the lover of violence is always to be trusted. These are supported by such a proverb, "Amala ya mwaume yashala ku cishiki." i.e., a man should fight to the last atom of his power (Lusaka Times, May 20, 2016).

Endnotes: Chapter One

[1] "Lacerda, Father Pinto, Gamitto and Livingstone are the most well-known of the early explorers and missionaries who have written in this area" (Werner 1971:3). See also Coxhead 1914 (in Whitely 1950:8).

[2] That, of course, does not imply that written accounts are inherently accurate, nor does it mean that oral accounts are to be treated with a note of caution per se. Rather, both modes of preserving history can contain an element of fake, manipulated, partial, incomplete, etc. data. Either way, the whole question of accuracy hinges on the human factor, that is, the person who writes or speaks history.

[3] Wendland, investigating sermons of the Malawian Evangelist Wame, speaks of the Malawian people as "still predominantly oral-aural, rather than print/script oriented, by nature" (2000:43-44). I take it that this would also be the general situation in Zambia and even more so among the Bemba people in the Northern Province. Maxwell also explicitly characterizes the Bemba "as an oral people" (1983:26).

[4] The major difference between the narrator of history and the writer of history lies in the fact that literate technology makes a person's mind withdraw into self-consciousness apart from tribal consciousness. Maxwell adds that "a writer works alone dissociating words from the total situation of the original dialogue" (1983:153). Ong says that a writer does not merely write words but analyzes elusive sounds into spatial components which are abstract. This in turn makes processes of greater analysis possible (in Maxwell 1983:153).

[5] The Bemba girl undergoing the *Cisungu* ceremony is called *nacisungu* (pl. *banacisungu*). "*Na*" is a female prefix. Because of the practice of teknonymy, women are called by the names of their daughters or sons. For example, *banaChanda* means "the mother of Chanda." The prefix "*ba*" is a second person plural personal pronoun and frequently used as an honorific.

[6] The Bemba Royal Charter tells of the three sons of Chief Mukulumpe Mubemba in the land of Kola whose anger was aroused against them when one of the three was held responsible for the death of many tribespeople. Katongo, the culprit son, was punished and blinded by his father. The two other sons, Chiti and Nkole, evaded punishment and escaped with their followers on a journey to the East, fleeing their father's wrath (see Maxwell 1983:37).

[7] In the East, the Bemba migrants found a place of refuge and a homeland for future generations (Hinfelaar 1994:3). The west-east axis also comes to light at death. Graves are aligned with the West-east axis. The head will always face the East.

[8] Ipenburg notes that the Bemba were "dreaded" by their neighbours. As an example of their reputation, he recounts an incident that happened to Rev. Dewar who tried to reach the Bemba in 1896. "In that year the Dewars had an encounter with a raiding party of Bemba, who had put human heads on poles to terrify them" (1992:30).

[9] Hinfelaar says that around 1830 the Bisa peoples were forcefully separated, as the Bemba drove a deep wedge into their territory stretching as far as the Chinama area of Mpika (1994:24).

[10] They were people of Khoisan extraction, and were called the *Bashimatongwa*, the aborigines (Hinfelaar 1994:2).

[11] About three kilometers East of Kasama, on the road to Isoka, cave paintings of "bushmen" origin can be visited.

[12] Interestingly, the history of the Luapula valley depicts an almost identical case. The original or earliest remembered inhabitants of a piece of land, the *Bwilile,* were remembered as *mwine wa mpanga* or *mushi wa calo,* "the owners of the forest/land." When the *Shila* and later the *Lunda* pressed in and imposed themselves, they would provide a "*mwine wa mpanga* in a political sense for every piece of country" from their own ranks. The *mwine wa mpanga*, the original settler, was the owner by the fact of being there first, and his ritual authority. The *mwine wa mpanga* imposed by the conquerors became the political owner "by right and might, or cunning or duplicity" (Cunnison 1951:14, 16).

Imiti Ikula - e Mpanga
trees increase the forest
(it is people who form community – nothing else)

Chapter Two

Umuntu – More than 'Existing'

The Bemba worldview is firmly rooted in their *history* of travel and conquest as shown in the previous chapter, with the theme of perpetuity as the centre thread woven into the fabric of historical events. History, however, is only one of the perspectives for exploring the worldview of a people.

How *society* is structured (e.g. matrilineal or patrilinear systems) is another, for it influences how power is brokered, how family and communal life is organized, how inheritance and descent play out, and how ritual and symbol inform all of them. Also, of interest is the kind of dynamics that inform the interplay between individual and communal. Kapolyo states:

> In Africa it is impossible to reflect on human beings apart from their cultural surroundings and identity. The society-based existence is evident everywhere. Not for us any 'I doubt, think or buy, therefore I am'. Rather for us it is: 'We are, therefore I am.' A Bemba proverb makes this point in its statement that umuntu ekala na bantu: uwikala ne nama, akaliwa (a human being lives with people or in the company of other people: he who lives with animals will be eaten). Note the seeming choices are between living with people and living with animals. Africans find it difficult to conceive of a solitary or highly individualistic or isolationist existence. 'I am because we are' is a very African attitude to life. Culture therefore is the best milieu for understanding human beings in most sub-Saharan African contexts (2005:18-19).

In relation to the neighbouring Malawian context, Bandawe reinforces this view by saying: "The very fabric of traditional African life centres on community and belonging to a community of people," further adding a Sotho saying: "*Umuntu ngumuntu ngabantu*" (A person is a person through persons)" (2010:17). Meiring asserts that "[a]n African is a being-in-community (Adeyemo 1998:374; Gerloff 1998:49; Ndungane 2003:102; Setiloane 2000:21; Tutu 1999:35" (Meiring 2007:735).

Maxwell (1983) draws attention to five pillars of Bemba religion (which in fact correlates with Bemba social life as such since there is no word or term for 'religion' in Bemba) stating that it is "traditional, communal, anthropocentric, vitally dynamic, and cosmically holistic" (1983:20).

Maxwell aptly comments:

> All Bemba religious practices seek to establish and maintain the central and regulative human place in the whole formed by the spiritual and physical universe. The Bemba are tenaciously terrestrial, and their vision of themselves -their life, their world and divinity- is determined by their earthly fixation. They are at once the image, the model and the integral part of the universe in whose cyclical life they are powerfully engaged but not overwhelmed (1983:22).

Language is yet another avenue for exploring the worldview of a people. *Umuntu* is the Bemba word which can mean "human being" but, as Oger points out, more accurately means "human person" (pl. *abantu* – human persons), "male or female, because what one sees you to be, e.g. someone else, an independent 'self', e.g. a human person, is more important than just 'existing'" (Oger 1993:39).

Man in the Universe

The Bemba worldview puts the person at the centre, for example, you always start with you: *ine na bantu bandi*, 'I and my people'. The individual is the important person, "the starting point from which to look around." Man is at the centre of the universe and "your position in the world is relational" (Oger 1993:39). The plural of *umuntu* is *abantu* (human persons). The communal and relational aspect of *abantu* is expressed in *Ubuntu* or *Ubuntunse*, which is "a *Bantu* ontological noun describing what it means to be a member of humankind" (Kapolyo n.d.:np).

There is much more to be said on the language aspect of a people's worldview regarding the Bemba. Oger (1993), a linguistic and long-time resident among the Bemba, furnishes valuable, detailed, and insightful linguistic and cultural data worth presenting here in its entirety (pages 39-46 in his manuscript). Inserts or comments added are put in brackets [...], so as to indicate the different source, hence no need to apply citation style for Oger's lengthy material.

'Being/Becoming'

There is no word in Bemba for the abstract term 'person'. The human person is pointed at either as I (me), You or We (us), and a personal name, [e.g.] Mulenga, Bwalya, or, failing the name, the right term of address in the group, like *mukwai* (sir, madam), *mune* (pl. *bane*) (friend, dear), *tata* (my father), *mayo* (my mother) ... One lives in this world and moves towards the future. This appears from the verbs 'to be', 'to have', 'to know' and 'to be intelligent' (1993:39).

'to be' (*ukuba*)

UKUBA renders the idea of 'being', but its first meaning is: to become. One is what she/he has become.

efyo naaba – usually translated by 'That is what I am', but the verbal construction *n-aa-ba* is as follows: The infix **-aa-** together with the stem ending **-a** indicates an event (action) of the past that resulted in a present situation or state. The literal translation runs: 'That is what I have become'. However, this sentence always has a negative connotation: *efyo naaba*, 'that is what I am' (I cannot help it). If I want to avoid this negative aspect, the sentence is *efyo nli* (*efyo n-li*, pronounced *ndi*). [The tense marker] **'-li'** is also a sign of past-present situation, which literally means 'that is what I happen to be now'.

efyo nleeba – (*n-lee-ba*, pronounced *ndeeba*). The infix **-lee-** points to the future, across the present, and the sentence becomes: 'that is what I am going to be' (in the process of becoming). There is no verb in Bemba which means: to become. The idea of 'becoming' is indicated by the verbal construction (alias 'tense sign') in the verb 'to be'. The verb *ukuba* needs an attribute and cannot stand alone (as, for example, in English, 'to be or not to be'). You are either a man or a woman, good or bad. And this is the result of an event or a process.

The important event is BIRTH, where you became what you are: - a male or female, - a genuine person (with visible powers which lead to the good of the community), or an unpleasant character (who may eventually turn into a witch or sorcerer with powers which lead to the destruction of the community), hence the **Birthname** and its importance. [Members] of the family spend much time in observing and analysing the signs so as to give the proper name to a child. This name can eventually be revealed in dreams. It is supposed to express the 'individuality' of a person, his/her well-being. It also expresses his/her link with the living-dead (ancestors). That is where the process of 'becoming' of a person is rooted. If the child often becomes sick, the name is changed. If, in later life, a person reveals himself/herself to be a witch or sorcerer, the evil power is believed to come from the ancestry.

Nicknames are also important but are only given at a later stage, when the person is accepted, or not accepted in society.

The verb 'to be' [is not used in reference to] the person. To introduce people, to identify them, and to point at yourself and at others, the verb 'to become-to be' is not used, but the 'set word' NI.

ni ine (nine)	It is I (me) (personal pronoun)
ni Mulenga	[It is Mulenga] (personal name)
nine Mulenga	I am Mulenga

This would imply that the identity of a person is out of the process of 'becoming'.

'to be with' (*ukuba na*) personal qualities or belongings

ukuba na - 'to be with' renders the idea of 'to have', either for a short time (mere association) or permanently. What was said about *UKUBA* also applies here. One was-not-always-with. There was a beginning, which can be birth, and even before birth, in the ancestry (inherited name, quality, witchcraft).

ukukwata – translates the idea of 'having', 'owning', but means first of all 'to acquire'. One has what one has acquired or gained. There is no verb in Bemba which means 'to acquire', 'to get'. The idea of 'acquiring' is given by the verbal construction one uses.

naalikwata - (*n-aali-kwata*). I long since have acquired the thing and I have it personally, permanently. It is part of me, part of my belongings.

efyo naakwata – (*efyo n-aa-kwata*). 'That is what I have'. The actual ownership is the result of the past event of acquiring. Pointing to the future one says:

nleekwata – (pronounced *ndeekwata*), 'I am going to have it; I am getting it today'.

ndeisakwata – (*nde-isa-kwata*) (*-isa*, meaning 'come', is added for emphasis).

'to be with intelligence, to be intelligent (*ukuba na maano*)

ukuba na maano – 'to be with brains.' The rules for '*ukuba*' apply here. There was a beginning, usually birth. It is an insult to tell someone: '*tamwaaba na maano*', 'you never had brains' or even '*tamuli na maano*' 'you have no brains.'

ukwishiba – renders the idea of 'knowing' but also first means 'to acquire knowledge', 'to get to know'. The same remarks regarding the verbal constructions can be made here.

nleishiba (pronounced *ndeishiba*) … never means 'I know' but rather 'I am going to know'.

ukucenjela translates 'to be intelligent', 'to be clever', 'to have brains'. This verb also enters into the category of verbs of 'becoming', of 'getting' and follows the rules given above.

nlecenjela (pronounced *ndecenjela*) rather means 'I am becoming clever' than 'I am clever'.

Verbs which result in a situation or state, like 'to be fat', literally mean 'to become fat', and follow the rules of the verb 'to be'.

> *A practical hint:*
> *When learning the language learn the 'basic' meaning of Bemba verbs. There are three categories: verbs of 'doing' (action), verbs of 'becoming, getting' (state), verbs of 'movement towards or away from'.*

'Belonging'

Umuntu belongs to a place, to a group. This appears from the verbs *ukuba* 'to become to be', and *ukwikala*, 'to sit', 'to live'.

'to belong to a place where one exists'

Ukuba is a mere abstraction. To make it meaningful one must add something (see above). One may add the suffix *-po* (on, at).

ukubapo - … comes to mean 'to exist', 'to be living', 'to be present', 'to dwell'. Hence the expressions:

epo naaba	that is where I live
epo ndi	here I am, present

ukwikala - [is the place where I 'sit'] at the time of speaking. The Bemba words 'to sit' and 'to live' are the same. One lives where he/she usually sits. It is primarily:

the soil, the earth	UMUSHILI
the village	UMUSHI
the chiefdom	ICAALO
the house (home)	IN'GANDA
the 'seat'	ICIPUNA

Where your *Icipuna* is, that is where you live. *Icipuna* also means 'authority'. The *Icipuna* of a chief is kept as a relic. It is a usurpation to sit on the *Icipuna* or 'chair' of one who has a higher 'status'. It is a real provocation. To sit on the chair of a deceased person during the mourning period is a sure sign of witchcraft.

Your place cannot be given away. It 'is' part of you, even after death. Anyone who disturbs your tomb is [a] witch or sorcerer. The same [is true] for the soil where ancestors are buried. It cannot be 'bought' or 'sold'. Formerly this applied strictly to the 'house'. It was usually destroyed after death.

> *A practical hint:*
> *When invited in, do not just take any chair. Wait for the owner's invitation to sit down.*
> *Do not allow anyone to sit e.g. on your desk chair.*

<u>'to belong to one group of people'</u>

The expressions are:

ukuba na	to be with (to live)
ukuba pamo	to be together
ukuba pamo na	to be together with

One is (lives) with people. Existing (*ukubapo*) or being present implies that one cannot exist without being at one place. One says:

ukuba pamo   (*ukuba pa-mo*; *-mo* meaning one place).

This *ukubapo pamo*, when speaking of people, always means 'to be together', 'to live together'. In other words: I exist

at my place	and nowhere else
at one place	only geographically
at one place	only socially, e.g. one has his or her place
in the group,	the family,

hence the importance of the terms of relationship, of addressing a member of a family with the proper term. The terms of relationships are meant to indicate where one belongs in the family network.

Your place in the family is a right of birth. The age does not affect the type of relationship, e.g. between a niece and her uncle, who might be ten years younger. In other words: relationship is based on blood.

> *A practical hint:*
> *Learn the terms of relationship. They are as important, and sometimes more, than personal names. This is the case when, for example, a mother is named after her first born NaMulenga, the mother of Mulenga.*

'Related to'

The belonging, [as briefly outlined above] implies relationship: my 'being' is 'to exist with, to be with'.

'I–with' in my group

The expression *naaba fye* (I just am) is in fact a cry of misery. The suffix *fye* adds finality. It means no people, no place where to live, no one who cares about you – [s]olitude, isolation, ostracism.

To be rejected by others and to be excluded from the group, is a curse (*li-shamo*). In order 'to be with' and guarantee good relations:

> I want to remain what I have become
> I want to become what I am expected to be
> I must have a vital and viable link with others
> I must lead a way of life approved by others

This means [that] traditions and customs, taboos, prohibitions and bans.

Relations and exchanges are not simply automatic in the sense that one is passive. Ways of living [must] be accepted. If they are contested, it must be done in the group in which everyone has the right and duty to speak. If they are to be modified, it must be by the chief, who has the last word, or by the pressure of circumstances. In practice, the following are vital:

> face to face relationships
> personal contacts
> greetings (establishing a contact rather than wishes)
> palavers [discussions] (share of the power of the spoken word)

obeying authority (the last word)
visiting (idle [casual] talk)

These good relations mean health, *UMUTENDE*; not merely the physical health and well-being of individuals, but also of the group. Another word for it is peace. This peace can be broken in various ways (see below).

<u>'I-with' in the lineage</u>

Relations are not broken by physical death. [The world consists of two parts]:

the visible	to be seen and touched
the invisible	[realm] of ancestors and spirits, to be [accessed] by symbols and rites, invocations and evocations.

In the visible one is remembered. [A person] who is remembered with love and veneration is an *UMUPASHI*: a protecting spirit after whom children are named, an ancestral spirit who continues to live in his/her descendants. One who is no longer remembered may be called an *INGULU*, an ethereal spirit, a stranger who comes to visit and possess people.

Therefore, one must have descendants so as to continue life thereafter. Death without offspring is a curse, a misery, a double death. 'No one will remember you and [have dealings] with you'.

Good relations with the invisible world demand *UKUPEPA*, 'to invoke' the ancestry, and *UKUPAALA*, 'to placate' it. This relating to the inhabitants of the invisible world can be called religion, that is, to link. This religion is mostly cultic and ritualistic (*LIPEPO*), aiming at securing good relations with the spirits.

'Broken Relations'

Relations can be broken. The negative is -*TA* and one hears the following expression:

tapali mutende   'there is no health, no peace, no well-being'.

This might mean deaths, epidemics, disasters, etc.

<u>The Ultimate Cause</u>
is always someone who is at odds with the group.

taaba bwino (*ta-aa-ba bwino*), 'he/she is no good, he/she is bad news. This means that he/she is an enemy of the group, or at least a danger to it.

aaba ne ciwa – 'he/she is with a bad spirit', e.g. the fallen spirit of a deceased (*ukuwa* – 'to fall'). This expression means that he/she is suspected of foul play under the influence of an evil ancestor. The more modern expression is *aaba ne cibanda*; *cibanda* refers to any bad spirit, even a stranger.

When this suspicion becomes a certitude, the person is said to be a 'witch' or 'sorcerer', UMULOSHI. Pointing at him/her one says:

ni ndoshi	meaning: 'he/she is a witch, sorcerer, wizard' (note that the use of *ni* for identity …renames identity)
muuloshi	meaning the same thing (the emphasised prefix *muu-* serves the same purpose as *ni*).

ubuloshi – wizardry, witchcraft, sorcery. One is a 'sorcerer' by nature, by birth. He/she by nature harms the group, consciously or unconsciously. This is expressed in the saying:

efyo aaba	'that is what he/she is'

This is confirmed by the common belief that such a person cannot change, nor repent, though he/she can check his/her ways. This is also confirmed by the fact that such undesirable characters were formerly done [away] with – killed, sold into slavery or exiled.

ubwanga – things used by 'sorcerers.' These are tangible proofs of someone's sorcery in which the witch-finder is most interested. The word is usually translated by witchcraft, witchcraft implements. Both renderings are correct. The expression is:

aaba no bwanga	he/she is with witchcraft things [implements]

One may be accused of witchcraft, even if nothing compromising is found on him/her or in the house. Then he/she is said to have UBWANGA BWA MPUPEENI, BWA CIKOLWE, travelling at night, experiencing bilocation, killing at a distance. Usually one uses 'things' like horns, leaves, bones, etc. [Oger is] inclined to translate '*ubwanga*' by simply a 'power' inborn in people and natural in things.

ng'anga – the restorer of good relationships. He is the expert in *ubwanga*, which he uses for good purposes, namely, to detect 'sick' or 'sickening' persons with evil power or purposes. He aims at restoring good relationships by pointing to an evil one in the group and neutralizing [that person].

This beneficial activity of '*nganga*' [says Oger] confirms [his] opinion that '*ubwanga*' should be translated by 'life-death power'. '*Ubuloshi*' would then exclusively mean the misuse, abuse, or manipulation of that power, consciously or unconsciously.

Suspicion
- anyone acting on his/her own is suspect
- to isolate oneself is a threat to others
- to use insults (*insele*), abusive language is a grave offence (abuse of the power of the word)
- to possess *ubwanga* [witchcraft implements] is a sure proof that one is evil
- to curse, threaten, cast a spell is perverse (misuse of the power of the word). In the case of an unexplained death this person will be suspected.

Excursus: The Verb *uku-ba (-li)*

As shown, the verb *ukuba* is a remarkably interesting and complex one since it expresses a process ('to become') rather than an abstract state of being ('to be'). Continuing with Oger (1993), here are some additional interesting features of this verb (:46-47):

uku-ba	become
	neeba bwino lelo, 'I'll get well today'
	ndi bwino, I am well now
uku-bapo	become – be present, exist, live
	ndeebapo leelo, 'I'll be here today'
	epo naaba, 'that is where I live'
uku-bako	become – present
	ndeebako leelo, 'I'll be there today'
	eko naaba, 'that is where I live'
uku-bamo	become – be contained in, e.g. a crowd
uku-ba na	be with, associated, have
uku-ba pamo na	be together [with]

Verb Extensions

Applicative:
ukubeela	become – be such

efyo naabeela,	'that is how I am'
	be in the usual place
eko naabeela,	'that is where I live'
	the reason to be, the reason why
cinshi aabeela ifi?	'Why is he/[she] like this?'
	be for, side for, obey
abeela abafyashi,	'he/[she] obeys his/[her] parents'

Passive:
    ukubeelwa   be obeyed

Reversive:
    ukuibeela   be distinct, different
    ukuibeelaibeela   be totally different

Intensive:
    ukubeelela   become and be accustomed to
    naalibeelela ukubomba, 'I am used to work'
    ndeebeelela incito, 'I'll get used to the job'

Perfective:
    ukubeelelela   become and be forever, permanent
    caabeelelela, 'it goes on forever'

Causative:
    ukubeelesha   cause to get accustomed, make familiar

Reciprocal:
    ukubeelana   live in good understanding

Causative/Reciprocal:
    ukubeeleshanya   to get accustomed to each other

<u>Verb Extensions with the Noun *Uluse* (mercy, kindness):</u>

applicative:	*ukubeelela uluse,* 'be merciful'
passive:	*ukubeeleelwa uluse,* 'be given mercy'
reciprocal:	*ukubeeleelana uluse,* 'be mutually merciful'
causative/reciprocal	*ukubeleshanya uluse,* 'forgive one another'

Nouns Derived from the Verb *Ukuba*

icibeelelo/Ifibeelelo (pl.)	custom, behaviour
umubeele/imibeele (pl.)	personal behaviour, habit
mbeela	habits of a person
icibeeleshi	habitual nuisance
(*umufuutatula*)	

Oger maintains the view that the examples provided

> are not mere linguistic acrobatics. The language shows that to be a person one has to be 'in relation with', 'with a place' and 'with the people of that place'. 'Just to be' is simply 'not to be at all' (une nonpersonne). Or, to put it in another way: one is worth what his relations are worth (1993:47).

Linguist and missionary educator E. Hoch in his Grammar book highlights other significant features of the verb *ukuba*.

> Depending on the tense, the verb either retains the verb stem '*b*', or changes into the verb stem '*li*'. The latter is only used in the present continuous/present progressive or pluperfect progressive tense. Used in present progressive tense, '*li*' expresses either a temporary or a permanent state.

> A temporary state is indicated when '*li*' appears in a nominal construction, that is, when it is joined with a noun, whereby the noun retains its pre-prefix vowel, e.g. *ndi umusuma* (the personal pronoun '*n*' fuses with the verb stem -*li* into ***ndi***) meaning, 'I am fine' (at the moment) or *tuli abalwele*, 'we are sick' (at the moment).

> A permanent state is indicated when '*li*' appears in a nominal construction, as shown in the previous example, whereby the noun drops its pre-prefix vowel, e.g. *uli mupupu*, 'you are a thief' (always, in a permanent way) or *tuli basuma*, 'we are fine, friendly, good natured' (always, in a permanent way).

> As shown in the previous section, *ukuba* is a mere abstraction. It always requires additional parts of speech, e.g. a suffix *-po*, *-ko*, *-mo* or a conjunction, e.g. '*na*'. When used with the conjunction '*na*' followed by a noun or a demonstrative pronoun, *ukuba na* attains the meaning of 'to be with' or 'to have', but never 'to

possess, to own'!, for example, *ndi ne citabo* (I am with [a] book', that is, 'I have a book with me') (n.d.:192-193).

Conclusion

It has been shown that the three avenues – history, society, and language – each give insight into the worldview of the Bemba. Their history of constant travel and conquest is less viewed as being an account in quest of adventure, but rather a quest for perpetuity. The legitimacy of lineages must be preserved and maintained in order to avoid chaos and disaster for the land and its people. Such is the extent of this concern that the powers of paramount chief Chitimukulu and the royal clan (*Beena Ng'andu*) are still socially upheld and institutionally manifest in *Ulubemba*, the land of the Bemba. Admiration and fear of the chief "cuts across ties of personal loyalty or kinship sentiment" (Richards 1936:1). Perpetuity of power and succession is the centre thread of socioeconomic life woven into the fabric of historical events as strongly emphasized in the Bemba charter myth, "a performance narrative" (Maxwell 1983:59).

In a similar way perpetuity is embedded in the girl's puberty rite (*Cisungu*) in the mouthing of the sacred emblems (*Mbusa*) and is

> meant to signify the Bemba appropriation of their oral culture. Bemba society's knowledge and ethics live in its oral cavities and will slip out of cultural consciousness unless they are constantly verbalized (1983:95).

That being the case, a human being, properly understood a human person, endowed with individual qualities is less measured by individual achievements than by what measure of contribution is made toward communal life according to the rank and social status one occupies. Society is much more than the sum total of all its individual members. The truth is rather: 'We are, therefore I am.' Religious practices order the social life of the community as well as the personal lives of its members. Human persons "establish and maintain the central and regulative human place in the whole formed by the spiritual and physical universe" (Maxwell 1983:22).

Language reinforces the communal – human – orientation of Bemba society. Being (*ukuba*) is more than existing. Every human person at birth joins the community of the living, lives in a certain place as a member of a certain community, and, eventually, departs from that community to join the community of the forebears. As Oger points out: "'Just to be' is simply 'not to be at all'. … Or, to put it in another way: one is worth what one's relations are worth" (1993:47).

However, it would be wrong to assume the individual can only be viewed and understood from the communal angle. The Bemba worldview is anthropocentric to the core; *umuntu* (human person) takes central place in the cultural universe where man is called not only to exist but to occupy a regulative place from where to act. This being the case, an individual does not therefore equate to a human person who is neither a passive member nor a puppet of a certain community. What elements are crucial in a Bemba vision of themselves as a human person? What insights can a semantic approach to *umuntu*, to being a human person, yield?

Mu nda ni Mwisano:
Tamuyako na Kamo na Kamo
the stomach is like the Chief's court
(you do not go there 'empty-handed')

Chapter Three

Umubili – More than 'Flesh and Bone'

Man – Biological and Social Realities

The integration of every individual person into family, community, clan, and society at large is at the same time an integration of a human body into physical space. Cultures set varying standards for how human bodies are integrated into physical space, for example, conventions on body appearance (a rich and interesting field of research for cultural anthropologists; see Thomas & Ahmed 2004; Cash 2012). Body appearance definitely matters in terms of prevalent beauty ideals, but more importantly, because "the surface of the body" acts "not only as the boundary of the individual as a biological and psychological entity but as the frontier of the social self as well" (Turner 2012:486).

Heidemann (2009) in his TV presentation "Körperbotschaften" (body messages) draws out a number of aspects on the human body of which the following is a brief English summary:

> Human persons are biological bodies as well as social bodies. The human body is always culturally defined, that is, how we experience, how we interpret, and how we modify it shows great cultural variations and differences across the globe. The modification of the body, for example, feeds a multi-billion industry worldwide such as beautification products, dietary articles along with fitness recommendations as well as other branches.
>
> Body concepts also include which body parts are displayed publicly and which ones cannot; they are subject to prevalent

cultural norms on certain clothes as well as clothing in general. Those norms also determine what part of the body a person can show to another person and even when this cannot be done.

The body is also a public manifestation of identity. For instance, tattoos are a permanent modification of the body, a worldwide phenomenon for a variety of reasons. Western countries allow for a very free expression of tattoos. It is like 'anything goes.' In many ethnic communities, tattoos function as identity markers signifying to the community a certain status or membership of a group.

Apart from tattoos there are other permanent modifications of the body, like the removal or perforation of certain body parts. For example, the custom of cutting off part of a finger serves to indicate to the community that a person is in mourning. In other cultures, the cutting off of a hand is a form of punishment for stealing as well as making a very definitive and permanent declaration about the offender to the community.

Every culture subscribes to certain beauty ideals which find expression in art or objects of daily use. The human body in particular manifests and transports a culture's beauty ideal, as can be seen, for example, in a certain style, such as the perforation of the ear lobe, the lip, the nose and so forth. It may also be revealed in elongated heads, the binding of feet to keep them small, the wearing of brass bracelets around the neck to lengthen it, or, as a more recent phenomenon, body building practices culminating in a real cult of presenting a particular type of body to the public.

In terms of what constitutes an ideal or a beautiful body, no universal formula or agreement exists, though basic notions of an ideal body may perhaps be found, such as a symmetric body or face, a homogeneous skin and a certain proportion of body parts.

Body parts also serve as metaphors in society, for example: "pulling the leg", "don't twist my arm", or "stepping on someone's toes."

Human persons possess a biological as well as a social, cultural body which is modelled, modified, and transformed and which will as such also be read by society. As human beings, we very effectively communicate with our body!

Heidemann omitted in his presentation notions of the body from a linguistic point of view. This is, however, an important perspective. Languages encode the view of the world. Inherent in language are also specific and significant ideas and assumptions about the human body. An attempt is made to provide a (limited) linguistic perspective on the body with reference to the Bemba of northern Zambia.

Umuntu requires corporeal existence: *umubili*, a physical presence in this world. To be what one has become, to be 'in relation with', 'with a place' and 'with the people of that place', one can only do so with *umubili*, a body.

Language brings to light perceptions and concepts of the human body. To gather vocabulary on body parts would therefore not only give insight into these perceptions but also into worldview and personhood in general. As Warren-Rothlin points out:

> Body part terms are some of the most productive nouns in many languages. That is to say, they contribute to a language much more than physical reference alone. Most importantly, their semantic range may be greatly enlarged by the culturally defined associations of the respective body parts, such as, in a range of cultures:
>
> *Spatial associations*: 'heart', 'stomach', 'eye' for centre; 'head' for up; 'hand' for side; 'lip' for edge; 'foot' for down; 'face' 'for front or forwards.
>
> *Functional associations*: 'hand' for acting, working, taking responsibility, owning; 'mouth' for speaking; 'eyes' for seeing.
>
> *Psychophysical associations*: 'heart' for feelings, love, thought; 'head' for thought; 'throat' for personhood; 'liver' for joy, courage; 'guts', 'semen' for courage; 'womb' for compassion; 'kidneys' for moral stature.
>
> *Superstitious associations*: 'right hand' for good, true, justice; 'left hand' for bad, sinister (2005:204-205).

Warren-Rothlin addresses a pertinent issue for a fuller understanding on personhood. A listing of body part terms merely establishes vocabulary whereas "culturally defined associations of the respective body parts" delves into a wide range of meaningful associations of which psychophysical associations attract the prime interest of this work. The heart of the matter (here we go!) concerns a detailed analysis of six areas: (1) notions of the body, (2) the seat of the emotions, (3) the intellect, (4) character attributes or personal behaviour patterns (traits), and (5) notions of the existence of the person after the death of the body, and equally important because relevant for many ethnic groups around the globe, (6) notions of a personal spirit being (spirit double) closely associated *with* the *person*, but *not* part of the *body* (Badenberg 2014). These areas will be explored in depth and unravelled in subsequent chapters.

Human Body

The most general term with which the Bemba language qualifies the human body in its entirety is the word *umubili*. However, *umubili* only refers to the body of living persons. A dead body is classified as *icitumbi* (pl. *ifitumbi*), a corpse, now in the noun class of 'things'! Also, all living animals have *umubili* and are divided into several groups. There are *inama* – also the word for meat – that is, animals with four legs. Then there is the category of *ifisenya* (insects), and the category of *ifyuni* (birds or animals that fly). There are two distinct sub-groups in the *inama* group: *inama sha mpanga*, that is, wild animals and game, and *ifitekwa*, domestic animals (literally, "the things that are ruled/governed").

Plants and trees do not possess *umubili*. The latter are often named after their characteristics. In general, things or objects (like bottles or tins) also do not possess *umubili* but are sometimes referred to as *umubili* when a part of an object is described emphasising shape. For example, *pa mubili wa cilimba*, lit. "at the body of the guitar", means "the neck of the guitar." This example is interesting because *umubili* does not refer to the "body", the hollow part of the guitar, the corpus, nor does it mean the neck itself. Rather, it describes a specific feature of the neck: the back of the fret, the rounded part of the lengthy guitar neck.

All spirit beings are without *umubili*. They are disqualified due to their nature (*Wesenhaftigkeit*). Their mode of existence prohibits physical properties. Only beings that allow physical contact have bodies, *imibili* (pl. of *umubili*). However, spirit beings possess the ability to appear in physical form such as in the shape of a snake, a streak of lightning or bright light, or in the form of a human being, an apparition a person sees in a dream.

The human body forms a domain[1] that incorporates all other parts of the body. Consequently, the term *umubili* forms a domain that incorporates all other terms that may themselves form a domain of their own. *Umubili* is sub-divided into eight categories or domains: *umutwe* (head), *umukoshi* (neck), *ifipea/amabea* and *amaboko* (shoulders and arms), *icitimbatimba* (chest), *ulufumo* (abdomen), *inuma* (back), *umusana* (waist), and *amolu* (legs). Each of these eight domains forms its own hierarchical structure or taxonomy. Terms of the lowest hierarchical level belong to the next highest level; and terms of that level again belong to the next highest level and so forth, until the top of the taxonomy, *umubili*, is reached. Despite the taxonomical order from top to bottom, term-inclusiveness applies from bottom to top but not vice versa.

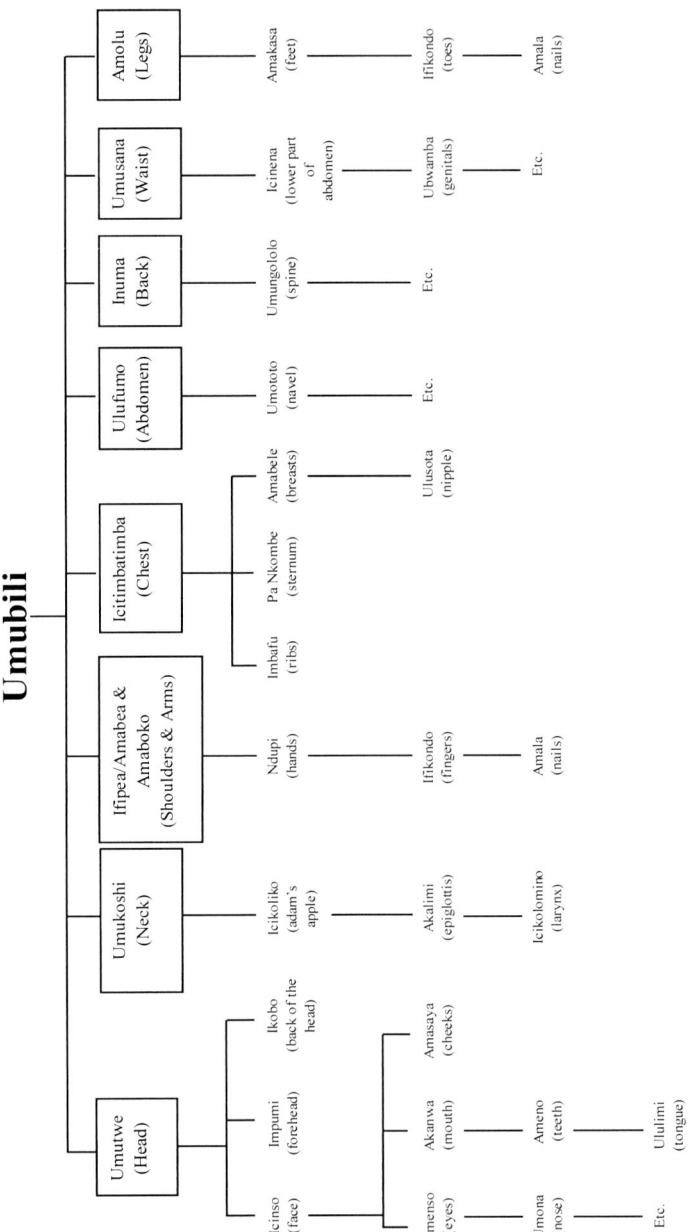

Figure 1: Umubili Taxonomy of Human Being
Source: Badenberg 2008:47

The order from left to right reflects the hierarchical structures of the terms in the cognitive perception of Bemba people in general, expressed by saying *ukufuma pa mushishi ukufika pa fikondo*, "from the hair to the toes," that is, "from top to bottom." For example, to look at the feet of a person for a long time is considered an act of improper behaviour. The above phrase is used in several contexts: (1) It is used to describe someone you know very well; (2) it is used to describe a stranger of whom details are only known for the purpose of finding out more about that person; and (3) it is used in the case of men eyeing women.

The Head: Umutwe

The word *umutwe* (pl. *imitwe*) is endowed with various meanings. Its primary meaning is associated with the anatomy of the body and denotes the head. Other meanings range from hair, intelligence, will-power/initiative, to sickness (fever or headache). Also, *umutwe* is used with language idioms and proverbs. Following are some examples for each of these strands of meanings:

1. *Umutwe* meaning Hair:
    - *asomo lusengo mu mutwe*, he/she stuck a horn in his/her hair.
2. *Umutwe* meaning Intelligence:
    - *ifwe mutwe walikosa*, lit., "us, the head is very hard", meaning 'we are very dull.'
    - *ukuba no mutwe ubi nangu uusuma*, lit., "to be with a head that is bad or good", which is said of a person whose bad or pleasant dreams/aspirations come true.
    - *aliba no mutwe wa maano* or *umutwe ulebomba,* lit., "s/he is with a head of wisdom" or "the head is working", meaning 'he or she has brains, is clever'. Said of a child that performs very well at school.
    - *umutwe walionaika,* lit., "the head is in a state of destruction/ruin", meaning 'a person lacks intelligence'. Said of a child that is dull, performs poorly at school.
    - *umutwe* meaning Will-power/Initiative:
      ico naasosa ni pa mutwe wandi naasosa, lit., "what I am saying, it comes from my head, I am saying it", meaning 'it is my idea, it is due to my initiative.'

3. *Umutwe* meaning Fever/Headache:
   - *ukulwala umutwe*, to be sick with fever.
   - *ndi no mutwe*, lit., "I am with a head", to have a headache.
   - *umutwe ulekalipa*, to have a light headache.
   - *umutwe naulepuka*, lit., "the head is in a state of shaking or refusal", meaning 'to suffer from severe headache.'

4. *Umutwe* in the Context of Idioms:
   - *umutwe we lyashi* or *umutwe wa lisambililo ili,* 'the headline,' or 'the headline of this particular lesson.'
   - *umutwe wa lukasu,* the knob of the hoe.
   - *ku mitwe ya busanshi,* at the ends of the bed; the end where the people put their heads.
   - *ku mutwe wa luputa,* at the end of the grave; the end where the head is.
   - *ulutwe ulu wa ntampo,* the end of a rope at either side.
   - *umutwe wa ng'anda,* the head of the house; the one who controls the family affairs.
   - *umutwe wa cilye,* chairperson (male or female).
   - *umutwe we bumba,* a group leader.
   - *umutwe wa cilonganino,* a church leader or leader of a political party.
   - *umutwe we spoke,* the nut of a spoke of a bicycle rim.
   - *umutwe wa nsunga,* the head of a nail.
   - *ulutwe lwe sumbu,* the ends of a fishing net.
   - *Mutwe wa museke,* the edge or the top of a basket.
   - *ali ku lutwi,* the first person in a queue.
   - *nseke ishituntulu mu mutwe,* the full grain in the ear of corn.
   - *umutwe,* the ear of corn.
   - *ukukusho muntu umutwe,* lit., "to enlarge, make a person's head bigger", meaning 'to shame, disgrace a person.'
   - *uyu mulandu wa mutwe wa ng'ombe,* lit., "this case is like the head of a bull," meaning 'this is an endless affair like a bull's head.'

- *ukukalifya umutwe,* to wear one out, to give one a headache.
5. *Umutwe* in the Context of Proverbs:
    - *amaano tayekala mu mutwe umo,* lit., "wisdom/intelligence does not live in one head only"; used when a person undertakes a project without consulting others and fails miserably.
    - *munshipingulwa: amaaano tayafula mu mutwe,* lit., "the one who is not advised does not have a lot of wisdom in his head"; applied to a person who denounced advice from others and then fell into trouble because of his stubbornness.
    - *uushili noko: takutonya mutwe,* lit., "the one who is not your mother does not feel your head", meaning 'only a mother has genuine concern and will not delay her help.'

The domain head includes various sub-domains such as *icinso* (face), *impumi* (forehead), and *ikobo* (back of the head).

Short Excursus on Hair

The Bemba language has a range of vocabulary on hair. For example, while the German language generally qualifies hair by a specific location (e.g., *Kopf-haare* [hair on the head], *Bart-haare* [beard], *Brust-haare* [hair on the chest], *Nacken-haare* [hair in the neck], *Scham-haare* [pubic hair] or by qualification like *graues Haar* [grey hair]), the Bemba language employs distinct words for hair at particular locations.

- *inkopyo,* only used for hair on eyebrows and eyelashes.
- *imishishi,* hair on the head.
- *imishishi ya mu matwi,* hair in the ears.
- *imishishi ya mu kwapa,* hair under the arm.
- *imishishi ya pa cifuba,* hair on the breast.
- *imyefu,* beard, moustache and the hair in the nose.
- *amapipi ya ku molu,* hair on the legs.
- *amapipi ya ku maboko,* hair on the arms.
- *amapipi ya kunuma,* hair on the back.
- *amaso,* pubic hair.
- *mfwi* (sg. *lufwi*), grey hair.

The Sense Organs[2]

Most of the sense organs (four out of five) are attached to the head. A closer look at the sense organs is therefore appropriate. The Bemba language has no term that could define the "five senses". Hearing, feeling, and tasting are all packed into the one word, *ukuumfwa*! Other terms to denote the two remaining senses are *ukumona*, to see (vision), and *ukununsha*, to smell (smell).

There is no expression in the language for the role of the "nervous system" and the brain regarding the origin and perception of physical sensations and emotions. Similarly, there is also no term for "nerve(s)". An approximation to "nerve" is "blood." Blood is thought to convey sensations like itching or the feeling of pain. All blood is pooled in and distributed from the heart. Signals of pain or other sensations are then transferred via the blood and eventually registered with the brain. The brain operates like a command centre receiving and sorting all incoming information.

The Eye: Ilinso

Ilinso is the word for the eye of a human being. Animals also possess *ilinso* (pl. *amenso*).

(1) The parts that belong to *Ilinso*:
- *inkopyo sha pamulu we linso,* the upper eyelashes.
- *inkopyo sha panshi we linso,* the lower eyelashes.
- *icikumbi ca pamulu we linso,* the upper lid.
- *icikumbi ca panshi we linso,* the lower lid.
- *amanongo,* eye pus.
- *ifilamba,* tears.

(2) *Ilinso* in the Context of Expressions:
- *ukushibata amenso*, to close the eyes.
- *ukutumbula amenso*, staring with wide open eyes.
- *ukushibashiba*, blinking with both eyes.
- *ukutoteka*, to squint.
- *ukufinya pa menso/ukukaka pa menso*, to frown (wrinkles on the forehead—a sign of disagreement).

- *akulebeleba kwa linso*, "frantic movement with the eye." *Alelebaleba*, said of somebody who is a suspected thief; one who moves his head vigorously so as to observe everything that is going on.

(3) *Ilinso* in the Context of Idioms and Figurative Speech:
- *pa linso lya lukasa*, the middle of the sole of the foot.
- *ilinso lye taba/amenso ya mataba*, the maize corn itself.
- *ilinso lya mushi*, the headman (one who keeps watch over the village).
- *ilinso lya nshindano*, the eye of the needle.
- *ukupima na menso*, to measure with the eyes.
- *pa linso lya cishilwa*, the centre point of a circle.
- *amenso ya sefya*, the holes of a sieve.
- *amenso ya mucetekanya*, a good judgment; someone who is usually right with his observations, judgments, or explanations.
- *ukulufyanya pa menso*, lit., "to do wrong at the eyes," meaning 'to look angry.'

Sense of Vision: The Verb *ukumona*

Ukumona is both a transitive and intransitive verb. Three principal meanings as well as some verb extensions are given below:

(1) to see:
- *namumona ku menso,* I saw him with my own eyes.
- *ifyo mfwaya ukumumona mwe,* how I desired to see you.
- *nshilamona,* that is not enough; it is not what the thing is worth.
- *mona mulelu,* to have a glimpse of …
- to perceive, notice:
  ulucelo namona isembe lyasendwa, in the morning I noticed the axe had been taken.

(3) to see, to find, to have, to see a way out:
- to find:
  nga fwaka ndemumona kwi? Meaning 'where shall I find some tobacco?'

- to have:
  Mwapoleni! Ati: nshimona mutende, meaning 'how are you?' He said: 'I have not seen health/I am not well.'
- to see a way out:
  Ntensha mundu wandi, nshimona ukuti nyende, I am taking care of a sick relative, I cannot see a way of getting out.

(4) to be in affliction, grief:

- *namone inshiku*, "I see days," meaning 'I am in affliction.'

(5) conjunction: when (synonym: *ukumfwa*)

(6) *ukumonwa* (passive extension of *ukumona*):

- to be seen, visible:
  ici cintu tacimonwa, this thing is not visible.

(7) *ukumonana/ukumoneshanya* (reciprocal extension of *ukumona*):

- to see or visit each other; to face each other:
  amayanda yamonana minshi, the huts are facing each other.

(8) *ukuimona* (reflexive extension of *ukumona*):

- *baimona fye ni filya fine cali na kale,* meaning 'they saw for themselves; they perceived that nothing had changed from former times.'

The Mouth: Akanwa

Etymologically, the noun *akanwa* has its root in the transitive as well as intransitive verb *ukunwa*, to drink. This etymological link signifies the primary task of *akanwa* (pl. *utunwa*); to be the agent facilitating the satisfaction of an elementary human need. The mouth as the organ from which thoughts proceed as sounds appears to be of secondary importance. That which enters the body via the mouth takes precedence over that which exits the body via the mouth. In other words, before one can speak, one has to live.

(1) The parts that belong to *Akanwa*:

- *umulomo* (pl. *imilomo*) *wa pamulu,* the lip and the part between the upper lip and the nose.
- *umulomo wa panshi,* the lower lip.

- *mumbali ya kanwa,* the corners of the mouth. (*Ifulo*—foam at the mouth).
- *ululimi (pl. indimi),* the tongue.
- *kalimba (pl. tulimba),* the frenum of the tongue.
- *amate,* saliva.
- *ifiponshi,* the gums.
- *ameno (sg. Ilino),* the teeth.

(2) Other contexts in which *akanwa* is used:
- *akanwa ka mupini,* the hole of a hoe where the blade is inserted.
- *pa kanwa ke botolo,* the opening of a bottle.
- *pa kanwa ka mpoto/ umupika,* the opening of a cooking-pot.
- *pa kanwa ka cilindi/ pa milomo ya cilindi,* the edges of a grave.
- *pa kanwa ka mbukuli,* the opening of a bag (term for all bags that can be closed).
- *pa kanwa ka museke,* the opening of a basket.
- *pa kanwa ka lukombo,* the opening of a gourd used as a drinking cup.

(3) *Kanwa* in Proverbs:
- *Icilya icibiye cikula umutwe,* lit., "that which eats the other should have a big head" (e.g. the pot which cooks the pumpkin should be bigger than the same) meaning 'one who is a leader must be wiser than others.'
- *Akanwa ka mwefu takabepa,* lit., "a bearded mouth does not lie," meaning 'a wise person does not lie; he has wisdom and maturity instead.' Also, 'the advice of an elderly person should not be neglected.'

The Teeth: Ameno

The teeth may further be qualified either according to the task they perform or the condition they are in:
- *insongwa,* the cutting teeth.
- *banaboya,* the molars.
- *imishila ye lino,* "the roots of a tooth." There is another word, *cabo* (pl. *fyabo*), which also carries the notion of roots in a variety

of contexts (e.g. *ifyabo fya meno*, the roots of teeth, *cabo fya ngala*, the root of a fingernail).
- *icipunda ce lino,* a hole in a tooth.
- *umucene,* the space between teeth.
- *umwangashima,* the space between the two upper big front teeth.
- *umuca,* toothache and swelling of the cheek (*ukufimba kwe saya*).
- *ubulwele bwa meno,* lit. "sickness of the teeth", meaning 'the loss of a tooth or teeth.'
- *ukusenganya na meno,* gnashing teeth.

The Tongue: **Ululimi**

Not only is the tongue, *ululimi* (pl. *indimi*), an important body part, it also appears in many different contexts. The tongue is an ambivalent organ because of its powers to build and to destroy. *Ululimi* turns thoughts into sounds and words. Words either build and confirm relationships or denounce and destroy personal and communal bonds. Bemba knows no word for "language" but uses instead *ululimi* to mean a different language. For some church communities, *ululimi* forms a key word in their sacrosanct vocabulary; *ukulanda mu ndimi ishalekana lekana,* "speaking in tongues," has become an object of much debate among churches of various denominations.

Here are some additional meanings of *ululimi.*

(1) *Ululimi* as a metaphor for cognitive associations:
- *ululimi lwe sembe,* the blade of the axe.
- *ululimi lwe lukasu / icilimi ca lukasu,* the blade of a hoe.
- *ululimi lwa mwele,* the blade of a knife.
- *ululimi lwa citenge / ululimi lwa citambala,* the piece/tongue of cloth which hangs loose after the knot.
- *ululime lwa supuni,* the part of a spoon to scoop with.
- *ululimi lwa cibampa,* the part of a ladle to scoop with.

(2) Other proper meanings of *ululimi*:
- *ululimi,* language.
- *ululimi,* a single flame.

- *ululimi lwa mulilo,* the flame/tongue of a fire. The whole fire is called: *ulubingu lwa mulilo.*
(3) *Ululimi* describing the character of a person:
    - *uwa ndimi shibili,* is a negative term! This expression is applied to someone who has a "split tongue." A person who cannot be trusted. His words say one thing but, in his heart, in his thinking he means otherwise. In Bemba such a negative character trait is called *umubele ubi,* a permanent negative psychic disposition.

Senses of Hearing, Feeling and Tasting: The Verb ukuumfwa[3]

The verb *ukuumfwa* is a remarkably interesting word. Its meanings are manifold. *Ukuumfwa* denotes *three* senses! It is a transitive and intransitive verb. Below are the three main meanings of *ukuumfwa.*

(1) to hear/listen, to understand, to take notice, to listen to advice
   - *uumfwa nkwebe ifyo natesha*, listen that I will tell you what I heard.
   - *toomfwa,* he or she does not listen or hear.
   - *ulya aloomfwa*, this one, this person listens.
   - *waumfwa?* do you understand?
   - *ukuumfwa mu menso,* to stare without listening.
   - *tuumfwe!* silence that we may hear!
   - *umfweni!* listen to that now! (sometimes expressing contempt).

(2) to feel, to perceive, to realize
   - *icikalipa cumfwa umwine,* what hurts, is felt or realized by oneself.

(3) to taste
   - *icakulya caumfwika shani?* The food, how does it taste?
   - *umucele tauumfwika iyoo,* the salt does not taste at all.

Sense of Smell: The Verb ukununsha

The sense of smell appears to be of lesser importance than the previous sense of vision and certainly inferior to the senses of hearing, feeling, and tasting. *Ukununsha* is a transitive as well as intransitive verb and has two principle meanings: (1) "to smell" indicating sniffing or scenting and (2) "to stink" with the meaning of annoying with an offensive smell.

- to smell, to scent:
  ndenunsha ifyakulya ifisuma filenunka mu kitchen, I am smelling good food in the kitchen.
  alenunsha bwema bwatula ku maluba, he/she smells the scent coming from the flowers.
- to stink:
  fumako, witununsha, go away (get out of here), do not stink us out.
- figurative expression:
  amununsha lya ikofi kumununsha, he made him smell his fist; he beat, thrashed him.

The External and Internal Chest Region: Pa Cifuba and Mu Cifuba

Pa cifuba denotes the external region of the chest starting from the top of the breastbone down to the bottom of the sternum (*pa nkombe*). Major features of this external region are the two breasts (*amabele;* a term that is used on females and males alike. Even animals possess *amabele*). The word *cifuba* in isolation refers to sickness, rather than the chest as such, like *ukuba ne cifuba,* which literally says "to be with a chest" but actually means "to have a chest cold," or "cough." One synonym is *ukulwala cifuba* literally "to be chest sick" which also means "to have a chest cold," or "cough."

By changing the locative preposition *pa cifuba* into *mu cifuba,* "in the chest," different meanings evolve. *Mu cifuba* in a very general way refers to the internal chest region or the internal organs of that region. In a narrow and specific sense, *mu cifuba* is a synonym of *mutima* (heart) or *mu mutima* "in the heart" (in more detail see subsequent chapter).

The Lungs: BaPwapwa

The word *bapwapwa* (sg. *pwapwa*) is an onomatopoeic term derived from the sound generated when breathing in and out. The task of *baPwapwa* is to act as an instrument pulling and trapping air (*ukutinta kola mwela; ukutinta* means 'to pull' and *ukukola* 'to trap'). The idea of "trapping" air is a concept that appears to exist in African as well as in Indo-Germanic languages. For example, in English the expression "to catch one's breath" conveys the same idea. The lungs "pull" and "trap" air and push it on into the liver (*ilibu*). There it undergoes a cleansing or washing process (*ukusamfya umwela*). From the liver the cleaned air goes to the heart which sets the breathing process into motion by pumping blood through the body.

The Stomach: *Icifu*

The stomach (*icifu*) acts like a storage chamber for the food entering the body. The gall bladder (*ndusha*) "melts" the food (*ukusungulula ifyakulya*).[4] This leaves the stomach with the task of separating and sorting out (*ukusobolola*) the good (*ifisuma*) ingredients from the bad (*ifibi*). The residue (*ifiseekwa*) leaves the body via the bowels (*amala*). The blood (*umulopa*) is responsible for taking (*ukusenda twala*) the digested food to all parts of the body. The primary task of this process is to strengthen the heart in order for it to perform its work well (*no kupeela amaka ku mutima pakuti ulebomba bwino*).

The Heart: *Umutima*

Umutima is the noun proper for the most important of all internal organs of the body. This is recognized by the phrase: *Abantu beshiba ukuti nafwa nga bamona umutima waleka ukutunta* (People know that s/he is dead if they perceive that the heart has stopped beating).

Grammatically, *umutima* is a Class Two noun (see appendix 2); it shares this noun class with other names for body parts, especially prominent ones, or other important features of a human person. For example:

umubili	body
umutwe	head
umushishi	hair (on the head)
umona (umu-ona)	nose
umukolomino	gullet
umunofu	flesh
umukoshi	neck
umungololo	spine
umutete we fumo	abdomen
umutoto	naval
umusana	loin, womb
umusula	rectum
umulopa	blood

Figure 2: Noun Class Two (umu- sg.) - Body Parts

Umutima is thought to be responsible for two principle tasks: (1) the breathing process! and (2) circulation of the blood to all parts of the body.

Linguistic Evidence Emphasizing Anatomical Aspects of *Umutima*

- *umutima usunga ubumi uwa mubili wapema*
  the heart keeps the life which is a body breathing
- *umutima ulenga ukupema*
  the heart causes breathing
- *umutima inga ulaleko ukubomba umulopa teti wende bwino*
  if the heart stops working, the blood will not 'move' nicely
- *umutima uli ukusalanganya umulopa elyo no kupeela amatontonkanya.*
  the heart scatters/disperses the blood and gives the thoughts.
- *umutima e ubomba mu kupêma. Pantu nga waleka ninshi umuntu kuti afwa.*
  the heart indeed it works in breathing. Because if it stops that is when a person can die.
- *kwena umwela ulaya mu mutima epakuti umutima uletunta.*
  certainly, breath it goes/ moves into the heart indeed so that the heart it beats.
- *umwela wingilila mu myona na mu kanwa no kwingilamo mu mutima.*
  breath enters in the nose and the mouth and enters into the heart
- *amabu e yatinta umwela elyo yatwala ku mutima.*
  the liver indeed - it pulls the air then it is taken to the heart.
- *umwela ulesalangana mu filundwa fyonse ifya mubili nga wafuma mu mutima.*
  the air is then spread/ dispersed in the all the parts of the body when it comes out from the heart.
- *nga amabu tayaletinta umwela, umutima uleka no kutunta. Umuntu kufwa.*
  if the liver is not pulling the air, the heart stops pumping. A person dies.

- *nomba umuntu nangu talesunkâna elyo baumfwa umutima uletunta baleshiba bati: acili mu tuuntulu.*

    now a person that is not swelling = rocking then they feel the heart; is it beating then they say: he is still in wholeness; complete, in good health.

In other contexts, *umutima* takes on a variety of meanings: the intestines; a character trait; conscience; intention, inclination, tendency; presentiment; emotions; will; and attention. This may suffice at this point as the next chapter will present a holistic description of *umutima*, more specifically by giving attention to the wide psychological spectrum of this term.

Excursus: Ukucite cupo - The Most Prominent Act

R. Kambole in his effort to preserve traditional knowledge for future generations also emphasizes the prominence of maturity, fertility/sexual capacity in Bemba culture. In his book *Ukufunda Umwana Kufikapo*,[5] he elaborates on these topics extensively in Bemba.[6] Kambole makes a strong plea for traditions being preserved. Otherwise, he says, there will be darkness over the land and forest; darkness over Zambia (*Pafiita ninshi, Pafiitila imitiikula, Pafiitila impanga yonse, Pafiitila Zambia*) (1980:vii). The Bemba text below[7] contains some teaching about traditional practice and perception of marriage and conjugal relations of man and woman (1980:96).

Kabili umbi ayipusha ati:	Then another [elder] would ask; he would say:
Nga umwana apangwa shani?	A child, how is it formed?
Umubiye ayasuka ati:	The fellow elder would answer and say:
Imwe mwebo tufishe, tamwakulayikala fye iyo.	You, whom we have wedded, you are not here on earth to merely live. No!
Mwakulabombo milimo uwacila pa milimo yonse ukucindama.	You are continuously to engage into the work/task that is beyond all tasks of honour.
Mwakulapanga icupo, kashita-kashita cila bushiku, mpaka uyu mwanakashi akemite.	You are continuously to engage in the marriage act (have sexual intercourse) a little while and again each night, until this woman conceives.

Ninshi aleka no kulaaba ku mpepo.	This is the time when she ceases to be "cold."
Baleeti fye ico bapombosa, Bayeba shibwinga na nabwinga.	Whatever they [the elders] wanted to say, they would say it to the bridegroom and the bride.
Babwekeshapo umo bacilandile umo umo.	They repeated it as the first one said it; one by one, they said it.
Kabili umbi ayipusha ati:	Again another (elder) said:
Bushe umwanakashi nga ali ku mpepo, kuti mwapilibuka nankwe?	When a woman is in the month (menstruating), can you turn around with her (can you have sexual relations with her)?
Iyoo, tecakwesha, kuti mwaikowesha.	No, never! That is not a thing to be attempted; you could cause yourself to become "contaminated" (become lean or sick).
Mwalwala icifuba ca makowesha.	You will contract the "cough of contamination" (technical term: tuberculosis).
We mwanakashi lyonse ilyo uli ku mweshi,	You woman every time when you are in the month (menstruating),
tauli nakufutatila umulume pa kusendama;	you are not in the position to be wetted (made wet by the sperm) when you sleep with your husband;
tauli nakwisalako iciibi;	you are not in the position to close the door (of your hut);
tauli nakwikata pe shiko;	you are not in the position to touch the studs of the fireplace (where you cook);
tauli nakwipika	you are not in a position to cook
no kulunga mu munani tecakwesha.	and to season (put salt in) the relish; that is not a thing to be attempted.

Figure 3: Bemba Traditional Teaching

Source: Badenberg 2008:65-66

Traditional teaching is quite explicit on the duty of a man and a woman and why they are here on earth. There is work beyond all work to be done: to continuously engage in the marriage act. It is the most prominent act of all! Even pregnancy of the woman cannot alter this maxim. Writes Tanguy:

> Among the Bemba, pregnancy even in its late stages does not constitute a reason for abstaining from the marriage act. The people think and are convinced that frequent intercourse is necessary to strengthen the feotus (pantu cileekosha fumo), and also to prevent abortion (1983:20).

The importance of the most prominent act in the Bemba worldview is also emphasised in the teaching of girls who undergo the *Cisungu* initiation rites. Two songs shall suffice for illustration purposes. They are taken from Rasing (2001) describing the *Cisungu* initiation rites in urban Zambia.

Song one goes with the drawing of 'The Sun' (one of the sacred emblems – *mbusa*) on the southern wall of the house were the initiation takes place.

> *Kasuba kawa nkonkele lumbwe* - The sun has gone down, I [need to] follow my husband.

> Interpretation: The research assistant's explanation was that when it is getting late and the husband is not at home, you should start worrying about whether he is with another woman. But you should not follow him. The nacimbusa adds: "The sun is daytime, you can prepare food, and medicine to prepare the body for the night. Wash your vagina, you can't do that at night when he wants to make love." The sun refers to a man. When the sun has set, the wife should prepare for intercourse with her husband (2001:159).

Song two goes together with another sacred emblem (*mbusa*), 'The Egret', *icembe*, a clay model of a bird or a bonnet of clay.

> *Icembe we mutwa nkwashi waipama pe ishiba lyakwe waipama-* Eagle, the pounder, pounds in the [its] pool, he pounds.

> Interpretation: The nacimbusa explains that icembe is an eagle but it refers to a man and the pool refers to the vagina. This is a song about intercourse (2001:160).

'Hot' and 'Cold': Euphemisms for Sexuality and "Access to the Divine"

In Kambole's teaching on cultural issues pertaining to sexuality, he makes mention of the woman to be in a state of "coldness." The opposite correlating metaphor would be "hot" or to be in a state of "hotness."

Hinfelaar (1994) relates the state of "coldness" and the state of "hotness" to the three seasons of the northern plateau. The months of May to August comprise harvest time; these months are cold and dry and symbolize the Feminine. August to November is the time of the hot season, which is more like the Masculine. The rainy season runs from November to April. These are the fertile months and characterize perfection as hot and cold merge. In the same way, sexual intercourse is seen as symbolizing the interaction of these three seasons. The perception of the cold state of the woman and her ultimate task of "receiving the divine gift of parenthood" needs the complementation of the "hot influence of the husband" (1994:7-8).[8] In merging "cold" and "hot" in marital intercourse, "Access to the Divine" is achieved (1994:8).

Maxwell (1983) sees water, blood, sex, fire and life as "root metaphors" of Bemba culture as they "set in motion their most sacred values" (1983:28). As regards sex (*icupo*), husband and wife can be potential threats to the family and the community at large. In fact, unsanctioned or non-sacralised sex is the cause of diseases and social tension within the community (cf. chapter four: "malnutrition"). Sex and fire constitute powers, which need utmost care and control. Once let loose, they can destroy the very life they are supposed to grant. The pollution of the fire on which sexually active persons who are not purified cook food, affects the life of the group that eats together (1983:31).

Richards (1956/1982) speaks of sex and fire as the "*idée maîtresse* behind most of the ritual behavior of the Bemba" (1982:30). Like the heat of the fire that poses danger if not carefully handled, so do sexual relations which make husband and wife "hot." This state can only be relieved of its danger by the purifying element of water. For this rite, a miniature pot (nuptial pot *akanweno*), the possession of the wife, is filled with water and put on the fire. The washing of hands with warm water from the pot after the conjugal act (*ukucite cupo*) "removes the condition of hotness from the body of man and wife" (1982:31). They are now free to touch the fire on which food is cooked without imposing ill effects on others, especially small children.

Another song from Rasing's *Cisungu* song collections underlines the importance of the 'hot' and 'cold' metaphors. The song is called 'The Moon' (*umweshi*); its symbol is the white crescent of the waning moon and is drawn on the opposite northern wall.

> *Umweshi nao auba ni mayo nga nshilila uwa kuti waya kabili wabwela nga nshilila wabwela* - If the moon was my mother, I would not cry, it goes and comes back, I would not cry).

Interpretation: The moon symbolizes the menstrual cycle and the menstrual period. The nacimbusa says: "Menstruation comes every month when the moon is waning. It goes with the moon, meaning that when the moon is waning, the woman's fertile period has gone. In the village the women do not tell their husbands that they are menstruating, they just draw the moon. It is like a funeral. If the mother is like a moon, she will come back, if my mother dies, she dies forever. The moon goes, after two weeks there is darkness, then the new moon appears, so it comes back. When a mother dies, she dies forever. But when the moon goes, she comes back again, like the fertility of a woman. Do not make love in the dark, when there is no moon." This song refers to the continuation of life, to the cycle of fertility and infertility (menstruation), of life and the cycle of life and death. Obviously, the sun and the moon symbolize the cycle of day and night, of the alternation of 'heat' and 'cold' (2001:159).

Other Euphemisms in Relation to Reproductive Biology

Bemba culture is very discreet about matters pertaining to sex within public settings. Despite the terrible effects of HIV/Aids in the communities, there is still reluctance to speak on these issues in public, especially in rural areas. One way this discreetness concerning sex or sexual matters becomes apparent is in the many euphemisms that are used to refer to sex, sexual parts, or reproductive biology.

Reproductive Parts

- *Bwamba* means nakedness but is also a euphemism for the sex organs (Richards 1982:188); a generic term for the sexual parts of human beings.
- *U/bwanakashi,* womanhood, derived from the noun *mwanakashi* (pl. *banakashi*) meaning "woman"; by implication, the "female sexual organs."
- *U/bwaume,* manhood, derived from the noun *mwaume* (pl. *baume*) meaning "man"; by implication, the "male sexual organs."
- *U/bufyashi,* parenthood; by implication (1) "offspring, progeny", and (2) "procreation."

- *Ulufumo*, the maternal womb. *Ulufumo* is derived from the verb *ukufuma*, "to come out". It also designates the trunk of a tree. A tree has three major parts. *Imishila*, the roots, *ulufumo*, the trunk, and *fibuula*, the branches.
- *Mu nda*, the maternal womb. *Twafyele mu nda umo*, we were born of the same womb.
- *Ubula*, the maternal womb. (pl. *amala*, primarily "the bowels").
- *Mfwalo*, the private parts, nudity. The etymological meaning is "the parts that must remain clothed."

Menstruation

- *Ukuwa cisungu*, to fall into maturity/puberty, meaning 'to have first menstruation.'
- *Akuba na mpepo*, being in a state of coldness, meaning 'to pass through the monthly period.'
- *Atiina mulilo*, fearing fire, meaning 'to pass through the monthly period'.
- *Ukuba mu mitanda*, to be in a shelter outside the village, to be in a liminal state, meaning, 'a woman during her monthly period' (Hinfelaar 1994:10).
- *Ukutaba*, "to move away (from the village)" (Hinfelaar 1994:10).
- *Ali mu minwe*, or *ukuba mu minwe*, "she is or is to be in the hands (of the forebears)" (Hinfelaar 1994:10), meaning 'a woman passing through her monthly period.'
- *Ali mu mweshi*, she is in a state of moving about, meaning 'a woman passing through her monthly period.'
- *Ali ku mweshi*, she is at the month, meaning 'to pass through the monthly period.'

Pregnancy

- *Muli pa bukulu*, lit., "you are at greatness, largeness" (physically) meaning "you are pregnant." *Kapiye ku cipatala no kupimwa lintu lyonse nga mwaishiba ukuti muli pa bukulu*, "Go to the clinic to be weighed regularly when you know you are pregnant."
- *Naimita umusuku*, I have conceived a foetus, I am pregnant.

- *Aba no musuku,* she is with a foetus", she is pregnant.
- *Ali ne fumo,* the term *l/ifumo* carries several meanings. In a general way it denotes the abdomen or belly. It also means womb, pregnancy, or foetus. Hence the expression *ali ne fumo* means: she is pregnant.

Social Body

Casting a trajectory from the human body to the social body is not that difficult to make as a linguistic excursion will show. For example, the phrase *ndi no mutwe* literally translates as "I am with (a) head." But the meaning of this phrase is quite different from what the literal translation suggests. The words explicitly mean "I have (a) headache." Another phrase is *ndi no cifuba,* literally translated "I am with (a) chest." Again, the literal meaning diverts from what the phrase means, namely, "I have (a) chest cold." These two phrases already reveal interesting features.

To begin with, the focus is squarely on the object noun, and not on an action done to the head or a condition to which it is subjected. It is the self! that is subjected to a certain condition. In other words, like in the former phrase, emphasis is not on the pain (as in English), but on the object that is affected, the head. It is the emphasis on the object proper which singles out the head from all other parts of the body, drawing attention to a disrupted wholeness. The phrase *ndi no cifuba,* "I am with (a) chest", puts stress on the malfunction of body functions (breathing problems, coughing, fever etc.) rather than descriptively referring to the anatomy of the body.

Dorothy Lee in *Freedom of Culture* (1959) says of the Wintu Indians in Northern California that their self is inseparably linked with the physical aspect of the individual. The Wintu have no word for body (!), but instead use and speak of the whole person (*kot wintu*). Consequently, there are no specific terms for the parts of the body; body parts "are aspects or locations" (1959:134). She furnishes the following example, among others: "I broke my arm" is expressed in Wintu by saying *"arm-broke-I."* The English language *separates* the person from the activity (i.e. the person's own action), putting emphasis on the verb in conjunction with a second personal pronoun highlighting an action. The Wintu draws attention to her as a *whole* person and qualifies a specific aspect or place/part of her (one could say *I-* the- *broke-arm*) thus highlighting a condition. Lee says the Wintu only separate the self from the part when a part of the body is no longer a physical part of a person (e.g. "this is *his* arm" means "the arm which was cut off, it is his") (1959:135).

Ubutuuntulu

The Bemba self, too, is holistic. But the Bemba have yet another way of contrasting the self. While the Wintu highlight a specific aspect or place/part of the self when, for example, an arm is broken, the Bemba do not. They stress the self to be in company "with" a specific part ("I am *with* head"). In so doing, a Bemba speaker particularizes the self, but – and this is important – s/he thereby indicates a *negative* disruption of the whole.[9] The explicit reference to the head at a particular time and in a particular situation does not mean a Bemba person lacks awareness of his head as being part of himself outside this situation. With the Bemba, the self assumes a separate self-awareness when the whole (health, well-being) undergoes *negative* influences or changes. When the self is "with" a particular part (head or chest) of the whole (body), then wholeness (health) is faced with a boundary. *Particularization threatens the whole*. To single out a specific body part and place it in the accompaniment of a particular part/location indicates a worrisome disruption of *Ubutuuntulu* (wholeness, completeness and by extension harmony). Hinfelaar has a more in-depth discourse on *ubutuuntulu* (1994:108).

Mu tuuntulu (*uli mu tuuntulu*) can operate as a compound adjective. *Mu* is a locative particle, but its value is prepositional and adverbial; *mu* may mean "in, inside, within, on" etc. The adjective *-tuuntulu*, means "whole, living, complete." The extension *mu tuuntulu* means therefore "to be complete, to be whole, to be in good health, to be in a state of completeness and health."

Mutuuntulu, as a nominal construction and a cognate of *ubutuuntulu*, may refer to a person who is in a state of completeness or may be used as a kind of title, as is the case with Emilio Chishimba Mulolani, the founder of the Mutima Church in Zambia, to whom his followers defer as *Mutuuntulu*, or "the Whole One" (Burlington 2008:16).

Umuntu utuuntulu (a whole, complete human person) reflects harmony covering the vegetative, emotional, affective, and rational functions as well as bodily well-being. To be *umuntu utuuntulu* is a highly treasured human condition in Bemba thinking. The idea of *tuuntulu* does not exist in isolation from other ideas expressing wholeness and health. For example, the greeting *Mwapoleeni*, "how are you, how do you do" is a predominant or quite common Bemba greeting. It specifically stresses the idea of wholeness. Clearly, the interest is in one's physical condition. The intransitive verb *-pola*, from which *mwapoleeni* is derived, expresses a specific and much desired state of well-being: good health. It is the state of *ubutuuntulu* (wholeness, completeness, health) that one wishes another person to enjoy in the *mwapoleeni* greeting (whether the greeting is meant to really communicate an individual's desire for someone else is, of course, not a matter of vocabulary alone).

Indeed, connecting the human body to the social body is not far-fetched. Bemba culture ascribes high value to communal bonds. Individualism – here I mean "independence" from the group – equals *particularization that threatens the whole* (social body). Individualism means that a person stands out from the rest of the community by, for example, putting in hard work and reaping a bumper harvest. Such situations upset communal norms and might create tensions among members of the community, such as envy and jealousy. Does this mean the "low value" for particularization and the "high value" for group conformity lead to an absence of, or a minimal degree of individuality, personality, or individual agency? No, not really.

On the contrary, an individual is not only affected by culture – subscribing to stereotyped behaviour – but individual agency also affects the cultural context, that is, actively moves toward particularization. Particularization does not necessarily mean a threat to the whole. Such a move toward particularization, however, is dependent on how that particularization succeeds in the process of integration. That is, how personality succeeds in integrating creativity and particularity into one's social group and society at large. Elsewhere I have presented a case study drawing out the mechanisms of how this works (Badenberg 2008).

Illness also particularizes, thus posing a threat to the whole. Illness disrupts *tuuntulu*. Illness threatens health. Not only this new condition of incomplete, disrupted *Ubutuuntulu* – that is the condition of ill health – but also the cause(s) of illness or ailments must be investigated. A theme which will, however, not be pursued here, as I have done so elsewhere (Badenberg 2008).

Excursus: Ukuumfwa – A Most Prominent Virtue

A Bemba proverb says:

> *Icuumfwa, maatwi; amenso, toomfwa* (ears are for listening; eyes do not hear)

Ukuumfwa is both a transitive and an intransitive verb. As shown earlier, it pertains to the senses of listening, feeling, and tasting! A noteworthy feature is the number of verb extensions that stress listening and its direct link to understanding and good relationships.

Ukuumfwana is the reciprocal of *ukuumfwa*

- to hear one another
  abapalamene mu mitanda baloomfwana
  those whose gardens are close together can hear one another
- to agree, come to an understanding, be on good terms with
  baloomfwana no mukashi
  he is on good terms with his wife

Ukuumfwanya – verb transitive and causative of *ukuumfwana*

- to cause to live on good terms

Ukuumfwika

- to be heard, understood, perceived
  mulandu waumfwika   (the case was heard)
  ishiwi lyaumfwika   (the voice/word was heard or understood)
- to be known, make known to
  mulandu waumfwika   (the case/affair was made known)
- to hear of
  baya kale nokuumfwika, iyo (they went away a long time ago and have not been heard of [since])

Ukuumfwikika (verb intransitive) intensive of *ukuumfwika*

- to be well understood
  amashiwi yaumfwikika   (the voices/words are well understood)

Ukuumfwikisha (verb transitive) intensive of *ukuumfwa*

- to be perfectly well understood

> *aumfwikisho mulandu* (s/he understood the case perfectly well)

The great emphasis placed on listening capacity goes far beyond acoustic hearing ability. The ear is the entry point of becoming a listening human person. Listening is a sign of respecting (*kucindika*) people, e.g. family, elders, and leaders. *Umucinshi* (respect, good manners, politeness, courtesy) is a virtue of great importance and one needs to have it in order to be considered socially acceptable, to be *umuntu wa mucinshi* (a polite person of good manners; a person who knows how to respect).

For example, '*Uyu muntu taakwata mucinshi* (this fellow has no manners [respect]' is seriously torpedoing a person's integrity and social standing. Such a statement labels you for good as unsociable, "as one who either does not know his place in society or ignores the rules of behaviour" (Oger n.d.:1). To be *umuntu wa mucinshi* also signifies to be a person with intelligence.

Says Maxwell

> The Bemba criterion of intelligence is not originality, but familiarity with the tradition […]. Compliance with the traditional wisdom enshrined in the formal songs and dances of the elders is a sure sign that one 'understands' (Kuumfwa, literally 'to hear'. *Munshumfwa sha bakulu* 'the one who does not obey/listen to the elders' is the proverbial butt of many jokes in the culture (1983:94).

The great emphasis on *ukuumfwa* (understanding) permeates all stages of *Cisungu*, the initiation rite of girls. Continuing with Maxwell, the importance of listening, of understanding! is

> … explicitly rehearsed in the Cisungu song Tumwe mafunde. "Let us listen to the teachings." Its accompanying Mbusa pot is slashed with dozens of small slits "like ears bent to hear" (Corbeil IV). The girls are to listen in silence, and not to be heard. So when the girls sit down on stools, they are immediately and dramatically chased away by senior relatives as the stools are signs of traditional speaking-authority (1983:94).

Conclusion

The human body is a viable source for staging an investigation into concepts of worldview and personhood. It literally embodies cognitive foundational structures through physical presence on the one hand in terms of individual self (a biological and psychological entity), and on the other hand as social self. This bi-polar 'body presence' opens up a wide area of other interconnected concepts like reproductive philosophy, rites of passage, sickness, and well-being, as well as others.

Following Warren-Rothlin, the sematic range of body parts, and most importantly their "culturally defined associations" (2005:204), truly furnish a much richer and accurate description of the bi-polar 'body-presence'. Taking into consideration the positive outcome of such an approach, a mere concentration on biomedicine would be nothing short of propagating reductionism.

Willis (2002) draws attention to this reductionist view and states:

> [w]hereas Western biomedicine since Descartes has developed a model of the human body as a complex, self-governing machine, non-Western cultures commonly conceptualize the physical body as the material expression of an invisible causative entity often called a 'soul' (:115).

In other words: *Umubili* – very much more than 'Flesh and Bone'!

Willis' 'invisible causative entity … soul' will be of major significance in the following chapters discussing essential aspects of 'soul' pertaining to Bemba anthropology.

Endnotes: Chapter Three

[1] "A domain is an area of conceptualization like space, color, the human body, kinship, pronouns, etc." (D'Andrade 1995:34).

[2] See the verbs *ukuumfwa*, *ukumona*, and *ukununsha* in the White Fathers Dictionary (1991 s.v. "*-umfwa*"; "*-mona*"; "*-nunsha*").

[3] The verb *ukuumfwa* is transitive and intransitive. The double "*uu*" is due to the full infinitive prefix *uku* and the verb stem *–umfwa*. Though vowels fuse in certain circumstances, the double "*uu*" indicates a stress in pronouncing the verb.

[4] *Ukusungulula*, a transitive verb, meaning: "to melt, to dissolve, to digest (food). *White Fathers, Dictionary* 1991, s.v. "*-sungulula.*"

[5] Joel L. Makopa translates *Ukufunda Umwana Kufikapo* to mean "Providing Complete Traditional Education to a Young Person."

[6] For example, Kambole says: *Icisungu calicindeme mu Lubemba; Embusa ikalamba yalimo, Entulo yabwanakashi; Ebwanakashi bwine,* meaning, "Maturity, female puberty [fertility] is the most significant, honourable, respectable tradition to the Bemba; indeed, it is the greatest sacred emblem there is; indeed, it is the source of womanhood (fertility); indeed, it is womanhood (fertility) itself" (1980:17-18).

[7] The translation into English is my own. However, I have counter-checked the text with Makopa's English translation of the same passage.

[8] Among the Bisa, a kindred group of the Bemba, the same idea of "hot" exists. Musonda writes that being in a "hot" condition is a dangerous condition since there is a "link between life and 'blood'" (1996:58).

[9] An alternative phrase to *ndi no mutwe* is *ndeumfwa mutwe,* lit., "I feel head", meaning "I have (a) headache." The latter phrase underlines the assumptions made above.

Iciteeko Mutima: Matwi
which rules the heart: it is the ears!

Chapter Four

Umutima – More than 'Heart'

Umutima – Most Prominent Organ

As outlined in chapter three, *umutima* is the noun proper for the most prominent of all internal organs of the body.[1] However, the richness of this word is less attributed to its physiological importance than to its significance as key psychological term. It is said man is a biological being, a cultural being, a social being, a moral being, and to add, also a psychological being. *Umutima* is the place where life is kept – certainly regarding the physiological-vegetative functions of this organ. Life is much more than physical existence; *umutima* is the place where true life resides. It unites physiology and psychology, thus being the most prominent organ and concept in Bemba anthropology.

Three Important Prepositions: pa, ku and mu

Each of these locative prepositions (*pa*, *ku* and *mu*) when used with *umutima* denote a difference in meaning.

(1) *pa mutima* describes a certain **condition** of the heart. It is often an expression that refers to a body function that is in disorder and feeling pain (e.g. *pa mutima palekalipa,* "at the heart there is pain," meaning 'I have a colic') or is used as a euphemism for sicknesses or ailments involving the intestines, *alwala pa mutima,* "s/he has diarrhoea;"

(2) *ku mutima* describes actions of external origin done or placed **towards** the "heart." *Cinshi ico musosela ku mutima wandi?* lit., 'why do you talk towards my heart,' meaning 'why do you talk to me?'

> *Ine kwali ku mutima wandi,* lit., 'I had it toward my heart,' meaning 'I had it upon my heart.'
>
> *mucibike na ku mutima yenu,* lit., "place it toward your heart," meaning 'take it to heart.'

(3) *mu mutima* speaks of what is going on ***in*** the heart; it is the place where emotions manifest themselves, and where intellectual processes occur.

> *wilapata munonko mu mutima obe,* meaning 'do not hate your brother in your heart.'
>
> *ilyo amwene, amusuulile mu mutima wakwe,* meaning 'when she saw him, she despised him in her heart.'
>
> *alepanga ifibi mu mutima,* meaning 's/he is devising evil, malicious things in his/her heart.'
>
> *alesosela mu mutima wakwe,* meaning 's/he spoke, thought, contemplated in his/her heart.'

Of special interest is the locative preposition *mu* which can be used with various word constructions. It alters the terms for things in such a way that they appear as a place in space or time. **Mu mutima references the 'inside' of the heart, and with the emphasis on space, it should more precisely be understood as a chamber wherein psychological and mental processes manifest themselves.**

Umutima as 'Psyche' – A Preliminary Definition

As a first line of argument it can easily be demonstrated that it is *mu mutima* where feelings and emotions are manifest, where they come to life, sometimes dispensing a profound sense of well-being, sometimes raging in battle. A second line of argument emphasises that even intellectual activities and cognitive processes are associated with *mu mutima*.

To undergird those two lines of arguments, contexts in which *umutima* features in language abound. The following 77 phrases are not really sorted or categorized in any way but serve to demonstrate the abundance of anthropological aspects of *umutima* as a chamber wherein psychological processes occur, hence its designation as 'psyche' (Badenberg 2002:58).

1. *kusoobolola ifyo mutima wa muntu upanga nefyo utontonkanya*
   to divide, sort what the heart of a person makes and what it thinks

→ to think, to plan
umutima upanga = the heart plans
amapange ya mutima = the plans of the heart
kelenganya = a diviser, designer; someone who is a planer

2. *pantu imwe mwafine mitima*
because of your heavy hearts
→ **because** you are unable to understand
ukufino mutima = heavy heart
imifinine ya mutima = the heaviness of the heart
→ e.g. holding back help; complacency, laziness; to shy away from work; to be very sluggish
uwafina mutima = a sluggard

3. *kulunguluka ku mitima*
to suffer pain toward the heart
→ *kulunguluka* v.i. = to suffer, to be ill at ease

4. *kulanda mu mutima*
to talk in the heart
→ to think, to ponder something

5. *umutima wakwe walambatile kuli Mulenga*
his heart was glued to Mulenga
→ he was insanely in love with Mulenga

6. *ilyo akakumona, kuti asaamwa mu mutima wakwe*
when she sees you, she will be joyful in her heart
→ when she sees you, she will be very happy

7. *ukutalamiko mutima*
to stiffen or paralyse the heart
→ to make someone to be stiff-necked
imitalamine ya mutima = the stiffness, paralysis of the heart (stiff-neckedness; stubbornness)
uwatalama = a stiff-necked, stubborn person

8. *Bamunyinefwe nabasungulule mitima yesu*
our brothers caused our hearts to melt
→ they discouraged us greatly
ukusungululo mutima = melting of the heart (to be soft, discouraged)
imisungulukile ya mutima = despair, hopelessness
kasungulula = a person in despair

9. *mucibike na ku mitima yenu*
place it toward your heart
→ take it to heart

10. *ukwishiba mu mutima*
    to know, understand in the heart
    → to have knowledge, understanding
11. *kupeela umutima uwatutuma*
    to give a shivering, shaking heart
    → to be frightened, to experience angst
    uwamwenso = a coward
12. *kubonsa kwa mutima*
    withering, paleness of the heart
    → to be very, absolutely discouraged; no inner drive
13. *alesosela mu mutima wakwe*
    s/he said in his/her heart
    → to think about, contemplate
14. *umutima wandi wayangila*
    my heart is joyous
    → to be joyful, merry
    uwayanga = a joyous person
15. *alamine ifyebo ifi mu mutima*
    s/he swallowed these words in the heart
    → to seriously consider, to accept, to take to heart
16. *elyo umukashi amwebele ifi fintu, nao umutima mu nda walifwile, kabili aisaba kwati libwe*
    as his wife told him these things, his heart died in his innermost and became like a stone
    → as his wife told him about these things, he lost all hope and fell into total despair
17. *umutima wakwe watutwime iciibi*
    his/her heart shivered, shook badly
    → he/she was very downcast
18. *alitambalalo mutima*
    he/she is of a straight heart
    → to be upright
19. *umutima nautambalala*
    the heart is straight, flat
    → to be care-free, without sorrows
20. *cali mu mutima wakwe*
    it was in his heart
    → it was his intention, he had it in mind

21. *ukupindululo mutima*
    a heart of altering direction
    → to reform; to transform behaviour
22. *muli bumpomfu bwa mutima*
    → in strength, in bravery or uprightness of heart
    uwashipa/uwampomfu = a mental giant; a hero of bravery
23. *umutima wakwe tawali uwa cishinka*
    your heart is not one of truth
    → not to be truthful; not telling the truth
    uwacishinka = a truthful person
24. *pa mulandu wakuti umutima obe uteku*
    because of your heart which is soft
    → to be receptive to teaching; to be attentive
    ubuteku bwa mutima = softness of the heart
    → teachability, attentiveness (often referring to children)
25. *ine kwali ku mutima wandi*
    I had it toward my heart
    → this is what I had in mind
26. *ici te cimbi kano icikonko ca mutima ku bulanda*
    it is nothing else but the knot of the heart because of sadness
    → because of sadness and sorrows one feels a certain way
27. *pantu abantu bali no mutima wa kubomba*
    because the people were with a heart of work
    → because the people were encouraged and liked to work
28. *pantu bamufiisha ku mutima*
    because they blackened him toward the heart
    → to insult; to anger
29. *ukfwa no mutima uwasashila*
    to die with a wounded heart
    → to die in bitterness
30. *ukulengo mutima ukufwe cipuupu*
    to cause the heart to die of a wind blow
    → to become weak; faint; unconscious
    ukufwa cipuupu [adverbial] = to die of a wind blow (unconsciousness)
31. *umutima wandi taunseebanya inshiku shandi shonse*
    my heart does not dishonour me all the days of my life
    → nothing to be ashamed of; to have a clear conscience

32. *eco nomba umutima wandi mu nda wasunguluka*
    that is why my heart is brought to melting point in my innermost
    → I am moved by pity
33. *bushe umutima wandi tawaikatilwe umubusu ubulanda?*
    has my heart not held itself firmly in the poverty of the needy?
    → have I not shown real concern for those in need?
34. *mwe bantu ba mutima wa mano*
    you people of a heart of wisdom
    → you wise and understanding people
35. *abantu ba mutima wa cine*
    people of a heart of truth
    → truthful, honourable people
36. *bumununu ku mutima*
    homelessness toward the heart
    → lewdness, to be wicked
37. *umutima wandi naufulunganiwa*
    my heart is broken, is gone
    → I am devastated, broken
38. *nga wafulwa mutima wafulungana*
    → when you are angry, your heart is broken, scattered in all directions
39. *ukuba na kafiisha mutima*
    to be with a blackened heart
    → to be in an awfully bad temper
40. *amatontonkanyo ya mu mutima wandi*
    the thoughts which are in my heart
    → the thoughts in my mind
41. *ntungilileni ku mutima wa kuitemenwa*
    please lead toward a heart of loving oneself
    → make me happy, joyful, loving myself
42. *washikimano umutima wandi*
    stand upright my heart
    → to be ready, to be confident
43. *ifya kutontonkanya fya mitima yabo fyalisansantika*
    what they are thinking in their hearts is shattered, full of holes
    → their thinking and talking is without substance
44. *ilyo wasashile umutima wandi*
    when my heart was sore, aching
    → when I was with anger, emotional, behaved badly

45. *natuntwo mutima, nafilwo kusosa*
    I am heart-beaten, I even fail to speak
    → I am so restless inwardly, I even fail to speak
46. *ndelolesho mutima tamuli*
    I am looking in my heart – in there, there is nothing
    → to look at something without interest
47. *pantu bapanda amaano umutima umo*
    because they counsel with one heart
    → because they counsel and cooperate in unity
48. *no kuleka tumone umutima wa mano*
    and let us see the heart of wisdom
    → let us be prudent and act with wisdom/foresight
49. *umutima uwapondama ufume kuli ine*
    a heart which is bent, twisted – it goes from me
    → a twisted mind – be it far from me
50. *awe bamufiishe ku mutima ku micitile yabo*
    they blackened him/her toward the heart by what they were doing
    → they angered him/her by their doings
51. *muleikala abaibukila, epali imitima yenu yalemenena ku mikalile ya buwelewele*
    you, live like people who are aware, lest your hearts they grow in a lifestyle of silliness or insignificance
    → be on your guard! Do not let yourselves become occupied with too much feasting and drinking and with the worries of this life
52. *imitima yabo yasunguluka ku bucushi*
    their hearts melted at the pain
    → they were in a state of pain and fear
53. *Ni shani imitima yamufuma mwalatwishika no kutwishika?*
    How can your hearts come out and you keep on doubting and doubt?
    → Why are these doubts coming up in your minds?
54. *umutima wakwe walishikimana*
    her heart is straight, upright
    → she is strong, confident, with self-belief
55. *umutima wakwe walitungililwa*
    his/her heart is being led, directed
    → to be confident; to be without fear

56. *umutima wandi wafungaulwa ku kufuluke*
    my heart is being broken in pieces on account of missing home
    → to be grabbed by homesickness; to long, grave for home
57. *pantu mukusho mutima wandi*
    because you widen my heart
    → to make someone happy, to comfort
58. *imitima yabo yainisha ngo munofu wa mafuta*
    their hearts are fatty like fatty meat
    → no compassion; to be unfeeling
59. *cine cine natalalika umutima wandi*
    indeed I have cooled my heart
    → *ukutalalika* v.t caus. of (-*talala*); to silence, to quiet, calm, to interrupt; to render peaceful, to appease, to comfort
60. *abapange fya bubi mu mitima yabo*
    those who plan evil in their hearts
    → to devise evil; to plan to harm others
61. *mutima naunjisalila*
    The heart has prevented me
    → my attention was drawn elsewhere
62. *umutima wandi walemba*
    my heart is limping
    → I am without strength; I am in despair
63. *umutima we libwe*
    the heart of stone
    → to be hard hearted; no feelings; insensitive
64. *umutima wa munofu*
    the heart of flesh
    → having feeling; understanding
65. *muntu wa mitimi ibili*
    person with two hearts
    hypocrite, double-minded, uncertain person
66. *mutima walunkonena*
    the heart of clinging on
    → a stubborn character; never gives up easily; to persevere
67. *mutima taunjebele*
    the heart has not told me
    → being unsure about something; not having one's mind made up

68. *ubupe bwa mutima*
    gift of the heart
    → talent, outstanding disposition
69. *umutima wakulowa*
    heart of bewitching
    → evil mind, hateful, unforgiving; interest in causing harm (to bewitch)
70. *umutima wakubomfya*
    heart of using
    → carefully using something; able to supervise; take care of other's property
71. *umutima wakufutuka*
    heart of changing
    → hypocritical; lacks confidence
72. *umutima wakalabana*
    heart of roughness
    → doing things hurriedly
73. *epo akobeke umutima*
    he has hung the heart there
    → to be crazy about something
74. *umutima ulya ico utemenwe*
    the heart eats what it desires, likes
    → no point in criticising another person's choice
75. *upali umutima obe apo ulemenwe we mwine*
    where your heart is, there your love is
    → will; being principled
76. *aleilwisha mu mutima*
    she fights herself in the heart
    → to be undecided what choice to make
77. *wifiitwa bwangu mu mutima obe, pantu ukufitwa kwikala mu fifuba fya bawelewele*
    do not be darkened quickly in your heart, because to be darkened [there] settles in the chests of dumb people
    → don't get angry easily, because angered people are dumb people

Umutima – Most Prominent Anthropological Term

The factual evidence establishes *umutima* not only as the major organ of the human body sustaining physical life, but as the central and most prominent anthropological term in Bemba thought *per se*. The relatively vague ideas on internal organs paired with vagueness on the internal anatomical complexities should not lead to the conclusion that little to nothing can be said about the 'inner man'. On the contrary! This vagueness is totally balanced through an intensive form of introspection (an observation Janowski confirms also for Hebrew thought during the classical period, 2015:9).

The term 'psyche' was merely chosen to bring to light this spectrum of *umutima* as the chamber where introspection takes place, the chamber that deals with emotions and intellectual/cognitive aspects of human life. In contrast to western conceptualisation (psyche vs. mind), these functions are not separate attributes, but merge or overlap *mu mutima* (in the heart), creating a common organic fixpoint (see Janowski 2015 and Greenstein 2020, who attests for biblical Hebrew the heart as an organ of speech).

At this point, however, it is necessary to discard the difficult and ambiguous term 'psyche' because of its deficiency in covering **all** significant dimensions of *umutima* adequately and comprehensively – feelings/emotions, intellectual, and cognitive or volitional processes as well as a third set of dispositions, the character attributes/traits more or less permanent in nature – and adopt the acronym (*SEIC*) introduced by Lothar Käser (2014:148; 2016:116). *SEIC* denotes the <u>S</u>eat of <u>E</u>motions, <u>I</u>ntellect and <u>C</u>haracter attributes.

Umutima as 'SEIC' – A Comprehensive Definition

Emotions, Intellect and Character attributes/personality traits are all **qualities** of *umutima*! **Emotions** are the 'feelings of the heart' (*Imyumfwikile/Imyumfwile ya mutima*). They are <u>temporary</u> qualities of *umutima* and come in two categories, positive and negative, or to be more precise, pleasant and unpleasant ones. The ***intellect*** is generally not associated with the mental power of the brain but is understood as a quality of the heart! A third aspect, (and this is why 'psyche' is an insufficient term as a comprehensive definition of *umutima*), consists of ***character attributes*** which are also reckoned as qualities, that is, <u>permanent</u> qualities of the heart, called *Imibeele*. They also come in two categories, as positive (pleasant) and negative (unpleasant) permanent qualities of the heart. Thus, the qualities of *umutima* make up its 'anatomy' as *SEIC* and can be illustrated as follows:

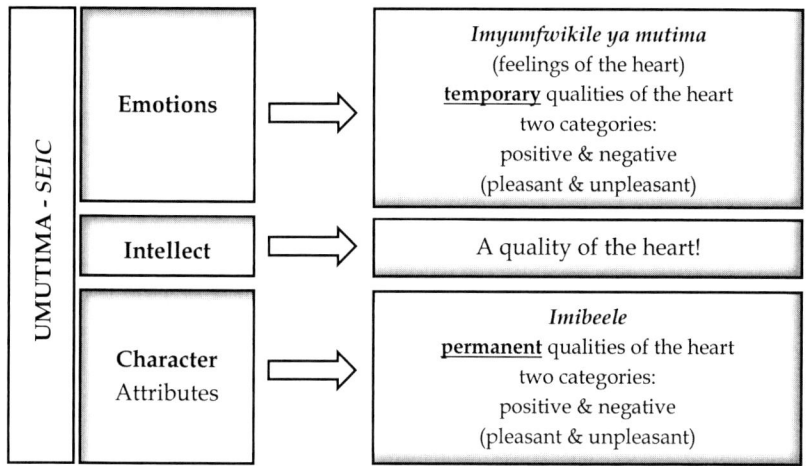

Figure 4: 'Anatomy' of Umutima as SEIC

Imyumfwikile/Imyumfwile – Feelings

Imyumfwikile, and its synonym *imyumfwile*, are derived from the verb *ukuumfwa*, 'to feel' (see previous chapter). When used with the human body there are two connotations: *imyumfwikile ya mubili* and *imyumfwikile ya mutima*. The former expression designates the 'feelings of the body', the latter the 'feelings of the heart'. The 'feelings of the body' are body sensations and can be felt over the *entire* body. But 'feelings of the heart' (emotions) are restricted to *one location only!*

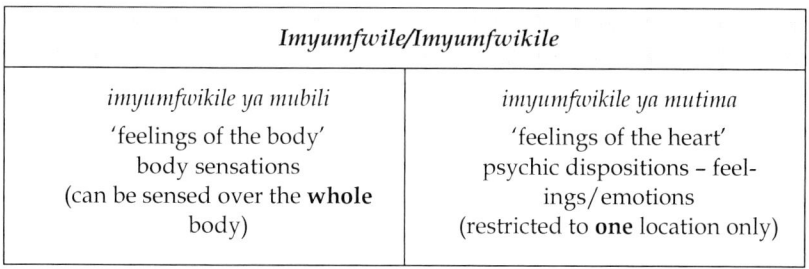

Figure 5: Imyumfwile/Imyumfwikile: Body Sensations and Psychic Dispositions

This one location blends partly with the English 'soul' or 'psyche' or the German 'Seele' or 'Psyche', but only partly and in insufficient manner, causing much ambiguity and confusion and should therefore be avoided. The acronym *SEIC* is a much better term.

In Bemba thought, *SEIC* is associated with a location inside the body or a specific internal organ and always in conjunction with the locative preposition *mu*. There are three terms which share certain aspects: *mu cifuba, mu nda* (*mukati ka mu nda*) and *mu mutima*. All three terms mean the same in certain circumstances but are differentiated when it comes to highlighting specific aspects of *SEIC*. However, contexts including *umutima* (*mu mutima*) are by far the most numerous.

The Term Mu Cifuba

Mu cifuba is an alternative term to both other terms. It focuses on the locality, on a concrete part or area of the body, and is associated with *SEIC* in its ability to desire or to have intentions, but in a less differentiated way than *mu mutima*.

> *Ankumbwa mu cifuba,* he desires me in his heart, he loves me. *Nshishibe ico waba naco mu cifuba,* I don't know what you are and what is in your heart, meaning 'I don't know what is on your mind.'

Due to the minor role the term *mu cifuba* plays where *SEIC* is concerned, and the fact that it has become a relatively rare term for expressing psychic motions, it will be omitted from further discussion.

The Term Mu nda

The term *mukati ka mu nda* or just *mu nda* characterizes *SEIC* as a "spot inside the belly, in the middle" and could be rendered as "the innermost."

(1) *na mu nda ya bawelewele muli ukufulungana,* meaning 'the innermost of fools is scattered, confused and full of chaos.'

(2) *moneni, icishinka ca mu fya mu nda eco mubwekelamo,* lit., "behold, the truth which dwells within you, you should return to it," meaning 'watch out for the truth; return to its principles, return to your convictions.'

The term *mukati* consists of two words: the preposition *mu* (*in*) and the word *kati* (*inside, into, in the middle of*). It denotes the "center core of a thing", "the middle between two points", or could mean "among" when used as preposition.

The word *mu nda* carries various meanings depending on the context in which it is used.

(1) *mu nda* is a compound noun prefixed with the locative preposition *mu*; *nda* without the preposition *mu* is a noun and means 'a louse (pl. lice).' The etymological link between the prefixed locative preposition and the noun proper is not clear.

(2) *mu nda* as a generic term denotes the whole internal region of the chest and abdomen. This assertion is confirmed by the expression: *Ishina lya mu nda lipilibula ifyaba mukati ka mubili onse,* meaning 'the word *mu nda* can also stand in place of the entire interior of the body.' *Umutima* can be said to be *mu nda*, meaning to be located 'in the belly' (inside the belly), but never the opposite way.

(3) more specifically, *mu nda* refers first to the organs *icifu*, stomach, and *amala*, bowels, intestines. But *mu nda* itself is not a body organ.

- Certain *imyumfwikile ya mubili* (lit., "feelings of the body") can be associated with *mu nda*.

  Imyumfwikile ya mu nda are 'stomach pains,' and *ukulwala mu nda* is "to be sick in the stomach, to have diarrhoea."

  To be with hunger is packed into the phrase *ndeumfwa insala mu nda*, "I feel hunger inside"; or *mu nda muli lubebeelu*, "my stomach is empty", meaning 'I feel hungry.'

  To gather strength through eating can be expressed by using the verb – noun construction *-ikasha mu nda*, lit., "to strengthen the stomach", meaning 'to strengthen oneself by eating food (e.g. *ukuya ku milimo kano naikasha mu nda)*, meaning 'I can't go for work unless I strengthen the stomach = unless I eat).

- *ndeumfwa ukwikuta mu nda*, is the equivalent of *ndeumfwa ukwikuta mu mala*, meaning, 'I feel satisfied in my stomach/bowels; I am full, have had sufficient food.'

- *mu nda mulecita macololo,* lit., "my stomach is doing *'cololo'* (the word *macololo* is onomatopoeic, an imitation of the sound when belching) meaning 'my stomach belches, eructates.'

(4) *mu nda* as a euphemism for the maternal womb

- *twafyelwe mu nda imo,* we were born from the same womb/mother.

- *wa mu nda nkalamba,* lit., "one of great womb," meaning 'a person of royal blood.'
- *akabufi kaba mu nda,* lit., "the lie is in your womb", meaning 'the proof of your adultery is in your womb.'

Mu Mutima vs. Mu nda

Mu nda and Mu Mutima: Collectivism vs. Particularity

Even though *mu nda* stands for thinking, thoughts, making plans, having intentions, character attributes, actions, and so forth, the usage of *mu nda* in connection with these appearances of *SEIC* is collective.

Mu nda: Collective Aspects of SEIC

Whenever a certain aspect of *SEIC* is expressed in a collective manner then *mu nda* **is** a synonym for *mu mutima*. For example, *amatontonkanyo,* thoughts; *amapange,* plans, intentions; *imibeele,* character attributes; *imicitile,* actions, deeds. All these collective categories can be associated with *mu nda.*

Examples where *mu nda* **is** a synonym of *mu mutima*:

(1) *ndetontonkanya amatontonkanyo mu nda* is equivalent to saying *ndetontonkanya amatontonkanyo mu mutima,* lit., "I think the thoughts in my psyche," meaning 'I am thinking.'

(2) *ndepanga amapange mu nda* is equivalent to saying *ndepanga amapange mu mutima,* lit., "I am making plans in my heart," meaning 'I am planning.'

(3) *mu mutima yabo batila abati: ico tucitile taciweme*, is equivalent to saying *mu nda shabo batila abati: ico tucitile taciweme,* lit., "in their heart they said, saying: what we did was not good," meaning, 'when contemplating the matter they realized what they did was not good.'

Mu Mutima: Particular Characteristics or Motions of SEIC

Specific characteristics or motions of *SEIC* are localized and associated with the heart, or to be more precise *mu mutima*, in the heart. For example:

(1) *insansa,* joy, happiness, and anger, *icipyu,* are specific emotions. One is positive and the other negative.

(2) *ukupeela,* to give, being generous, is regarded as *umubeele uusuma,* a good character attribute.

(3) *ukwiba,* to steal, is regarded as *umucitile wibi,* a bad action, or bad deed. Emotions, character attributes, and deeds have their origin *mu mutima,* in the heart.

Examples were *mu nda* **cannot** be used as a synonym of *mu mutima*:

(1) *ndeumfwa insansa mu mutima,* I feel joy in my heart, I am joyful, happy cannot be substituted by saying: *ndeumfwa insansa mu nda.*

(2) *ndeumfwa icipyu mu mutima,* I feel anger in my heart, I am angry cannot be substituted by saying: *ndeumfwa icipyu mu nda.*

(3) *ndeumfwa ulupato mu mutima,* I feel hate in my heart, I am hating cannot be substituted by saying: *ndeumfwa ulupato mu nda.*

(4) *ndeumfwa ukutemwa mu mutima,* I feel love in my heart, I am loving cannot be substituted by saying: *ndeumfwa ukutemwa mu nda.*

(5) *alikwata umutima wa kupeela,* s/he has a heart of giving, meaning "s/he is a giving, generous person cannot be substituted by saying: *alikwata mu nda ya kupeela.*

(6) *aba no mutima wa cikuuku,* he/she is with a *SEIC* of mercy, kindness, tenderness, meaning 's/he is a kind, merciful, tender person' cannot be substituted with *aba no mu nda ya cikuuku.*

Though it has been shown that three terms feature in referring and ascribing *SEIC* to one location or one spot, Bemba psychology is firmly anchored to **one** location, the internal organ *umutima.*

Mu mutima characterizes *SEIC* as the centre of those psychic-intellectual activities which primarily focus on the origin of intentions, exercising of will-power, thinking, the seat of character attributes (permanent psychic dispositions, *imibeele*), the acts (*imicitile*) and attitudes of a person, and, finally, the seat of emotions (temporal psychic dispositions, *imyumfwikile ya mutima*).

The findings are briefly summarized in the following illustration.

```
                    ┌────── Imyumfwile / Imyumfwikile ──────┐
                    │      (physical sensations & psychic dispositions)      │
                    ▼                                                        ▼
```

Imyumfwikile ya mubili
"the feelings of the body"
= physical sensations

(can be sensed over the <u>whole</u> body)

Imyumfwikile ya mutima
"the feelings of the heart"
= psychic dispositions
(feelings & emotions)

(can be sensed at only <u>one</u> location;
three terms are available for it):
mu cifuba/ mu nda/ mu mutima
⎵⎵⎵⎵⎵⎵⎵⎵⎵⎵⎵⎵⎵⎵⎵⎵
SEIC

1. These three terms describe *umutima* as the <u>S</u>eat of the <u>E</u>motions, the <u>I</u>ntellect and <u>C</u>haracter (*SEIC*).
2. All three terms have the same basic meaning, but are <u>not always</u> interchangeable
3. Each one emphasises specific aspects of the *SEIC*.

   mu cifuba ("in the chest cavity")
   - aspect of the physicality of the *SEIC*
   - not used extensively in connection with *SEIC*

   mu nda ("inside, in the abdominal cavity, the innermost area")
   - not an organ; indicates the whole inner abdominal cavity, including the stomach and intestines e.g. *casungulula mabu mu nda* (lit.: 'that made my liver melt right inside')
   - a euphemism for the female lower abdomen

   mu mutima ("inside the heart")
   - aspect of *SEIC* in relation to a person's qualities (emotions, intellect, character or personality traits)

(*mu-* a prefix with a variety of applications. It characterises objects such that they appear as locations in space and time).

Figure 6: Imyumfwikile ya Mubili and Imyumfwikile ya Mutima

Source: Badenberg 2014:112

Mu mutima pinpoints the location/spot where intellectual processes take place, temporal psychic dispositions (feelings and emotions) and permanent psychic dispositions (character attributes) are manifest. The latter category receives primary attention in Bemba thought and is called *imibeele* without which true humanness cannot be attained. A human person (*umuntu*) is called to embody and display a certain set of *imibeele* (e.g. respect, humility, patience, ability to listen, maturity, wisdom, sharing and others) in order to claim a place in the intricate net of social bonds and communal living.

Imibeele – Character Attributes

The term *imibeele* is derived from the intransitive verb *ukuba*, 'to be' or to be more precise, 'to become'. The applied form of this verb is *ukubeela*, as in: *efyo naabeela*, 'that is how I am'.

A derivative of the applied form of *ukubeela* is the Class Two noun[2] *umubeele* (singular) and *imibeele* (plural) respectively. The term *imibeele* can be used of persons, plants, animals, or objects. It mostly occurs in the plural form and refers, when applied to a person, to his or her individual behaviour, that is, how a person acts and behaves toward people in a habitual or kind of permanent way. For example, someone's laughter is one distinct feature distinguishing a person's idiosyncratic way of laughing from that of someone else.

Imibeele are categorized in two groups: *imibeele iisuma* (good or positive *imibeele*) and *imibeele iibi* (bad or negative *imibeele*). **Imibeele are permanent psychic dispositions; they constitute a major characteristic of the quality of SEIC** – a theme to be continued in more detail at a later stage.

Noteworthy is the way *imibeele* are used in speech because this, too, provides a little window into Bemba thought world, the interesting, and at times idiosyncratic features, of their conception of *SEIC*.

Perceptions of Imibeele: Language Expressions

The column on the left contains *imibeele* expressions followed by a column with a plus or minus rating (good or bad *imibeele*). The right column contains *imibeele* expressions which constitute opposites of the left column, also carrying a positive or negative marker (good or bad *imibeele*).

How *imibeele* manifest	+ or -	Opposite	+ or -
ukulanga imibeele v.t. (to show *imibeele*)	+	*ukufisa imibeele* v.t. (hide, conceal *imibeele*)	-

81

ukutampa imibeele v.t. and intr. (begin, start *imibeele*)	-	*ukupwisha imibeele* v.t. and intr. (completely consume, use up *imibeele*)	-
ukutendeka imibeele v.t. (begin, commence *imibeele*)	-	*ukuleka imibeele* v.i. (stop, cease *imibeele*)	+
ukuonaula imibeele v.t. int. (totally destroy *imibeele*)	-	*ukuwamya imibeele* v.t. causative (improve, repair, beautify *imibeele*)	+
ukukuula ne imibeele v.i. (grow with *imibeele*)	+	*talekuula ne mibeele* (not grow with *imibeele*)	-
ukusebanya imibeele v.t. (dishonour, shame *imibeele*)	-	*ukucindika imibeele* v.t. (honour, respect *imibeele*)	+
ukufulunganya imibeele v.t. (confuse *imibeele*)	-	*ukulungika imibeele* v.t and intr. (rectify, straighten *imibeele*)	+
ukupata imibeele v.t. (hate, detest, dislike *imibeele*)	-	*ukutemwa imibeele* v.t. and intr. (love, like, be content with *imibeele*)	+
ukusalanganya imibeele v.t. caus. (dislocate, scatter *imibeele*)	-	*ukulongaanika imibeele* v.t. caus. (gather, accumulate *imibeele*)	+
ukulufya imibeele v.t. (lose, forget *imibeele*)	-	*ukusanga imibeele* v.t. and intr. (find, retrieve *imibeele*)	+
ukusunga imibeele v.t. (take care, keep *imibeele*)	+	*ukulufya imibeele* v.t. (lose, forget *imibeele*)	-
ukwikata imibeele v.t. (catch, hold *imibeele*)	+	*ukulekelesha imibeele* v.t. (neglect, leave *imibeele*)	-
ukulungika imibeele v.t and intr. (rectify, straighten *imibeele*)	+	*ukuonaula imibeele* v.t. int. (totally destroy *imibeele*)	-
ukucimfya imibeele v.t. (overpower, suppress, conquer *imibeele*)	+	*ukufilwa imibeele* v.i. (fail, be incapable *imibeele*)	-
ukufwaya imibeele v.t. and intr. (want to, wish *imibeele*)	+	*ukulufya imibeele* v.t. (lose, forget *imibeele*)	-
ukutamfya imibeele v.t. (drive away, exclude *imibeele*)	-	*ukwita imibeele* v.t. (call, summon *imibeele*)	+

ukuputula imibeele v.t. (cut off, break off *imibeele*)	+	*ukulunda imibeele* v.t. (increase, add on, add to *imibeele*)	+
ukukosha imibeele v.t. (harden, strengthen *imibeele*)	+	*ukunasha imibeele* v.t. caus. (make tired, soft, exhausted *imibeele*)	−
ukukusha imibeele v.t. caus. (enlarge, broaden, grow up with, cause to grow *imibeele*)	+	*ukwipaya imibeele* v.t. (kill *imibeele*)	−
ukukaana imibeele v.i. (refuse *imibeele*) v.t. (refuse, decline *imibeele*)	−	*ukusumina imibeele* v.t and intr. (believe, affirm, accept, agree *imibeele*)	+
ukwishiba imibeele v.t. and intr. (know, understand, recognise *imibeele*)	+	*ukuluba imibeele* v.i. and trans. (disappear, get lost *imibeele*)	−
ukuolola imibeele v.t. (make straight *imibeele*)	+	*ukupetamika imibeele* v.t. causative (bend, subdue *imibeele*)	−
		ukukongamika imibeele (curve *imibeele*)	
ukucita cipya cipya v.t. (renew *imibeele*)	+	*ukuleka fye imibeele* v.i. (cease, stop *imibeele*)	−
ukusansamusha imibeele v.t. (make happy, cheer up, delight *imibeele*)	+	*ukulenga ubulanda* (sadness) *imibeele* v.t. and i. (cause, inflict *imibeele*)	−
ukukonkomesha imibeele v.t. (instruct, confirm *imibeele*)	+	*ukusuula imibeele* v.t. (despise *imibeele*)	−
ukwipaya imibeele v.t. (kill *imibeele*)	+	*ukukula ne mibeele* v.i. (grow with *imibeele*)	+
ukulesha imibeele v.t. and intr. (prevent, stop *imibeele*)	−	*ukusuminisha* v.t. and intr. Int. (hold fast, believe, approve, completely affirm *imibeele*)	+
ukukaka imibeele v.t. and intr. (bind, guard carefully *imibeele*)	−	*ukukakula imibeele* v.t. rev. (untie, open *imibeele*)	+
ukukola (trap, to copy) *imibeele* v.t. (catch, collect, copy *imibeele*)	−	*ukulufya imibeele* v.t. (lose, forget *imibeele*)	−
ukupekanya imibeele v.t. (prepare, put in order, hold ready *imibeele*)	+	*ukulekelesha imibeele* v.t. (neglect, abandon *imibeele*)	−

ukukwata imibeele v.t. (have, acquire *imibeele*)	+	*ukuonaula imibeele* v.t. int. (totally destroy *imibeele*)	-
ukukanya imibeele v.t. (decline, dissuade, forbid *imibeele*)	-	*ukusuminisha imibeele* v.t. and intr. Int. (hold fast, believe, approve, completely affirm *imibeele*)	+
ukulunda imibeele v.t. (increase, add to, append *imibeele*)	+ -	*ukuputula imibeele* v.t. (cut off, break off *imibeele*)	-
ukulekelesha imibeele v.t. (neglect, abandon *imibeele*)	-	*ukupekanya* v.t. (prepare, put in order, hold ready *imibeele*)	+
		ukusunga imibeele v.t. (to keep, look after *imibeele*)	
ukufusha imibeele v.t. caus. (increase *imibeele*)	+ -	*ukucefya imibeele* v.t. caus. (reduce, diminish *imibeele*)	+ -
ukwangusha imibeele v.t. (make light, reduce, diminish *imibeele*)	+	*ukufinya imibeele* v.t. (overload, overtax, overpower *imibeele*)	-
ukukonka imibeele v.t. and i. (follow *imibeele*)	+	*ukuula imibeele* v.t. (despise *imibeele*)	-
		ukukaana imibeele v.i. (refuse *imibeele*)	
		ukukaana imibeele v.t. (refuse, decline *imibeele*)	
ukukumbinkanya imibeele v.t. caus. (unite, assemble *imibeele*)	+	*ukupasaula imibeele* v.t. int. (scatter, squander, completely eradicate *imibeele*)	-
ukutinya imibeele v.t. caus. (alarm, threaten scare *imibeele*)	+	*ukusuminisha imibeele* v.t. and intr. int. (hold fast, believe, approve, completely affirm *imibeele*)	+
ukucena imibeele v.t. (wound, strike *imibeele*)	-	*ukusansamusha imibeele* v.t. (make happy, delight, cheer up *imibeele*)	+
ukusambilila imibeele v.t. and intr. (learn, acquire, familiarise *imibeele*)	+	*ukukaanaishiba imibeele* (refuse to recognise, to know *imibeele*)	-

ukucincisha imibeele v.t. (encourage, stimulate *imibeele*)	+	*ukulekelesha imibeele* v.t. (neglect, abandon *imibeele*)	-
ukushukuka imibeele v.i. (to become unearthed, meaning to dig out, to 'resurrect' *imibeele*)	+	*ukushiikama imibeele* (completely forgotten *imibeele*) v.i. (completely covered up, totally forgotten)	-
ukwanguka imibeele v.i. (be easy, transparent, rapid/active *imibeele*)	+	*ukufina imibeele* v.i. (be hard, grim, slow, sluggish *imibeele*)	-
ukusekela imibeele v.i. appl. (happy, content *imibeele*)	+	*ukufulilwa imibeele* v.i. (be discontented, disgruntled *imibeele*)	-
ukuposa imibeele v.t. (throw away, get rid of *imibeele*)	-	*ukubwesha imibeele* v.t. make return, bring back, give back *imibeele*)	+
ukuleka imibeele v.i. (stop, cease *imibeele*)	+	*ukutampa imibeele* v.t. and intr. (begin, commence *imibeele*)	-

Figure 7: Imibeele – Language Expressions

Certain verb-noun constructions in reference to *imibeele* are **not** possible. They are non-applicable *imibeele* designations and are equally important as reference points for another nuance of the nature of *imibeele*. A small sample-set below.

Non-applicable Imibeele Designations

ukubelama imibeele (to hide *imibeele*)	*ukufuuta imibeele* (to exterminate, wipe off *imibeele*)
ukukuula imibeele (to build *imibeele*)	*ukwendesha imibeele* (to hurry on, to push-start *imibeele*)
ukubonsa imibeele (to dry up *imibeele*)	*ukupoka imibeele* (to receive *imibeele* – like receiving a gift, a visitor)
ukutantika imibeele (to begin *imibeele*)	*ukupeelwa imibeele* (to be given *imibeele*)
ukusalanganya imibeele (to scatter *imibeele*)	*ukupetula imibeele* (to unwrap, wind up *imibeele*)
ukusunka imibeele (to push *imibeele*)	*ukulimbula imibeele* (to transplant, translocate *imibeele*)
ukutinta imibeele (to pull *imibeele*)	*ukufumya imibeele* (to remove, take out *imibeele*)
ukulosha imibeele (to direct, point *imibeele*)	*ukulima* (to plant *imibeele*)
ukuumfwa imibeele (to feel, sense *imibeele*)	*ukuteeta imibeele* (to mutilate *imibeele*)
ukusanika (to light *imibeele* – like lighting a fire)	*ukulepula imibeele* (to tear, tear apart *imibeele*)
ukukama/ukutinta imibeele (to pinch, squeeze *imibeele*)	*ukufwanta imibeele* (to injure, wound *imibeele*)

Figure 8: Non-applicable Imibeele Designations

Umutima – 'Key term' in Bemba Psychology

Without *umutima* physical life is impossible. However, without *umutima* as *SEIC*, understanding a human being as a social, emotional, and psychological being is deprived of truly expressing the human condition. The quality of life is inseparably linked to certain 'qualities of the heart'. These qualities do not come to a human person in a full and complete set in the birth-event and, for analytical purposes, should be viewed as dispositions of the *SEIC*.

Introductory Description of Umutima as SEIC

Dispositions of the Seat of Emotions, Intellect und Character attributes (SEIC) – *umutima*				
Permanent psychic dispositions *imibeele* 'qualities of the heart' (character attributes)		Intellect planning, thinking, remembering, etc.	Temporary psychic dispositions *imyumfwikile ya mutima* 'feelings of the heart' (emotions)	
positive *imibeele iisuma*	negative *imibeele iibi*		pleasant *imyumfwikile ya mutima iisuma*	unpleasant *imyumfwikile ya mutima iibi*
graciousness, etc.	greediness, etc.		joy, etc.	unwillingness, etc.

Figure 9: The Structure of Bemba Terminology of Dispositions of the SEIC

To further elaborate on the above structure as an illustration of the nature of *SEIC*, 10 examples of each column and sub-column will be given starting from the left with permanent positive psychic dispositions (*imibeele iisuma*).

Permanent Positive Psychic Dispositions (imibeele iisuma)

Noun and Infinitive verb composites (u=prefix with a=binder → *ua* (fusion of the vowels = *wa*). Noun composites (u=prefix with a=binder → *ua* (fusion of the vowels = *wa*)

Umutima wa ku-bomba	willing to work, someone eager to work (if carried to the extreme – workaholic)
Umutima wa ku-umfwa	one who listens, listens to others; one who carries out what s/he was told (obedience); one who pays attention to what is told to him/her

Umutima wa kwampana	one who desires closeness; one who cares for others or wishes to work together (team worker)
Umutima wa kucululuka	one who is used to sufferings, who does not easily complain; one who shows resilience through suffering in prolonged periods of difficult circumstances
Umutima wa kuboko	one who easily gives, assists; generous behaviour (*Kuboko* designates the arm or the hand with which one helps or harms, e.g. steals. A person who is *ukuba no kuboko* may either mean a generous person or a thief)
Umutima wa bufuma cumi	one who advocates interests; who is trustworthy and can be relied and counted on
Umutima wa munofu	one who is very understanding; who has empathy, is able 'to walk in someone's shoes'
Umutima wa cikuuku	one who cares for others without complaining, grudging; a loving, kind, compassionate, mild, caring person
Umutima wa mucetekanya	one who shows insight and understanding; who is intelligent and attentive, wants to know the facts; not forgetful
Umutima wa matwi	one who listens (to advice, counsel); someone who is not stubborn

Figure 10: Permanent Positive Psychic Dispositions

Permanent Negative Psychic Dispositions (imibeele iibi)

Umutima wa kusongelekanya	someone who is always looking for a quarrel; someone who cannot be trusted, who provokes disputes; a troublemaker; a brawler. Synonym: *umutima wa kulwikanya*
Umutima wa kufutuka	someone who easily makes a promise but does not keep it, who superficially gives his word, easily contradicts himself, all too quickly retracts a

	promise, a consent. Then, someone who has little assurance, not much self-confidence, quickly opts out
Umutima wa kuitu-umika	someone who is always 'puffing himself up' in front of others; a braggart
Umutima wa kufutika	someone who deceives, betrays others; willing to commit fraud; a 'cheater', 'pulling the wool over the other's eyes'
Umutima wa kusonsomba	someone who likes to pester others, annoy them; someone who is always causing trouble, quick to 'fly off the handle'; a troublemaker
Umutima we libwe	someone who has no feelings, especially lacks empathy; someone who keeps things to themselves, shows no participation or interest and wants nothing to do with anyone
Umutima wa buwelewele	a stupid person; someone full of meanness; a fool
Umutima wa uma	someone who lacks feeling, can act callously; pursue a course of action without scruple. It can also indicate a heart that is not at peace, someone who is easily unsettled; a further meaning is: to have a premonition about something
Umutima wa bubifi	a liar, cheat
Umutima wa kaso	a miser; a jealous fellow

Figure 11: Permanent Negative Psychic Dispositions

Dispositions of the SEIC which are Cognitive (Intellectual) Activities

Umutima upanga	*alefwaisho kwishiba ifyo mutima wandi upanga nefyo utontonkanya*, s/he wants to know what my heart plans and thinks (s/he wants to know my plans, my intentions)

Ukulanda mu mutima	*Ine ncili nshilapwo kulanda mu mutima wandi …*, I hadn't finished conversing in my heart Synonym: *ukusosa mu mutima* = to speak in the heart (think, think about, ponder over something)
Ukubika ku mutima	*tawabikile mutima obe pa fikali ifi*, when it mattered, you did not place it toward your heart = at the decisive moment you were unmindful, imprudent
Amapange ya mutima	*nkasuke nkafishe amapange ya mutima wandi*, whatever – I will bring the plans of my heart to an end, meaning: I will finish what I set out to do
Ukuiwamya umutima	clean out of the heart, meaning: to tidy up in the heart = to undergo self-examination.
Ukwimina mu mutima	*Kabili tacaimine mu mutima wandi*, it never stood up in my heart = it never crossed my mind
Ukupanda amaano kwa mu mutima	*ukupanda amaano kwa mutima wa muntu menshi ayashika*, the way the human heart confers, decides what to do, is like deep water (unfathomable)
Kuli ku mutima	*Ine kwali ku mutima wandi*, I had (directed) it towards my heart = to have thought about it, turned it over in thought, had it in mind
Umutima taunjebele	My heart has not yet told me = I haven't yet come to a decision; it is not yet decided
Umutima ukwishibila	*Iwe nawishibo bubi bonse ubo umutima obe waishibila, ubo wacitile*, = you know about all the bad stuff your heart is familiar with/what it is used to, what you have done = you are aware of all the bad things you have done; you are aware of it.

Figure 12: Dispositions of the SEIC - Cognitive (Intellectual) Activities

Temporary Pleasant Psychic Dispositions (imyumfwikile ya mutima iisuma)

Umutima nawisuka	beginning to understand a thing, a person; to have come to accept advice at this moment
Umutima nautwa	to have reached a point of great willingness to carry out work of any kind.
Umutima nawima	to have understood, comprehended sth.; to make sense out of the confusion surrounding a matter; to have woken up from the slumbers of ignorance, unawareness, etc., if necessary, through the help or advice of another; feeling on top of things
Umutima naukosa	to have mental strength to continue an undertaking, a plan; feeling of bringing something to its fulfilment; to be confident
Umutima nawipaiwa	to be insanely in love with someone; be mad about a woman or man, to be blind with love and to be totally unable to think about something else
Umutima nautambalala	to be care-free, without sorrows; feeling of inner peace
Umutima nausansamuka	being joyful, happy; feeling of contentment (having experienced something good, beautiful, having enjoyed a good meal, etc.)
Umutima nawanguka	feeling of relief; no longer being burdened
Umutima naucilimuka	being frightened, to be positively astonished, 'grabbed by the heart'
Umutima nautungililwa	feeling of support (*umutima wakwe walitungililwa*, his/her heart is braced), meaning: being comforted, nothing to fear

Figure 13: Temporary Pleasant Psychic Dispositions

Temporary Unpleasant Psychic Dispositions (*imyumfwikile ya mutima iibi*)

Umutima naunyongaana	to have worries, to be nervous about something; to have had great concern also: not to be doing what one was told to do, to act contrary to what was arranged
Umutima naufuupa	refusing to continue with something; to have lost all interest in pursuing something, to be not in the mood of trying again at all
Umutima nauluba inshila	to have no awareness of what is happening, what is going on; to be in a condition of having forsaken that which is good and acceptable, e.g., morals, good behaviour; to have gone astray
Umutima naunaka	feeling of tiredness; worn out after a task; to feel emotional fatigue: to be emotionally drained immediately after a long discussion or argument; longing for peace and rest, able to put one's feet up
Umutima nausendwa bunkole	to (have to) submit to authority; to (have to) consent to someone's leadership; feeling of defeat
Umutima ulekalipa	feeling of resentment after an insult, feeling cross after being insulted
Umutima ulekunta	to be nervous (before taking a test, writing an exam; stage-fright, etc.)
Umutima watutwime iciibi	feeling of extreme despair
Umutima watuntwa	feeling beaten; feeling of being restless inside
Umutima naufungaulwa	feeling of great sadness; strong longing for something or someone

Figure 14: Temporary Unpleasant Psychic Dispositions

Umutima – Vibrant Chamber

Looking at the vast corpus of linguistic material in which *umutima* prominently features one can appreciate the incredible richness of the language to describe and speak about the human condition. Stated differently, without *umutima* hardly anything can be said about it and there is truly little that people could say about themselves and what it means to be human. The sheer abundance and incredible richness of the term *umutima* shines forth in the wide spectrum and complexity of internal states of human beings from a Bemba language perspective. And more than that! Languages encode the view of the world – in this case linguistic investigation reveals that *umutima* encodes a Bemba view of the world with the main actor *umuntu* in the centre.

Comprehensive Description of Umutima as SEIC: Psychic Dispositions in Metaphorical Categories

It would be beyond reasonable scope of a monograph of this nature to include the entire corpus of available data pertaining to *SEIC*. Especially with regard to the immensely numerous metaphorical expressions of permanent and temporary psychic dispositions, I had to settle for a selection of them while including enough linguistic data for fair representation.

The previous section presented *SEIC* more from an analytical perspective, slicing it up into categories of permanent and temporary dispositions with positive and negative quality markers. This section deviates from the strict analytical path and looks at the extremely 'colourful' facets of the chamber (*mu mutima*) as the centre hub for *SEIC* bringing visibility to its interior in catching the 'colours' in metaphorical categories – a tremendously rich and colourful vibrant chamber indeed. Metaphors, Warren-Rothlin argues, "are in fact the more 'primitive' form of language" and stand "not for an equivalent term but for a whole bundle of semantic features" (2005:200). And "Paul Ricoeur has asserted that metaphor, which plays a significant role in indigenous uses of language, not only provides an aesthetic form of expression but is capable of redefining the nature of the world" (Ulin 2001:38).

Permanent Psychic Dispositions (*imibeele iisuma* and *imibeele iibi*)

1. Metaphors of Form

SEIC is large, big (*-kulu* [adj.] /*ubukulu* [noun]):

umutima ukulu: positive quality of character; someone who thinks things through, plans meticulously, and then achieves good outcomes; a successful person (business, career, etc.); a thinker.

umutima wa bukulu: negative quality of character; someone who behaves like an elderly person, always complaining about something, is never content.

ubukulu bwa mutima: anatomical: the size of the heart.

SEIC is small (*-nono* [adj.] / *ubunono* [noun]):

umutima unono: 1. Anatomical: "smallness of heart" (small size of the heart). 2. Someone who is a "lame duck"; who never makes a success of anything; of little intelligence, can never complete a task, unable to do even simple jobs.

umutima wa bunono: negative quality of character; someone who behaves like a child (older and younger persons); who is reckless; who does not think of others, e.g. a father who squanders his money and brings none home (an idiom mostly used by women referring to their husbands). Then also clumsy, etc.

ubunono bwa mutima: The "smallness of heart" = the small size of the heart (in the anatomical sense); no other meaning.

SEIC is deep (*ukushika – v.t. + i.*):

umutima uwashika: positive quality of character; someone who thinks deeply about things, who is successful on the basis of thorough preparation, reflection; someone who can face up to even difficult problems and solve them, and hence is also asked for help and advice, who is entrusted with difficult situations (such people then often hold office or become village leaders, etc.).

umutima walishika: synonym for *umutima uwashika*.

SEIC is flat (*ukutambalala – v.i.*): (to be straight, to be flat, to stretch out flat):

A cloth is *ukutambalala,* when it is spread out; to be *ukutambalale fumo* to have a flat (slim) stomach; by contrast to be tall and slim *ukutambalalo mubili*. In relation to *SEIC*:

umutima walitambalala: positive quality of character; someone who is not easily weighed down with cares and worries, etc.; someone who despite those things is of good cheer, remains assured; someone with poise.

Synonym: (*ukololoka – v.i.*)

SEIC is straight, upright (*ukololoka – v.i*): (to be straight, upright):

ukololoka: be straight (a building, a roof rafter etc); be upright (to stretch and straighten up).

umutima wololoka: positive quality of character; integrity; not involving hidden motives. Holding one's opinion clearly and unambiguously; someone who helps others out of difficulties, who helps someone to be rehabilitated into society.

umutima walyololoka: someone who is known for not achieving what they want by lying, who does not deceive or behave dishonestly, who does not cheat others; someone who can be trusted (such a *SEIC* is demanded of treasurers, administrators, etc.).

SEIC is bent, twisted, (*ukupondama – v.i.*):

umutima uwapondama: negative quality of character; someone with dishonest intentions, who pretends to be what he is not; lack of integrity.

SEIC is twisted (*ukunyongaana – v.i.*):

umutima walinyongaana: negative quality of character; someone who on principle behaves to the contrary, who basically does the opposite, is absolutely unreliable when depended upon to achieve something.

SEIC is bent (*ukupetama – v.i.*):

This kind of bentness of the *SEIC* has to do with being "compliant". A person with such a *SEIC* has attained a certain quality, e.g. being acquiescent, obedient. Such a *SEIC* is valued as an educative goal for children.

umutima uwapetama: positive quality of character; someone who is not too quick to do wrong, cause harm; someone who does not act rashly, does not have a short fuse.

umutima walipetama: see above.

SEIC is wide open (*ukwisuka – v.i.*):

umutima waliisuka: positive quality of character; someone who is always ready to take advice and accept criticism; but also quick-witted (the right word for the right situation; the word in season).

SEIC is linked together (united) (*ukwikatana – v.t. rec.*):

umutima wa kwikatana: positive quality of character; someone who is always prepared to work with others, values maintaining unity and is active in helping to achieve unity and consensus in the community; someone who can always keep a secret or a confidence; who can be "as silent as the grave".

SEIC is diluted, is thin, slim (*ukusongoloka – v.i.*):

A somewhat many-layered concept. On the one hand the focus is on a quality: the *SEIC* is diluted (like juice with added water). Then again, the emphasis is on the appearance: the *SEIC* is thin (lacks substance) or slim (like someone with a slim body).

umutima walisongoloka: quality of character; someone who can only concentrate or deal with one thing; but also, someone who can often not cope on their own; totally one-sided in terms of talent (in one area a genius, in others a non-starter).

SEIC is known (open) (*ukwishibikwa*):

umutima walishibikwa: quality of character; someone who is totally open and transparent. In a negative sense: someone who is known to be always up to something, planning some mischief.

2. Metaphors of Quality

SEIC is good (*uusuma – adj.*):

umutima uusuma: a very comprehensive term, containing all positive qualities of character and capacities of the intellect, all good and agreeable mental emotions and dispositions; someone who possesses decency; who is always ready to help, always doing good, friendly to all those around him.

ubusumo mutima: the goodness, beauty of the *SEIC* (revealed in attitude to others).

aliba no mutima uusuma: a good and generous person.

ubusuma bwa mutima: "goodness, beauty of the *SEIC.*"

SEIC is beautiful (*ukuyemba – v.i.*):

umutima waliyemba: positive quality of character; a good-hearted person.

SEIC is bad, ugly (*ubi –adj.*):

umutima ubi: the opposite of a *umutima uusuma*. This term contains all the negative qualities of character and capacities of the intellect, all bad and disagreeable mental emotions and dispositions; someone without decency, unwilling to accept any advice; someone who basically has an unfriendly attitude towards others.

ububi umutima: "the badness, distortedness" of the *SEIC* is visible, e.g. in attitude to others.

ububi bwa mutima: "the badness, distortedness" of the *SEIC* (the severity of the affected *SEIC*).

wa mutima ubi: negative quality of character; a villain, a wicked person (synonym: *umubi*).

SEIC is light (*ukwanguka – v.i.*):

umutima walyanguka: someone who is at ease with their basic disposition; someone who harbours and cherishes nothing bad in their *SEIC*.

ukwanguka umutima: positive quality of character; someone who is quick on the uptake, grasps things easily and quickly; someone who shows understanding and is accessible; someone who is easy to talk to, approachable.

Is also used in a negative sense, meaning "quick to react", "liable to fly off the handle" (*alianguko mutima nga kasonto*, he/she is so irascible, with a reflex like a mouse).

In another connection *ukwanguko mutima* refers to a person who can get drunk without much persuasion; someone who is easily influenced, quick to change opinion and reluctant to take a firm stand on an issue.

SEIC is sharp (*ukutwa – v.i.*):

umutima walitwa: positive quality of character; someone who is always "on fire" and willing to get stuck in and help.

SEIC is blunt (*ukufuupa – v.i.*):

umutima walifuupa: negative quality of character; someone who is totally "blunted", above all to do with work; a lazy-bones; someone who only shows readiness if there is enough stimulus; never does anything of their own volition; not co-operative; unwilling to show any community spirit.

Synonym: *ukutompoka umutima:* to lose inner resilience (like the string of a bow); to become soft, yielding; wanting to give up the effort for something, have no more energy to carry on.

SEIC is hard (*ukukosa – v.i.*):

umutima walikosa: negative quality of character; someone who cannot be convinced, whether for a good or ill purpose; a really stubborn person. One synonym is *umutima buumankonso*: to be adamant; such a person withdraws from being influenced by any good words or arguments.

ukukosa umutima: a pig-headed person.

SEIC is soft (*ukunakanaka – v.i. red.*):

umutima walinakanaka: positive and negative quality of character; a good-natured and mild-mannered person, or someone who easily yields to whatever wind is blowing, is too easily softened or persuaded.

(*-teku* – adj.):

umutima uteku: someone who is receptive both to suggestions and to criticism; including when he is accused of something.

SEIC is tough (*ukushangila – v.t. + i.*):

umutima uwashangila: positive quality of character, someone who doesn't give up, who braves wind and weather; who allows nothing to derail him, who holds fast to one issue, who shows toughness; who on no account "throws in the towel."

SEIC is tame (*ukuteeka – v.t.*):

umutima uteeka: positive quality of character; someone who has and demonstrates qualities of leadership; someone who approaches a task with prudence and reflection; someone who is not rash or precipitate. A person with self-control.

ukuteeka umutima: to exercise self-control, restrain oneself, be patient, be calm.

SEIC is wild, fierce (*ukukalipa*):

umutima wa bukali: negative quality of character; someone who goes off the deep end at the slightest provocation, who is quick to get angry, who quickly gets in a huff.

SEIC is clear (*ukulengama – v.i.*):

ukulengama umutima: behind this is the idea of transparency. Someone who is transparent in their actions, whose motives are clear. It is pleasant to be connected with such a person.

SEIC is white (*ukubuuta* v.i.):

ukubuuta is to be white, e.g. skin colour (*ababuuta* = the Whites, the Europeans).

umutima uwabuuta: to be bright, light, free; someone who is cheerful, buoyant.

alibuuta ku mutima: open-hearted person; someone who is not picky; able to take criticism; having humility; takes a liking to people: *uyu alimbuutila ku mutima*, this person has made me white to the heart = I have lost my heart to him/her; I have locked him/her in my heart.

SEIC is cold (*ukutalala*):

If something is *ukutalala*, it is fresh, cold (mountain water, temperature, glowing iron that is cooled, etc.); in the metaphorical sense it indicates someone who, after completely wearing themselves out emotionally, is able to calm down, has "cooled off".

umutima uwatalala: positive quality of character; someone who acts calmly, in a considered manner.

SEIC is heavy (*ukufina – v.i*):

ukufina umutima: negative quality of character; someone who is slow, who takes a long time to do something or understand an issue ("slow on the uptake"); someone who has a ponderous heart = is hard, of iron.

umutima uwafina: a grumpy person.

SEIC is adorned, embellished, is refitted, does good (*ukuwamya – v.t. caus.*):

ukuwamya is one of those terms with a very wide breadth of meaning. It can mean adorn, beautify, improve, repair, or do good.

umutima uuwamya: positive quality of character; an entertainer.

ukuwamya umutima: is used to convey that it is time to end disputes with others or clear up problems.

ukuiwamya umutima: "beautifying action" of the *SEIC*; tidying up the heart = submit to a self-examination.

(*ukuwama – v.i.*):

waliwama umutima: positive quality of character; to have a beautiful *SEIC*, e.g. to have manners; able to behave oneself.

SEIC is turned round, reversed (*ukwaluka v.t. + i.*):

umutima walyawike: to get totally obsessed; then completely turn away from an activity or a person and give total attention to something else; to allow oneself to be attracted or enraptured.

The literal meaning of *ukwaluka* is to turn round, turn away towards something. The metaphorical sense indicates a change of mind; follow a new line of thought, adopt a new attitude.

SEIC **is different, distinct (***ukuibela v.i.***):**

umutima waliibela: negative quality of character; someone who sets himself apart from others; a loner.

SEIC **blazes (***ukwaka* **– v.i.):**

ukwaka means to burn, ignite, blaze (flames).

umutima uwaka: positive quality of character; to radiate and spread happiness; a cheerful soul.

SEIC **is fatty (***ukwinisha***):**

umutima wainisha: negative quality of character; someone whom you can't impress; Things glide off him like water on a duck's back; immovable in his attitude, opinion, indifference.

imitima yabo yainisha ngo munofu wa mafuta, their hearts are fat like the fat on meat, their hearts are like fat = they are insensitive, lack feeling.

SEIC **is stiff, lame (***ukutalamika***):**

ukutalamika umutima: someone who is absolutely unwilling to listen; stubbornness and complete refusal of any suggestions or advice, even despite the danger of ignoring serious consequences; totally fixated on something.

SEIC **is molten (***ukusungulula***):**

ukusungulula umutima: to lack confidence or courage, be despondent. The basic meaning of *ukusungulula* is to melt iron in the fire. A *SEIC* which is molten loses its stability.

SEIC **is rotten, decayed (***ukubola***):**

umutima ubola: negative quality of character: someone who has permanently lost all his/her good qualities, lost all sense of justice; who is unable to do good. Such a *SEIC* is almost beyond cure.

SEIC **is cowardly (***ukuba no ca mwenso***):**

umutima uca mwenso: a coward, chicken-hearted.

SEIC **is pure (***ukusanguluka* **– v.i.):**

umutima uwasanguluka: having no ulterior motives; having clear intentions; abstaining from evil deeds and being cleansed from them; to be cleansed (acquitted) of guilt.

3. *Metaphors of Rest*

SEIC **has sat down (***ukwikala***):**

umutima waikala: the *SEIC* is sitting; to have come to rest; be content; able after great excitement to breathe quietly; be no longer anxious.

Synonym: *umutima watalala:* when after a storm calm returns, after a storm on the sea the water is still again, then the world is *ukutalala*. When applied to the *SEIC*: after great tension, great anxiety, and emotional shock, finding peace and relief again.

SEIC is composed, complete, whole (-*tuuntulu*):

umutima utuuntulu: to be in a good frame of mind; to feel complete, that life is good; feeling of inner wholeness and harmony.

4. *Metaphors of Motion*

SEIC is turning (*ukupilibuka*):

umutima wa kupilibuka: negative quality of character; someone who turns this way and that; someone who is always doing something different (continually changing his opinion, his career, his work, etc.).

SEIC is fizzing (*ukusabuka – v.i.*):

ukusabuka also means to sparkle, e.g. someone who surprises another by his smart clothes, causing amazement (*kwena mwasabuka,* "you look enchanting").

umutima usabuka: positive quality of character; someone who often "sparkles, lights up, effervesces"; someone who gives good and rapid answers, finds solutions. Has ideas, suggestions etc.

SEIC is falling down, falling over (*ukuwa – v.i.*):

umutima uwa: negative quality of character; someone who is always falling, falling over" = who is always doing something stupid, always talking nonsense, never displaying seriousness; someone whose *SEIC* has lost its stability.

umutima waliwa: following a certain moment in the past no longer being able to think and act clearly; no longer able to act for himself in the normal way.

An interesting idiom is *umupashi waliwa* = *umupashi* has "fallen down or over" and means that someone has lost their reason; it serves to denote a psychic illness ('a mad person').

SEIC is vibrating (*ukutetema – v.i.*):

umutima utetema: negative quality of character; someone who quickly loses their inner equilibrium, who quickly/always/ trembles inwardly at the smallest thing; someone who is quickly thrown off course; who reveals nothing on the outside but is inwardly totally unsure.

SEIC is not aligned with the direction of movement (*ukukaana lungama – v.i. + v.t.*):

umutima ushalungama: syn: *cumbu munshololwa* = bent like a sweet potato. If you try to straighten it, it breaks. Someone like that cannot be corrected without hitting back.

(*umupashi ushalungama* = polite way of saying that someone has "lost" his *umupashi*).

umutima walikaana lungama: negative quality of character; someone who is obstinate, twisted, not pointing the right way; whose actions cannot be controlled by others; someone who is very conceited, always thinks he is doing the right thing.

The opposite is being *uwalungama*; an upright, honest, just person.

SEIC has left the path (*ukuluba inshila – v.i. + t.*):

umutima uuluba inshila: negative quality of character; someone who is always deviating from the path (e.g. who is always making mistakes in his speech; who is always digressing in his talk etc.).

umutima waliluba inshila: following a particular moment in the past has lost that which is good, acceptable (e.g. someone who has always been blamed, corrected, beaten by his father and is then no longer able to respect him).

umupashi waliluba inshila: paraphrase for *umupashi,* who became a *cibanda/ciwa* [a malevolent spirit being].

(*ukupindulula*):

ukupindulula umutima: to leave the good path; not behave according to the prescribed norms and hence go the wrong way; to turn away from a matter or a person, cease to trust in someone.

SEIC has lost its way (*ukuluba – v.i. + t.*):

umutima waliluba: negative quality of character; someone of little intelligence; has no idea at all; is "lost" as regards all areas.

SEIC changes, alters, turns round (*ukwalula – v.t.*):

umutima uwalula: positive quality of character; someone who can change positively, who can bring about positive changes; an adviser in the best sense; someone who uses their influence to put people back on the right path, lead them to behave according to the right norms.

SEIC is always in a state of change (*ukupilibuka pilibuka bwangu – v.i.*):

umutima uupilibuka pilibuka bwangu: negative quality of character; someone who is fickle, like a weathervane, who says one thing to one person, and something different to another; someone who cannot commit, takes no position; switches camp depending on how things develop etc.

SEIC is slow to change; only "turns" from time to time (*ukupilibuka pilibuka limo limo – v.i.*):

umutima uupilibuka pilibuka limo limo: quality of character (in positive and negative sense); someone who is obstinate, never easy to persuade, has his opinion and is very reluctant to shift; someone who cannot be easily swayed, etc.

SEIC runs away (*ukubutuka – v.i. + t.*):

umutima uubutuka: (1) negative quality of character: a coward, a timid person; someone who always runs away (from the new job, from school, etc.) (2) positive quality of character: someone who is always quick to carry out tasks, who is eager to know and ready to learn.

SEIC runs around (*ukwenda – v.i.*):

umutima uwenda: positive and negative quality of character; someone who has a fabulous memory, who can remember lots of things even from a long time ago.

ukwenda kwa mutima: the memory capacity itself; clarity of memory; detailed remembering; ability to recall facts, events, etc.

umutima wa kwenda or *aliba no mutima wa kwenda:* positive and negative quality of character: someone who loves travel, is always on the move; then also someone who is restless, who cannot/will not settle down; a nomad etc.

SEIC is active, lively, swift to respond (ready to dive in) (*ukusupa – v.i.*):

ukusupa umutima: adjectival use: be lively, active, quick to respond.

(*ukusupila – v.i. appl.*):

umutima usupila: positive quality of character; always being active, always working on a project; someone who is always eager for new challenges and completes them; someone who loves adventure.

SEIC is standing up, raises itself (*ukwima – v.i.*):

umutima waliima: positive quality of character; someone who understands things clearly, analyses correctly; someone of strong will; then also someone with a strong need to participate, to be actively involved in whatever is going on.

SEIC is upright, vertical (*ukushikimana* – *v.i.*):

umutima washikimana: a house is *ukushikimana* if it is not leaning; a person who is standing upright is likewise *ukushikimana*. A *SEIC* which is *ukushikimana* describes someone who is prepared, who is braced for the event and not anxious; someone who can await something unpleasant with equanimity.

SEIC is lying down, lying flat on the ground (*ukulambalala* – *v.i.*):

umutima walilambalala: negative quality of character: someone who can only be entrusted with simple tasks, who has limited ability.

SEIC is lifted high (*ukusansabala*):

ukusansabala umutima: in real terms *ukusansabala* means to sit in the place of honour, to raise someone up to a position. Applied to the *SEIC* it is tantamount to being committed to something, have firm convictions; not easy to be shifted from something.

SEIC is exalted (*ukutakalala* – *v.i.*):

ukutakalala umutima: the verb *ukutakalala* means to have no needs, well off, to possess a good and honourable position; to be enjoying life, because you can afford things.

Applied to the *SEIC:* a negative quality of character; it denotes someone who is haughty, proud and boastful (*pantu walitakalele umutima wakwe*, because of being exalted, lifted to elevated position his/her heart = because of his/her boastfulness).

SEIC orients itself (*ukulungamika* – *v.t.*):

umutima uulungamika: positive quality of character; someone who helps others to find direction, to turn from the bad to the good; someone who is able through advice to "orient" others towards something definite.

SEIC surrenders itself (*ukukupukula v.i.* / syn: *ukusokolola*):

umutima uukupukula: positive quality of character; someone who is always ready to share knowledge with others or pass on skills to others; who pours out his whole reservoir of ability for good or ill on behalf of others (e.g. a teacher, etc.).

umutima walikupukula: positive quality of character: someone who is openhearted, giving gladly of oneself.

SEIC **withdraws, takes back, breaks a promise** (*ukufutuka – v.i.*):

umutima wa kufutika: negative quality of character; someone who makes promises easily but does not keep them, who gives their word superficially, who easily contradicts himself, takes back a promise, a pledge, all too quickly. It can also mean someone who has little confidence, scarcely trusts himself and quickly backtracks.

5. Metaphors of the Human Body

SEIC **is strong, powerful** (*ukukosa – v.i.*):

umutima walikosa: quality of character; in a positive sense it denotes a person who is not easily intimidated, who is mentally resilient; possesses courage, endurance, remains calm under danger, is used to austerity. In a negative sense it denotes someone who cannot be persuaded, who is obstinate, cannot be told anything, is strong = immovable (pig-headed).

SEIC **is weak, gives in** (*ukunenuka – v.i.*):

umutima wa kunenuka: negative quality of character; someone who does not complete things, projects; someone who has not the endurance to "see something through"; someone who also influences others to give up.

SEIC **is lifeless, exhausted** (*ukutembuka – v.i.*):

umutima walitembuka: someone who continually says he does not have or cannot do; a condition which can lead to depression and even to illness.

SEIC **is tired, exhausted** (*ukunaka – v.i.*):

umutima walinaka: negative quality of character; someone who is always claiming he cannot do it, who is always "tired", who always refuses and does not help or want to help others.

ukunaka umutima: positive: to be meek; attentive; obedient; to submit; negative: unprepared even to lift a finger.

SEIC **is hungry** (*insala* – **noun**):

umutima wa nsala: negative quality of character; someone who is always wanting, continually demanding, (e.g. a glutton; insatiable in his wants and demands).

SEIC **is thirsty** (*icilaka* – **noun**):

umutima wa cilaka: to always want something, covet, thirst for something, (house, woman, car etc.).

icilaka wa mutima: feeling of wanting, desiring (continuous or temporary, weak or strong).

SEIC is injured (*ukucenwa* – *v.i. pass.*):

umutima ucenwa: negative quality of character; someone who is easily vulnerable; who has no defence mechanisms.

SEIC is hurting (*ukukalipa* – *v.i.*):

umutima wakalipa: the *SEIC* is hurting (mentally affected by a physical illness).

umutima wa bukali: negative quality of character; someone who is always complaining, in a rage over even small mistakes; a bad-tempered person.

SEIC has eyes, can see (*ukumona* – *v.t + i.*):

umutima walimona: positive quality of character; someone who can look ahead (a planner, a visionary).

(*ukulinda*):

A further nuance of seeing contains the word *ukulinda*. It refers more to the sphere of watchfulness, showing care, taking on responsibility for people.

umutima ulinda: positive quality of character; watching out for someone; to be caring; taking on responsibility for a person; being dependent on someone and hence being able to find comfort.

SEIC is blind (*ukupofula* – *v.i.*):

umutima walipofula: negative quality of character; someone who has little intellectual capacity, who is ignorant.

SEIC has ears, listens (*ukuumfwa*):

umutima uumfwa: positive quality of character; someone who hears, listens to others, is obedient; someone who does what he has been entrusted with; someone who listens when something is being explained; one of the outstanding qualities of *SEIC* as understood by the Bemba.

umutima wa kuumfwa: as above

(*ukukutika*):

umutima ukutika: A *SEIC* that is *ukukutika* is distinguished above all by its capacity to hear or to listen (e.g. student, counsellor, or pastor).

SEIC enjoys good health, is at peace, is restful (*umutende* – noun):

umutima wa mutende: positive quality of character; someone who is always concerned for peace, who always wants to keep the peace; a "peacemaker".

SEIC is ill (*ukulwala* – *v.t. + v.i.*):

umutima walilwala: negative quality of character; "never looking on the bright side"; someone who only knows sorrow and care.

ukulwala kwa mutima: disease of the SEIC that leads to certain outcomes (sudden irrational acts – "blowing a fuse"; mental collapse).

SEIC is infected (*ukwambukila – v.t. + i.*):

The verb *ukwambukila* means primarily "to spread" (like fire over the plain) or "disseminate" (of news). In relation to the SEIC it contains the meaning of "to infect" (influence and incite to imitate).

umutima walyambukila: quality of character; someone who is inclined to be easily influenced (above all in a negative way); to imitate another person, to emulate (in a positive and negative way).

ukwambukila kwa mutima: the infection of the heart manifests itself in the consequences of imitation and emulation (in both positive and negative respects).

SEIC is alive (*umi*):

umutima umi: to feel active and enterprising (even if risk is involved).

umutima wa bumi: positive quality of character; someone who is enterprising, accepts challenges, not averse to risk; a leader.

SEIC consumes (*ukulya – v.t + i.*):

umutima ulalya: positive quality of character; someone who is "insatiable", always wants to know more, shows interest.

umutima wa kulya: someone who enjoys eating and is therefore voracious, tucking in beyond measure, serving himself quickly and with the best of the food.

SEIC is weeping (*ukulila – v.i.*):

umutima ulalila: negative quality of character; someone who is always "crying out", always complaining, always feels at a disadvantage, always wails or breaks out in tears ("cry-baby").

umutima wa kulila: as above.

SEIC is crying out (*ukukuta*):

umutima ulakuta: to ask for help; to utter a cry for help out of great need, to call out in pain.

(*ukupanda*):

umutima wa kapanda: someone who always feels the need to shout out loudly (an announcer; "noisy brat").

SEIC is swallowing (*ukumina – v.t. + i.*):

umutima walimina: quality of character; in a positive sense: someone who "holds their tongue", under no circumstances gives anything away (secret); in a negative sense: people who always keeps things to themselves (e.g. news, knowledge, special offers at such and such a place etc.).

ukumina mu mutima: someone who takes words to heart, swallows them into his *SEIC*. It means taking a matter, a circumstance, situation so to heart that it leads to a resolution or decision.

SEIC is asleep (*ukulala – v.i.*):

umutima walilala: negative quality of character; someone you cannot rely on, who does not think matters or situations through. Euphemism: being dead.

ukulala kwa mutima: completely inactive, moved by nothing. Great apathy, lack of interest.

SEIC is lying down, sleeping (*ukusendama – v.i.*):

umutima nausendama: physical feeling; metaphorical idiom for describing fainting.

umutima walisendama: euphemism for death.

SEIC is growing (*ukukuula*):

ukukuula is a key concept in describing the *SEIC*. It can be seen as one of the central quality traits for personality characteristics.

umutima walikuula: positive quality of character; a mature person; to some extent the attainment of an ideal of adulthood.

ukukuula kwa mutima: the growth of the *SEIC*; indicates the process someone goes through in order to become a mature person (e.g. through instruction or through personal experience, personal study).

umutima wa kukuula: positive quality of character; to possess a *SEIC* of maturity; to be a mature, adult person. Can also be expressed as a desire (desiring to be old, because then the *SEIC* is fully unfolded and developed).

SEIC is old (*ukukota – v.i.*):

umutima walikota: negative quality of character; someone who feels old throughout their whole life.

ukukota kwa mutima: the state of being old is seen in the *SEIC* above all in its activities (e.g. being slow. Sleeping a lot, stiff muscles after working, etc.).

umutima wa kukota: someone who is always talking about age.

SEIC **of childhood (***ubwaice* – *noun***):**

umutima wa bwaice: someone who behaves like a child; to be childish.

ubwaice bwa mu mutima: someone who tries to be "young".

6. Metaphor of a Different Kind

SEIC **as a knot (***icikonko* – **noun):**

icikonko ca mutima: icikonko is a tree or bamboo knot. The metaphorical use can mean: someone is crushed by a load. More frequently with a negative connotation, e.g. *ukwenda ne cikonko ku mutima*, to run around with a knot in one's *SEIC* = to harbour a grievance against someone.

ukufwe cikonko mu mutima: to die with a knot in the *SEIC* = to die with hate or a grudge.

kukamba kwa mutima: impertinence, impudence, rudeness.

ukumanama kwa mutima: angst, terrified.

7. Metaphors of War or War Activities

SEIC **is making an attack (***ukusansa* – *v.t.***):**

ali no mutima wa kusansa: negative quality of character; someone who is planning evil; who is quarrelsome, who is always intent on doing harm to others.

SEIC **is fighting (***ukulwa v.i.***):**

umutima uulwa: quality of character; positive: someone who does not let go; to fight to the end for someone, for a cause; negative: to seize every opportunity to provoke a quarrel.

SEIC **is totally destroyed (***ukonaulwa* – *v.t. int. pass.***):**

umutima walionaulwa: to have lost control over oneself (as regards speech or action). Someone who has lost every criterion for living a good life.

SEIC **inflicts harm (***ukucena* – *v.i.***):**

umutima ucena: negative quality of character; someone who deliberately does other people down; person who on principle is always out for revenge or retribution.

umutima wa kucena: see above.

SEIC **plunders, robs (***ukutapa* – *v.t.***):**

umutima wa kutapa: negative quality of character; squeezing information out of people while under duress from others; someone who also uses violence in order to find out what he wants to know.

SEIC conquers, overpowers, subdues (*ukucimfya* – *v.t.*):
umutima wa kucimfya: positive quality of character; a conqueror; someone who will not be intimidated despite obstacles.

SEIC is conquered, overpowered, subdued (*ukucimfiwa* – *v.t. pass.*):
umutima ucimfiwa: negative quality of character; always easy to persuade; a person of no backbone; someone who submits all too easily to the demands of others.

SEIC kills (*ukwipaya* – *v.t.*):
umutima walipaya: quality of character (positive and negative); someone who can solve problems, who knows ways of surmounting difficulties.

umutima wakwipaya: quality of character; someone with the "killer instinct" when it comes to solving problems or surmounting difficulties. In a negative sense someone who "tramples over the bodies of others" and does not even recoil from murder.

SEIC has been killed (*ukwipaiwa* – *v.t. pass.*):
umutima walipaiwa: negative quality of character, someone who is not self-determined, who has no opinions of their own, who is controlled or directed by others.

SEIC tortures (*ukulungulusha* – *v.t. caus. int.*):
umutima wa kulungulusha: negative quality of character; someone who deliberately and with pleasure annoys others, makes them sad, inflicts mental pain.

SEIC is spying (*ukulengula* – *v.t. + i.*):
umutima wa kulengula: negative quality of character; someone who is always trying to get information from others; an "eavesdropper"; a spy.

umutima ukuilengula: positive quality of character; someone who keeps an eye on themselves; practises self-control; acts and speaks with prudence.

SEIC interrogates (*ukwipusha ipusha* – *v.t. repl.*):
umutima wa kwipusha ipusha: positive quality of character; always interested in what is being discussed; always wanting exact information.

SEIC gives orders (*ukupeele fipope* – *v.t.*):
umutima wa kupeela ifipope: quality of character (positive or negative): a director, a commander etc.

umutima walipelwa ifipope: quality of character; aware of a sense of duty; keeping to the rules and regulations; executing a task; honouring an agreement.

SEIC defends (*ukucingilila – v.t. and i.*):

umutima ucingilila: positive quality of character:someone who is always ready to mediate; someone who is prepared to defend the weak against the strong, the attacked against the attacker; someone who tries to reconcile two opposed parties; someone who tries to get the person who has suffered wrong to make peace; someone who can produce and mediate lasting solutions.

umutima wa kucingilila: as above.

SEIC is defended (*ukucingililwa – v.t. and i. pass.*):

umutima wa kucingililwa: negative quality of character; negative and declining attitude, unwilling to admit error; someone who always runs to his "big brother"; becomes weak and cowardly; someone who needs support or back-up.

SEIC saves, gives back, "disarms" (*ukupokolola – v.t.*):

umutima wa kupokolola: positive quality of character; someone who is concerned to protect others from harm; a mediator.

SEIC withdraws (*ukufuntuka – v.i.*):

umutima wa kufuntuka: negative quality of character; an insecure person; a coward.

SEIC hides itself (*ukubelama – v.i.*):

umutima walibelama: negative character trait; on the one hand a coward, but also a self-serving person; an egotist.

SEIC takes up arms (*ukwipangasha – v.t. refl.*):

umutima ulaipangasha: always armed, always equipped at all times, ready to face danger/ threat/ challenge, etc.

umutima waliipangasha: someone who is equipped and prepared to face any situation, (a teacher who can impart his subject at any time or place, however inconvenient – in school, en route, with or without book).

umutima wa kwipangasha: intentionally prepared for things, affairs, situations or people; feeling of confidence, security in making the best of any situation.

SEIC chooses the weapons, the method of defence (*ukusala ifyanso – v.t.*):

umutima walisala: positive quality of character; someone who knows how to defend himself at any time and in any situation and is equipped to endure it.

umutima wa kusala ifyanso: positive quality of character; someone who does not want things to be unclear, facts etc. twisted or skewed; someone who knows how to manage and cope even in the most difficult situation.

imisalile ya fyanso: the manner in which someone organises his defence.

SEIC aims, shoots, (and hits target, wounds) (*ukulasa – v.i.*):

umutima wa kulasa: positive quality of character; someone who always faces up to a situation; someone who always sets sights on something new.

SEIC measures off, weighs up (*ukupima – v.t. and i.*):

ukupima as a transitive verb means: to gauge or weigh something. As an idiom it also carries the meaning of to fathom, get to the bottom of something.

umutima wa kupima: positive quality of character; a planner; someone who always explores the options, even if it seems impossible to achieve (e.g. set sights on a particular car and wants to buy it without having the necessary finances to own it).

SEIC misses (the target) (*ukupusa – v.t.*):

umutima ulapusa: always being wide off the mark with an opinion or an approach.

ukukwata umutima wa kupusa, someone who is always off beam, does not grasp the essence of a matter or keeps producing defective work and is not aware how to avoid doing it.

umutima wa kupusa: negative quality of character; someone who, while always making a start with things, assumes that it will come to nothing, that his efforts will be fruitless.

SEIC is amenable (*bupete – noun*):

umutima wa bupete: someone who submits to orders, instructions and wishes. The quality is particularly valued with children. It can also mean someone is loyal, devoted, or willing and serious in what they do.

SEIC elevates itself (*ukusunsa pa cifulo*):

cifulo is the location where someone has their regular home, where one is happy (*cifulo ca mpomfu*). *Ukuba ne cifulo* conveys that someone has a fixed place, has established himself there. It also means to occupy a position. A misuse of position or power, e.g. enrichment, profiteering, is found in the idiomatic expression *ukulila mu cifulo*.

In the expression *umutima ukuisunsa pa cifulo*: a person who elevates himself.

umutima walisunsa pa cifulo: negative quality of character: a braggart, a boaster, a show-off.

umutima walisunswa pa cifulo. The opposite of the above. Someone with a sensible, wise heart and hence also receives honour and esteem. Such qualities are valued in political dignitaries (chiefs) or others in a position of leadership.

SEIC is taken away, frog-marched away (*ukusendwa – v.t. pass.*):

umutima wa kusendwa: positive quality of character; someone who lives for a particular cause or programme.

SEIC is frog-marched away (in prison) (*ukusendwa bunkole – v.t. pass.*):

umutima walisendwa bunkole: negative quality of character; a weak personality; someone who can easily be led astray, is easily influenced and is unable to make own decisions.

SEIC marches together (*ukwenda capamo*):

umutima wa kwenda capamo: positive quality of character; a friendly person; a sociable person, not a loner; someone who likes to participate.

SEIC makes peace (*ukupanga icibote*):

umutima wa kupanga icibote: a peacemaker; someone who looks for peace even if it exposes him to attacks or opposition.

umutima wa cibote: a *SEIC* of peace; a peace-loving person; as above.

8. *Metaphors of Permanent Psychic Dispositions which match Western Categories*

<u>Positive traits: Imibeele iisuma</u>

SEIC of straightness (*ukutambala*):

ukutambalala kwa mutima: uprightness, honesty, trustworthiness.

SEIC of mercy (*luse*):

umutima wa luse: to be merciful, empathetic; to have kindness.

SEIC of not lying (*ukubepa*): *umutima ushibepa:* a promise-keeper, keeping to the truth, telling the truth (e.g., in the court room).

SEIC of mildness, gentleness, humility, respect (*ubufuuke*):

umutima wa bufuuke: a mild, gentle, humble person; someone who has respect for others.

SEIC of work (*ukubomba*):

umutima wa kubomba: willingness to work, a workaholic.

Negative traits: Imibeele iibi

SEIC of duplicity (*wa mitima ibili*):

muntu wa mitima ibili: person of two *SEIC's* – a double-minded, uncertain person; a hypocrite.

SEIC of prosperity, honour (*ukutakalala*):

ukutakalala kwa mutima: pride, boasting.

SEIC of cleverness (*ubucenshi*):

umutima ucenjeshi: a cunning character.

SEIC of dryness (*wa buuma nkonso*):

umutima wa buuma nkonso: obstinacy, stubbornness.

9. *Metaphors of Psychic Disposition which match Western Categories to a lesser Degree*

Positive traits: Imibeele iisuma

SEIC – being widened (*ukukuusho*):

ukukuusho mutima: someone who comforts and arouses joy; in a more particular way helping to shape, to guide the behaviour of a person into adult behaviour.

SEIC – being pliable (*ukupetamo*):

ukupetamo mutima: to be still, quiet, noiseless; a more specific meaning has this expression in the context of obedience, submission. A child is expected "to bend its heart" that is, to be obedient to its mother.

SEIC of mildness, friendliness (*wa cikuuku*):

umutima wa cikuuku: in the specific context of someone who looks after somebody else without complaining or murmuring; someone who regards it a privilege to render this particular service.

Negative traits: Imibeele *iibi*

SEIC of avarice, of stinginess (*ukuba na kaso*):
aliba na kaso mu mutima: someone who is stingy or greedy especially when food is concerned.

SEIC of 'little talking' (*ukweba*):
mutima kaebele: someone who does not need the advice of others, an independent, self-reliant person. Someone like this is feared, because this is the character of a wizard who is not in need of any counsel and therefore poses a great threat to the community.

Homeless in the SEIC (*ubunununu*):
bunununu mu mutima: someone who has no dwelling place, a vagabond. For this reason, he has potential to pose a threat, since his *SEIC*, that is, his behaviour is not known.

Whimpering in the SEIC (*ukutefya*):
ukutefya mu mutima: a whimpering person; to be impatient, to act without much thinking beforehand, attracting the laughter of others.

Permanent and Temporary Metaphorically and Non-metaphorically Designated Mental Dispositions: Intellectual Processes

SEIC of thoughts:
umutima wa kutontonkanya: a thoughtful person; someone who acts after due deliberation and consideration, who processes everything in the mind; a thinker.

umutima uutontonkanyapo: to be careful; approach things step by step, think things through in the smallest detail.

balatontonkanya mu mitima yabo = they thought about it, deliberated on it in their hearts.

amatontonkanyo ya mutima wandi: the thoughts of my heart.

SEIC of drive, energy, wanting:
umutima wa kufwaya: to have strength of will (in the sense of carrying through to the end what has been started, planned); a doer (positive and negative); negatively: always wanting to do everything.

Then also "a wishful *SEIC*": always glad to participate actively; willingly make a contribution, get involved; wanting the best for oneself and others.

ukufwaya kwa mutima wa iko mwaliipeela = the heart's own wanting, desiring – you grant it to yourself.

SEIC of strong drive, strong wanting:
umutima wa kufwaisha: to be very strong-minded, great willpower.

SEIC of consideration, of compassion:
umutima wa kulanguluka: a considerate person; someone who does not act precipitately or plunge in; also a compassionate person.

Planning, conceptualizing, imagining in the SEIC:
ukupanga mu mutima: to "build" in the *SEIC*: plan, imagine, work things out in the mind.

SEIC of planning, conceptualizing:
umutima wa kupanga: someone who plans every detail, who considers and prepares everything (also when the matter presents itself unexpectedly or urgently).

ukupanga fya bubi mu mitima: to plan evil in the heart.

SEIC of leaning on what it speaks:
umutima wa kushintilila ifyakusosa: someone who thinks well before speaking.

wingashintilila ifyakusosa: do think before talking.

Synonym: *ukushinikishe fya kusosa*: to think before talking.

SEIC of understanding, insight, intelligence:
mutima wa mucetekanya: someone with insight, who has understanding, goes about things intelligently.

no kwalwilo mutima obe ku mucetekanya: bend, turn your *SEIC* toward understanding.

SEIC of understanding, listening:
umutima wa kuumfwa: someone who is intelligent; quick on the uptake; grasps things quickly.

SEIC of hope:
umutima wa kusuubila: someone who is optimistic, who sees the good, who has hope; a hopeful person.

SEIC of forgetfulness, absent-mindedness:
umutima wa cilafi: a forgetful person.

SEIC of trusting:

umutima wa kucetekela: positively: someone who fundamentally trusts people; negatively: a gullible person; a rash person.

SEIC of refusal:

umutima wa kukaana: a repudiator, a gainsayer; someone who is always opposed.

SEIC of refusing love, fondness:

umutima wa kukaanatemwa: "someone who always refuses to be liked", a difficult person.

SEIC of refusing consent, agreeing:

umutima wa kukaanasuminisha: "someone who always refuses to agree", wilful, self-centred.

SEIC of urging on, encouraging:

umutima wa kucincisha: a motivator; someone who encourages people (also without being asked).

SEIC which expounds, explains:

umutima uupelulula: someone who can present issues, can give guidance; who can give people a lead, introduce them in precise detail to a subject; an interpreter, an instructor; an adviser in the best sense.

SEIC is expounding, explaining:

umutima ulepeelulula: planning something minutely, considering every detail and aspect.

cali ku mutima = it is toward the heart, meaning: to have something in mind.

ukupekanya kwa mutima kwa buntunse = the intentions of the heart of man.

ukupanda amano kwa mu mutima wa muntu menshi ayashika: the advising in the heart of a person is like deep water (what a person contemplates, wishes, wants is like deep water).

SEIC which suspects (without sufficient reason), surmises:

umutima uutunganya: always having certain assumptions, always harbouring suspicions; to suspect with no good reason, proceeding from conjectures; questioning all explanations and statements; a mistrustful person; a pessimist.

SEIC which agrees, believes:

umutima uusuminisha: a "yes-man"; someone who is always in agreement (in a good or bad sense)

SEIC which spies out:

umutima uulengula: wanting assurance before letting oneself in for something; undertaking research before offering cooperation or help; someone who first ponders and then acts; a cautious person.

'Self-spying' of the *SEIC*:

ukwilengula umutima: to find, discover one's *SEIC*: to examine one's motives, one's conscience.

SEIC which imagines, invents, devises:

umutima uwelenganya: someone who is never short of ideas; a designer, developer, an inventor.

Negatively: someone who invents, fabricates issues, who proceeds from pure imaginings.

SEIC which is 'self-made'; self-assured:

umutima uuishinina: to "make" one's own *SEIC*: similar to self-assurance (e.g. unwilling to get into an argument because "you know on which side your bread is buttered"); to think and act independently.

SEIC which differentiates:

umutima uulekanya: someone who can differentiate, able to make distinctions.

SEIC which acts decisively, judges well:

umutima uupingula: "a *SEIC*, that can cut across, cut through"; someone with decisiveness; someone who can effect decisions.

SEIC which 'wakes itself', remembering:

umutima uwibukisha: "a SEIC which brings things to the surface"; a 'reminder'; (historian, story-teller, family custodian, etc.); someone who has an incredible memory – even the most minute details – and can bring to life the past, even in great detail.

SEIC is always in a state of change (*ukupilibukapilibuka bwangu – v.i.*):

umutima ulepilibuka pilibuka bwangu: to be continually changing one's opinion, intentions, plans; never able to come to a decision about something.

SEIC is suspecting, supposing:

umutima uletunganya: suspecting, imagining, supposing something; to see something is 'brewing up'.

SEIC is checking, verifying:

umutima ulelengula: checking, verifying if something is the way it appears to be.

umutima ulelenganya: just now imagining something, to picture something in the mind.

Temporary Psychic Dispositions (*imyumfwikile ya mutima – iisuma and iibi*)

Temporary psychic dispositions denote a present condition of the *SEIC*, and are expressed using the Present Perfect Tense.[3] However, as Janowski (2015) also notices for the heart in Hebrew thought, *umutima* as *SEIC* is not the source of positive and negative feelings and emotions, but rather the place where they manifest themselves. Again, the numerous metaphors language provides for denoting emotional states may be an indication of the 'need' a people group has to express these states in a very differentiated manner.

1. Metaphors of Form

SEIC is wide open (*ukwisuka – v.i.*):

umutima nawisuka: present condition – to be about to understand a thing or person; to have come to accept advice at this moment; feeling of openness.

SEIC is twisted (*ukunyongaana – v.i.*):

umutima naunyongaana: present condition – to have worries, someone who is anxious, troubled, bothered about something, to be nervous about something; to have had great concern; not to be doing what one was told to do, to act contrary to what was arranged.

ukwinyongo mutima: to distort one's own *SEIC* = be worried (discontented for whatever reason, be in a bad mood, get worked up over small issues).

SEIC is twisted, wrung (like wringing out clothes) (*ukupota – v.t.*):

umutima naupota: condition of being wrung out, to worry about something or someone.

SEIC is flat (*ukutambalala – v.i.*) (to be straight, to be flat, to stretch out flat):

umutima nautambalala: feeling of contentment, free of care, because for the time being there is no problem to face, no mental oppression; feeling good after a problem has been successfully solved.

SEIC is bent (*ukupetama – v.i.*):

umutima naupetama: someone who in given situations does not draw precipitate conclusions or get entangled in matters, who considers the facts sufficiently, keeps calm.

SEIC is known (open) (*ukwishibikwa*):

umutima uleshibikwa: someone who cannot keep his true self secret, is open through his speech or actions.

umutima nawishibikwa: whatever has come to light about someone's intentions or plans, his true personal nature has been revealed in it.

SEIC is linked together (united): (*ukwikatana – v.t. rec.*):

umutima nawikatana: someone who is so at one with himself that he has the courage to keep secrets, even when facing torture; feeling of being strong, of a desire to "keep shtum".

SEIC is blunt (*ukufuupa – v.i.*):

umutima naufupa: someone who simply has no desire to do something, to get drawn into a task, to devote himself to a matter; feeling of disinclination; someone who is lazy; apathetic, unreceptive of advice, suggestions etc.

SEIC is straight, upright (*ukololoka – v.i*): (to be straight, upright):

umutima naololoka: present condition – has integrity, does not deceive, deals honestly, does what one has been entrusted with in a particular situation.

SEIC is collapsed, shapeless (*ukukopoka*):

Metaphorically describes the 'collapsed' breasts of women after they have lost their form and texture.

umutima naukopoka: present condition – A 'collapsed' *SEIC* speaks of someone who is angry, and some other person is likely to feel his/her anger.

SEIC is diluted, is thin, slim (*ukusongoloka – v.i.*):

umutima nausongoloka: present condition – only thinking of one issue, totally preoccupied by one matter; only one particular issue on one's mind (have a beer, a particular girl, etc.).

SEIC is deep (*ukushika – v.t. + i.*): (to be deep)

umutima naushika: state or condition: having thought about something very deeply, having thoroughly considered it.

SEIC is shattered in pieces (*ukufungaulwa – v.t. pass.*):

umutima naufungaulwa: condition of great sadness (*umutima wandi wafungaulwa ku kufuluke,* my heart is shattered in pieces because of feeling home sick); strong longing for something or someone.

SEIC is closing, locking (*ukwisalila – v.t. appl.*):

umutima naunjisalila: present condition – feeling of being closed in, of having attention drawn elsewhere; being absent-minded.

Synonym: *umutima nauncilikila*

SEIC is being suppressed, absolutely devastated (*ukutitikishiwa v.t. pass.*):

umutima nautitikishiwa: condition of being suppressed (kept under, not getting a chance, not getting a chance to speak even though one has a good contribution to make).

ukutitikishiwa = to be oppressed; to be crushed down (by sickness or mental health issues).

SEIC has superposed me, 'has patched me up' (*ukwilikila v.t. appl.*):

umutima naunjilikila: my heart has blocked me, feeling of not going somewhere/ doing something.

2. Metaphors of Quality

SEIC is light (*ukwanguka*):

umutima nawanguka: to be relieved after dealing with a problem, to be free of worry, no longer feeling burdened, able to breathe again.

SEIC is heavy (*ukufina*):

umutima naufina: to feel weighted down, unhappy about something or someone, fear something which has not yet materialised, be concerned.

SEIC is sharp, pounding (*ukutwa – v.i.*):

umutima nautwa: present condition – to have reached a point of great willingness to carry out work of any kind.

SEIC is blunt (*ukufuupa – v.i.*):

umutima naufuupa: to be in a condition of refusing to continue with something; to have lost all interest in pursuing something; also to be not in the mood for trying again at all.

SEIC is cooled off (*ukutalala*):

umutima nautalala: present condition – after great tension, great anxiety and emotional shock, finding peace and relief again; feeling of being calmed down, 'cooled off' after completely wearing themselves out emotionally.

SEIC is rotten, decayed (*ukubola*):

umutima naubola: present condition of rot, decay; someone who is losing his/her good qualities, losing sense of justice; being unable to do good; endangering *SEIC*, to be beyond cure.

SEIC is melting, dissolving (*ukusungulula v.t.*):

umutima nausungulula: feeling of being moved, touched by something or someone. Also: being discouraged.

SEIC is dissolved (*ukusunguluka*):

umutima nausunguluka: present condition – to be discouraged, disheartened, drained = to be totally overcome by worries (*umutima nausunguluka, uli ngo ufwile,* your heart is completely drained, you are like a dead person) = completely full of anxiety.

SEIC is hot (*ukukaba*):

umutima naukaba: present condition – to be hot: to really go for something, to be 'on fire'; also: to be really agitated, to really say your piece ('spit fire').

Walikabile umutima wandi mu nda yandi – my *SEIC* is hot, caught fire in my belly (innermost).

SEIC is 'blackened' (*ukufiishiwa*):

umutima naufiishiwa ku mutima: condition of having been blackened to the core = incensed because of things said or done.

SEIC is clear (*ukulengama – v.i.*):

umutima naulengama: someone who shows that they are transparent in motive and intention in whatever situation.

SEIC is hard, strong (*ukukosa*):

umutima naukosa: someone who is able to carry on, continue to pursue a task, to cope with a situation, have a fighting spirit, pursue something with tough determination.

SEIC is tough (*ukushangila – v.t. + i.*):

umutima naushangila: a feeling of strength to approach any and every problem, feeling of confidence to be able to cope with whatever stands in the way.

SEIC is hurting (*ukukalipa*):

umutima naukalipa: condition of being angry, of being insulted for a brief time.

SEIC is blossoming, budding (*ukupuuka*):

umutima ulepuuka: feeling of creating something, to have, develop ideas.

SEIC **is supported, braced; a '*SEIC* brace' (*ukutungililwa*):**

feeling of support (*umutima wakwe walitungililwa,* his/her heart is braced, meaning: being comforted, nothing to fear).

SEIC **blazes (*ukwaka – v.i.*):**
umutima nawaka: to be happy, visibly in a state of bliss.

SEIC **cause to get accustomed, become familiar (*ukubeelesha – caus.*):**

umutima naubeelesha: to have got used to something for the time being, have come to terms with a situation, able to agree concerning a certain matter, to endorse a certain matter.

SEIC **becomes and is accustomed to (*ukubeelela – int.*):**

umutima naubeelela: to have got used to a person, matter or animal, so that one is no longer afraid of it; to have overcome initial fears, fears of contact.

SEIC **is beyond, at the end of brains (wisdom) (*ukupeshiwa amaano*):**

umutima naupeshiwa amaano: condition of perplexity: completely at a loss, not knowing what to do, even after much thought, being at wit's end.

SEIC **is inhospitable, hardhearted, selfish (*ukukaluka v.i.*):**

umutima naukaluka: condition of not being willing to forgive; bearing a grudge, even prepared to take someone to court, although the deed is hardly worth mentioning.

SEIC **is tired of, disgusted with, fed up (*ukutendwa v.t. and i.*):**

umutima nautendwa: condition of boredom: to be bored; having nothing to do; also, being bored with an activity (e.g. doing the same thing year after year, not having a change, etc.).

SEIC **is being suppressed, absolutely devastated (*ukutitikishiwa v.t. pass.*):**

umutima nautitikishiwa: condition of being suppressed (kept under, not getting a chance, not getting a chance to speak even though one has a good contribution to make).

ukutitikishiwa = to be oppressed; to be crushed down by sickness or mental health issues.

3. Metaphors of Rest

SEIC **is straight, flat (*ukutambalala*):**

umutima nautambalala: to be care-free, without sorrows; feeling of inner peace.

SEIC is resting, ceasing from activity (*ukutusha*):

umutima nautusha: resting, feeling of inner relaxation.

4. Metaphors of Motion

SEIC is standing up, raises itself (*ukwima – v.i.*):

umutima nawima: present condition – to have understood, comprehended something; to make sense out of the confusion surrounding a matter, to have woken up from the slumbers of ignorance, unawareness, etc., if necessary, through the help or advice of another, feeling 'to be on top of things.'

SEIC is leaving the path, is lost (*ukuluba inshila – v.i. and t.*):

umutima nauluba inshila: present condition – to have no awareness of what is happening, what is going on; to be in a condition of having forsaken that which is good and acceptable, e.g., morals, good behaviour; to have gone astray.

umutima nauluba: present condition – not knowing what to say or do, "be lost" in relation to what is going on around one; (e.g. looking for a solution as regards a particular matter and being totally at a loss = the more you look, the more you are surrounded by mysteries.

SEIC is astonished, shaken by a fright, 'jumping aside' (*ukucilimuka*):

umutima naucilimuka: present condition – to be positively astonished, 'grabbed by the heart' (e.g. *bushe, imitima yesu tayacilacilimukila mu nda shesu?*, did our hearts not 'jump aside' in our belly = did not our hearts burn within us?)

SEIC is scattered, confused (*ukufulungana*):

umutima naufulungana: condition of being flustered (feeling all over the place because of so much that has happened, not knowing any more whether you are coming or going).

SEIC is turning (*ukupilibuka*):

umutima naupilibuka: present condition – to turn, meaning not wanting to carry on, owing to fear or discouragement.

Synonym: *umupashi naupilibuka*

SEIC is thundering, shaking (*ulekunta*):

umutima naukunta: to be nervous (before taking a test, writing an exam; stage-fright, etc.).

SEIC is being beaten, aggravated (*ukutuntwa* – v.t. pass.):

umutima nautuntwa: condition of being restless inside (*natuntwo mutima, nafilwo kusosa*, "I am so restless inside, feeling beaten: I cannot even speak").

SEIC is fizzing (*ukusabuka* – v.i.):

umutima ulesabuka: answers, comments, proposals etc. simply effervesce out of the person.

umutima nausabuka: present condition – it has already sparked, ignited; a suggestion, idea, contribution, answer, has already burst forth (exam passed, etc.).

Also: *kwena mwasabuka* = someone who surprises others with the way he is dressed, "you look magnificent."

SEIC oscillates (*ukupeeleela*):

umutima ulepeeleela: working on a difficult aspect of a problem, the successful solution to which is still uncertain, the possibility of failure still exists, along with not knowing if it is going to work.

SEIC is falling down, falling over (*ukuwa* – v.i.):

umutima nauwa: present condition – no longer able to think correctly, everything one starts thinking about, reflecting on, having a negative effect.

umupashi nauwa = someone who is about to die.

SEIC is vibrating (*ukutetema* – v.i.):

umutima uletetema: to be moved inwardly, tremble inwardly, be uncertain (fear etc.) but not outwardly visible, not able to be perceived by others (*ukututuma* is stronger, because that mentality manifests itself outwardly, is visible – a shivering, shaking).

SEIC is happy, joyful, merry, contented (*ukusansamuka*):

umutima ulesansamuka: to be happy, be glad about something or because of something; (a good meal, a good experience, etc.).

umutima nausansamuka: momentary condition of joy, of being happy; being in a rejoicing mood (having experienced something good, beautiful, having enjoyed a good meal, etc.

SEIC is joyous, jubilant (*ukwanga*):

umutima uleyanga: to be enthused beyond all measure by something, to lose control over something and over oneself, possibly leading to problems; or by chance hitting on the right thing, on what has been sought, and being enthusiastic about it.

umutima nawanga: momentary condition of being enthused (still doting over it, really crazy about it, owing to a particular occasion or inducement).

SEIC is lighting up, shines (*ukusaamwa*):

umutima ulesaamwa: to be really elated, quite full of joy because of having experienced so much that is good, beautiful, etc.; to be happy beyond all measure.

umutima nausaamwa: momentary condition of happiness (because something good has been introduced, presented, etc.).

SEIC is praising (*ukulumbanya*):

umutima ulelumbanya: to praise, to give praise to someone (for what was done); in religious language to praise God).

SEIC is merciful (*ukubeelela uluse*):

umutima naubeelela uluse: condition of having forgiven; having already forgiven someone, shown mercy; having forgiven after being begged for forgiveness.

SEIC has (acquired) mercy (*ukukwata uluse*):

umutima naukwata uluse: condition of willingness to forgive, to forget even when someone has deliberately inflicted harm on one.

SEIC is overwhelmed, startled (*ukusunguka*)

umutima nausunguka: condition of being overwhelmed, startled.

SEIC is loving (*ukutemwa*):

umutima nautemwa: condition of love, fondness (for something or someone).

SEIC is hating (*ukupata*):

umutima naupata: condition of hatred, contempt (because of something that happened in the past; to be unable or unwilling to forgive someone for something and hating or despising that person ever since).

SEIC is angry, disgruntled, dissatisfied, annoyed (*ukufulwa*):

umutima naufulwa: condition of being disgruntled: annoyed because of some event (having been mocked, not taken seriously, scorned, etc.).

SEIC changes, alters, turns round (*ukwalula – v.t.*):

umutima nawalula: a person with a mental attitude that wants to change others (the people around him are all farmers, but he wants to change them all to become fishermen, etc.).

SEIC is running around (*ukwenda – v.i.*):

umutima uleenda: to have lots of ideas and thoughts all at the same time; to be full of one's ideas and plans, but not wanting to share them with others.

SEIC is made to reach (reaches) (*ukushinta – v.t.*)

umutima naushinta: present condition – being determined to go ahead, to do something.

SEIC orients (*ukulungamika – v.t.*):

umutima naulungamika: present condition – to have helped someone who has behaved badly to know what right behaviour is, to help someone back on to the right path.

SEIC reveals (*ukukupukula – v.i.*):

umutima naukupukula: present condition of being open-hearted, to have disclosed, communicated to another what someone knows either through words or deeds.

Synonym: *ukusokolola*

SEIC is drawn to, attracted to (*ukukondela v.i. appl. (-konda*):

umutima naukondela: to be drawn to, attracted *(umutima wakwe naukondela ku mwana wenu*, his heart is drawn to your daughter).

5. Metaphors of the Human Body

SEIC is strong, powerful (*ukukosa – v.i.*):

umutima naukosa: present condition – to have mental strength to continue an undertaking, a plan; feeling of bringing something to its fulfilment; to be confident.

SEIC is weak, flabby, limp (*ukutompoka – v.i*):

umutima nautompoka: present condition – feeling of slackening, being weak; lost all energy, lost courage.

SEIC is weak, without strength (*ukutentuka – v.i.*):

umutima nautentuka: condition of oppression: having little mental energy, feeling oppressed because of something bad that has occurred (quarrel, slander, insult etc.). It is difficult to entertain or cheer up someone in such a condition.

SEIC is tired, exhausted (*ukunaka – v.i.*):

umutima naunaka: present condition – feeling of tiredness: worn out after a task; to feel emotional fatigue: to be emotionally drained immediately after a long discussion or argument; longing for peace and rest, able to put one's feet up.

SEIC is irritated/ itches (*ukubaba – v.t. and i.*):

umutima naubaba: present condition – feeling of annoyance, feeling which rises up when one does not know how to pin down a remark, something which feels odd and easily irritates or 'itches.'

SEIC is hurting (*ukukalipa – v.i.*):

umutima ulekalipa: present condition – feeling of resentment after an insult, feeling cross after being insulted (a consequence of *ukubaba*).

Synonym: *umutima naulunguluka*: state of being uneasy; to suffer, to be ill at ease.

umutima naukalipa: present condition of being angry: angry about something (e.g. someone who has set your house on fire, etc.).

umutima naukalipa sana: present condition of being annoyed: having been vexed, insulted in the worst possible way and extremely enraged; to be beside oneself; to lose control over oneself (scream, go around roaring and even becoming violent).

SEIC is feeling pity, misery (*ukuumfwa ubulanda*):

umutima uleuumfwa ubulanda: to feel pity for someone, have empathy (if someone is in torment, lost a relative, etc.)

umutima nauumfwa ubulanda: state of feeling empathy (feeling empathy following a particular experience: also feeling sorry for oneself).

SEIC is lifeless, in a faint, exhausted (*ukutembuka – v.i.*):

umutima nautembuka: momentary state, feeling of powerlessness, feeling of having to let go of something which gives security.

SEIC is restored (*ukupuputuka – v.i.*):

umutima napuputuka: momentary condition – feeling of being refreshed; feeling alive again after some encouragement, preparation, mentally stable again, agile, mentally re-energised.

Anatomical: return to consciousness after having fainted.

SEIC swallows (*ukumina – v.t. and i.*):

umutima naumina: present condition – 1) to have understood (swallowed) something, be in the know about something, be in the picture 2) to know something but be unwilling to disclose it.

SEIC is eating (*ukulya*):

umutima naulya: present condition – feeling of being satisfied with what one wanted (news, a particular matter, etc.).

SEIC is 'satisfied' (*ukwikuta*):

umutima nawikuta: present condition – to be content, feeling of being "full": taking over an idea from someone that turns out extremely well, carrying out a proposed plan or advice with success, to "feed oneself" with ideas, proposals, plans, etc.

SEIC is injured (*ukucenwa – v.t. pass.*):

umutima naucenwa: momentary state of being insulted; also having suffered psychological harm.

SEIC sees (*ukumona – v.t. and i.*):

umutima ulemona: someone who, after a warning or advice, understands an issue and thus can appreciate what is happening; to be able to foresee something in its early stages.

umutima naumona: state of perception = to have so understood an issue that one knows what is about to come or apply, state of knowing, foreseeing or planning in advance.

SEIC is blind (*ukupofula*):

umutima naupofula: present condition – someone who is not in the position to understand or grasp an issue or situation, even if assistance is offered (explanations, being shown, etc.).

SEIC hears (*ukukutika – v.t. and i.*):

umutima ulekutika: someone who is keen to listen, who does not always want to add their own comments, or already claim to know what it's all about, what the solution is; someone who is interested in the other person, because the latter wants to give sufficient help, who only wants to listen.

umutima naukutika: state of having understood what it's all about, who has grasped what has been presented in the way the other person has intended, who is in the picture but has not said anything, not offered any comment.

SEIC is listening (hears) (*ukuumfwa – v.t. and i.*):

umutima naumfwa: present condition – to have understood, grasped what has been said; also, to feel something: pain, joy, etc.

SEIC is talking, speaking (*ukulanda*): *umutima ulelanda:* someone who is prompted to do or say something; also, to say what is on one's heart after having considered something, been advised or warned.

umutima naulanda: present condition – having said what was to be said (reflections, advice, warnings, encouragements, etc. which have already been expressed).

SEIC is speaking (*ukusosa v.t. and i.*):

umutima ulesosa: to express, make known reflections, plans, thoughts, warnings, advice, etc. *umutima nausosa:* present condition – to have decided, to be clear about something, to have fixed on a plan etc. which now only needs implementing.

SEIC is sleeping (*ukulala*):

umutima naulala: momentary state of absent-mindedness, not thinking seriously about anything, having no plans; also, being "a bit dim" (at times as a disease or a condition).

SEIC is weeping, crying (*ukulila*):

umutima ulelila: to be very full of worries; be very despondent; if nothing can be done about it, it can lead to suicide (extraordinarily strong emotion).

umutima naulila: present condition – feeling one has when something like that has befallen one, momentary state of cheerlessness, dismay, etc.

SEIC is gasping for air (*ukucilimukila – v.i. appl.*):

umutima ulecilimukila: to be mentally unstable; quickly becoming anxious again and again or be thrown off course.

umutima naucilimukila: present condition – to have been gripped by fear a short time ago or have experienced a fright.

SEIC is ill, sick (*ukulwala – v.t. and i.*):

umutima ulelwala: inability to be happy (e.g. because something has been stolen from you or you have suffered an insult, etc.).

umutima naulwala: present condition – feeling one has when something like that has happened, momentary state of cheerlessness, affectedness, etc.

SEIC is inflamed, infected (*ukwambukila – v.t. and i.*):

umutima nawambukila: present condition – 1) someone whom another person has stimulated with an idea etc., someone who has let themselves been affected by the good behaviour of someone else; 2) someone who has allowed themselves to be negatively influenced, someone who has taken on too much of something that is not really for them, not suitable for them.

SEIC is well, healed (*ukupola – v.i*):

umutima naupola: present condition – whatever problem or mental burden it was, psychological equilibrium has been restored, one feels good again, (e.g. someone obtained what was wanted, needed, etc.).

SEIC is growing (*ukukuula – v.i*):

umutima ulekuula: somewhat who is outgrowing childish behaviour, someone who shows maturity of behaviour, action, speech; but it can also refer to an illness (the heart is becoming bigger).

umutima naukuula: present condition – someone who shows maturity in a situation, whose maturity is visible and recognizable; who also feels they have grown up.

SEIC is old (*ukukota v.i.*):

umutima naukota: present condition – someone who can no longer do what they used to or would like to do; someone feeling their age; feeling of becoming old.

SEIC is on the point of becoming weak, is sagging (*ukunenuka – v.i*):

umutima naunenuka: state of wanting to give up (shopping trip – not finding what one is looking for); to give up the search for something, not wanting to continue.

SEIC is tired, weak, flabby (*ukuleeba, ukuleebela – v.i.*):

umutima nauleeba: present condition – to be weary, feeling exhausted, worn out (after difficult times, hard exams, difficult problems; after hard physical effort (the state arrived at after *ukunenuka*).

SEIC is depressed, dejected, tired out as sick person (*ukubongoteka v.i.*):

umutima naubongoteka: condition of being dejected, depressed; tired out due to sickness.

SEIC is tasting (*ukusonda*):

umutima nausonda: present condition – to have an idea, a notion, an inkling of what is in the air; to have a foretaste of something (first love; gathering first experience of something, get first taste of something).

6. Metaphors of War or War Activities

SEIC is killed (*ukwipaiwa – pass.*):

umutima nawipaiwa: present condition – to be insanely in love with someone, to be mad about a woman or man, to be blind with love and to be totally unable to think about something else.

SEIC **is frog-marched away (in prison) (***ukusendwa bunkole – v.t. pass.***):**

umutima nausendwa bunkole: present condition – to (have to) submit to authority; to (have to) consent to someone's leadership; feeling of defeat.

This phrase mostly refers to men, when under the thumb of their wives, who have no say at home; who have yielded to the leadership of their wives; men whose wives' wishes are their commands.

SEIC **has peace (***ukukwata icibote***):**

umutima naukwata icibote: present condition of freedom from care: to feel free from worry, have peace of mind again; sense peace again after a difficult time.

SEIC **is being attacked (***ulesanswa***):**

umutima ulesanswa: having problems or difficulties one after another within a short period of time.

umutima nausanswa: present condition – troubled mind, to receive worrying information, be disheartened, disillusioned, can lead to depression.

SEIC **defends (***ukucingilila – v.t. and i. pass.***):**

umutima ulecingilila: to speak up for someone, defend someone using words and arguments (feeling a desire or obligation to step in).

umutima naucingilila: to have stepped in (by speaking up) after a dispute and providing someone with support, help.

umutima naucingililwa: 1) anatomical; 2) someone who has received protection and support from someone (now feeling safe).

SEIC **takes up arms (***ukwipangasha – v.t. refl.***):**

umutima uleipangasha: to arm oneself for a purpose, to gear oneself up for a particular issue or task; sense of getting prepared, arming oneself.

umutima nauipangasha: present condition – to be armed, fitted out, feeling armed for dealing with something, someone who is expecting difficulties and has equipped himself, is geared up.

SEIC **chooses the weapons, the method of defence (***ukusala ifyanso – v.t.***):**

umutima ulesala ifyanso: to (continue to) reflect on how to defend oneself against something, what words to say, what tactics to employ, what facts, knowledge etc. to bring to bear.

umutima nausala ifyanso: present condition – having already come to a decision about how to defend oneself, how to build one's defence strategy.

SEIC inflicts harm (*ukucena* – *v.i.*):

umutima ulecena: 1) someone who persists in wanting to do harm = saying bad things about someone, having evil intentions towards him, insulting him, etc.; 2) who keeps on inflicting harm on someone (stealing, doing damage, etc.).

umutima naucenwa: present condition – to be harmed, seriously insulted, upset.

SEIC kills (*ukwipaya* – *v.t.*):

umutima nawipaya: present condition – to have successfully solved a problem, successfully surmounted something, etc.

SEIC has been killed (*ukwipaiwa* – *v.t. pass.*):

umutima ulepaiwa: someone who continues to be obsessed by someone, engrossed in something, and can then think of nothing else.

umutima nawipaiwa: present condition – someone who is in love, blind with love, can think of nothing except him/her.

SEIC misses (the target) (*ukupusa* – *v.t.*):

umutima naupusa: fail to see things clearly; fail to carry out properly what you wanted to do; be wide of the mark, fall short of a set target, miss the actual essence of an issue.

SEIC aims, shoots, (and hits target, wounds) (*ukulasa* – *v.i.*):

umutima naulasa: present condition – what you undertook has been achieved, has been attained through corresponding activity (someone wants to buy a goat or a car and succeeds by good financial planning; to be successful in what one has undertaken).

SEIC is being tortured (*ukulungulushiwa* – *v.t. pass.*):

umutima ulelungulushiwa: is being annoyed, plagued within a short time by what people have said and done, having had to get worked up about it and hence being unsettled, etc.

SEIC is destroyed, (spoiled) (*ukonaula*):

umutima naonaula: being in a state of destruction; great dismay - what you undertook was not successful, could not be realised, was shattered, destroyed, etc.

SEIC is being destroyed (spoiled) (*ukonaulwa*):

umutima uleonaulwa: become ruined (someone who has allowed himself to be infected with bad behaviour, bad habits, thereby ruining, "destroying" his or her character).

umutima naonaulwa: being in a state of ruin – someone who has ruined his character by what he has done.

SEIC plunders, robs (*ukutapa – v.t.*):

umutima uletapa: someone who within a short period of time tries to extract information etc. from someone, not even afraid to use violence (torture etc.).

umutima nautapa: present condition – someone who has got what he/ she wanted after using violence.

SEIC makes peace (*ukupanga icibote*):

umutima ulepange icibote: someone who is working at a peace plan, trying to bring about peace (e.g. by forgetting what was done to him, willing to be reconciled, etc.).

SEIC which spies out (*ukulengula*):

umutima naulengula: present condition – someone who is in possession of certain information, knowledge, and is keeping it secret till a later time, then making use of it to personal advantage (e.g. someone who is in love with a girl and finds out things about her – what she likes to eat, wear etc.).

umutima ninengulwa: present condition – I sense that someone is spying on me, snooping on me.

SEIC interrogates (*ukwipusha ipusha – v.t. repl.*):

umutima uleipushaipusha: to ask oneself if one is rightly prepared for something etc.; to "interrogate" oneself in order to assure oneself about something; then also to inquire of others, ask for advice, etc.

umutima nawipusha: present condition – to be already put in the picture, already knowing what is going on, already knowing the truth.

SEIC withdraws (*ukufuntuka – v.i.*):

umutima naufuntuka: present condition – to draw back from something, take back what was said, refrain from putting a plan into action.

SEIC measures off, weighs up (*ukupima – v.t. and i.*):

umutima ulepima: to find out if one is on target in what one is undertaking to do, to sound out what someone else's opinion or intention is; to question oneself critically, examine one's conscience.

umutima naupima: present condition – to complete one's findings and know what one needs to do a certain task, be able to fight a battle etc., end one's reflections and move to action.

***SEIC* walks together (*ukwenda ca pamo*):**

umutima uleenda ca pamo: mind and body in agreement; harmony between the desires, appetites of body and mind.

***SEIC* saves, gives back, "disarms" (*ukupokolola – v.t.*):**

umutima ulepokolola: to persuade someone verbally, dissuade him from what he intends, get him to change his mind (e.g. someone wants to divorce his wife, but is persuaded not to, etc.).

umutima naupokolola: present condition – to be disarmed = no longer able to carry out plans, ideas, intentions, because someone has found out about them and gone public about them; hence to be wary of implementing them, because punishment is sure to follow.

***SEIC* conquers, overpowers, subdues (*ukucimfya – v.t.*):**

umutima naucimfya: present condition – to have mastered a problem, successfully promoted an opinion or view (e.g. two people put forward a proposal about something but only one is successful, is accepted).

umutima naucimfiwa: present condition – to have been conquered = to have suffered a setback, suffered a defeat; then also to have been persuaded to do something negative (steal, deceive, etc.).

***SEIC* is active, lively, swift to respond (ready to dive in) (*ukusupa – v.i.*): (*ukusupila – v.i. appl.*):**

umutima ulesupila: to pursue something adamantly (how and where one can get hold of money), to cling like a limpet to something, not give up, pursue something with single-mindedness, simply have to possess something (a drinker wanting a beer).

umutima nausupila: present condition – to have attained something that one has unrelentingly pursued (someone who wanted to be a teacher and has stuck with it until he achieved it).

umutima nausupilwa: present condition – to divulge something under threat or pressure, hand over (money source, hidden income, etc.); to have something squeezed out of you.

***SEIC* hides itself (*ukubelama – v.i.*):**

umutima naubelama: present condition – to hold something back or keep hidden, out of shyness or shame; someone who is very reserved about sharing ideas etc. with others; then also to plan something bad, have evil intentions and conceal them from others (*naabelamika matontonkanyo* – he/she is hiding thoughts).

umutima naubelamikwa: present condition – someone who up till now has managed to keep himself hidden, either through cleverness or because of fear (because evil intentions are apparent).

SEIC withdraws (takes back, breaks a promise) (*ukufutuka* – *v.i.*):

umutima naufutuka: present condition – someone who has made known the intention of another, brought it to light (either with a desire to do him harm or in order to prevent something bad).

umutima naufutukwa: present condition – to have been betrayed, to have heard from people who knew nothing about it something that would not have been revealed publicly; to be aware that matters discussed within the group are not being kept secret.

SEIC keeps a secret (*ukusunga inkama*):

umutima nausunga inkama: present condition – to have resolutely kept a promise, a secret (where someone had kept their money, where there are good hunting grounds, etc.).

SEIC gives orders (*ukupeele fipope* – *v.t. and refl.*):

umutima naupeela ifipope: present condition – to overcome oneself, urge oneself on to do something; to brace oneself despite tiredness in order to work at something (even when it means to do something bad (to steal, etc.).

umutima naupeelwa ifipope: present condition – to be subject to a directive; to summon oneself to do something; to have a choice of two options (to do this or be punished).

umutima nauipeele fipope: present condition – to encourage oneself, give orders to oneself = force oneself to do something; pull oneself together.

SEIC elevates itself (*ukusunsa pa cifulo*):

umutima nausunsa pa cifulo: present condition – feeling, momentary condition 1) of "feeling important" (strengthened under the influence of alcohol) 2) to feel good, feel honoured.

umutima nausunswa pa cifulo: present condition – to have an honour bestowed on one; to have been praised because of a wise decision, clever and wise thinking and acting; to have good ideas and plans.

SEIC is fighting (*ukulwa* – *v.i.*):

umutima ulelwa: to strive with all means to attain one's objective, resist a temptation, solve a problem.

SEIC is spying itself (*ukuilengula – v.t. + i. refl.*):

umutima nauilengula: present condition – to have controlled oneself, reflected and weighed carefully before doing or saying anything.

Psychic Dispositions: Metaphors of Unusual Kind

Language truly provides its users with a tremendously well-stocked toolbox with which speakers may create wonderfully ornamented pieces of art. Metaphors are such pieces of art. What Bemba speakers may be able to create with and from their language for the benefit of the world around them has been shown in the previous passages. To underline this further, a set of rather peculiar metaphorically illustrated conditions of the *SEIC* are added.

ukutapwo mutima: **to enslave the *SEIC***
- unable to give up something, especially bad habits
- a spoiled person

ukwandiko mutima: **to oil the *SEIC***
- to cause mental illness, especially through witchcraft

ukusaamo mutima: **to suspend the *SEIC***
- be vexed, be annoyed
- an impatient person

ukushimo mutima: **to dim (douse – like dousing a flame) the *SEIC***
- to be sluggish, phlegmatic

ukuumo mutima: **to dry out the *SEIC***
- to be pitiless, stubborn

kubonsa kwa mitima: **a withered, dried up *SEIC***
- to despair, be absolutely discouraged

ukubaila umutima: **to level the *SEIC***
- to be inconsistent in what one says

ukusakana umutima na mafi: **to mix the *SEIC* with faeces**
- be vexed, uncontrollably angry
- to go away with a temper

ukucenuno mutima: **to chip/ chop up the *SEIC***
- hurt someone unexpectedly but sharply

umutima ulesalaba: **a wriggling *SEIC* – like cut tail**

- to have some anxiety, causing restlessness

ukobeka umutima: **to hang the *SEIC*** (like clothes on a hook)
- to be crazy about something or someone
- *epo akobeke umutima:* s/he has hung the heart there

umutima wa kubomfya: **a *SEIC* of use (usefulness)**
- to be able to supervise
- to take care of other's property

umutima ulya ico utemenwe: **the *SEIC* eats what it likes**
- no point in criticizing another person's choice

wampita mu mutima: **'you passed me by' in the *SEIC***
- you enchanted me, totally captured my attention, thoughts

bunununu mu mutima: **homeless in the *SEIC***
- someone who has no dwelling place; a vagabond!

wakungumanina we mutima: **plaintive, languishing appearance of the *SEIC***
- someone who is in misery, emotional pain (*ukukungumana* is used to refer to someone who is sick and sits with crossed arms across the chest)
- *cinshi ico wakungumanina, we mutima wandi?* (why is your appearance so miserable, sickly oh you my *SEIC*?)

ukutuuma kwa mutima: **the full-to-bursting *SEIC***
- someone who is proud (in a negative sense), arrogant, very boastful
- *ukutuuma kwa mutima kutangililo kuipununa* (the full-to-bursting *SEIC* – it will lead to its fall)

ukubulwa mutima wa mano: **to receive a *SEIC* of wisdom**
- someone who accepts advice
- *abulwo mutima wa mano uufunkana mu minwe* (who receives a heart of wisdom – greets himself, congratulates himself)

isha wasansamuko mutima: **causing the coming of happy, rejoicing, contented *SEIC***
- *lelo isha wasansamuko mutima mutebeto wa pe:* those who cause the coming of joy to the heart enjoy a perpetual feast, (to be in good spirits is a perpetual feast)

Umutima – Judicial Chamber

The Bemba language has no technical term, no lexeme for 'conscience' (though this word has its own difficulties across the spectrum of the social sciences – the psychological literature in particular). The fallacy, that because a language does not provide a word for a certain thing, object, living being or state of being, and its conclusion that this thing, object, living being or state of being does therefore neither exist in the physical world nor in the minds of people, must certainly be avoided. In other words, because a certain language is devoid of an equivalent word, for example, 'thank you', does that mean people who operate within the framework of that language are not thankful? Or in a language where there is no word for death,[4] as with the Unangan people of the Aleutian Islands, does that mean these Islanders do not experience death? Does absence of word equivalence mean absence of concept, absence of experience? Most certainly not!

Every culture provides for its members a local theory of life and death, of norms and values by which life is navigated through the rough terrain of living the human life. That being the case, a human person must then first acquire knowledge about these norms and values, align him/herself with these norms and values, and finally be able to judge, evaluate oneself in reference to them in order to be in a position to re-adjust, re-align oneself accordingly whenever that may be necessary (either self- induced or foreign-induced).

Swinging back to the absence of a lexeme for conscience in the Bemba language, how else could one capture the internalization of the norms and values, the process of assessment, judging and alignment with, and the realignment with the same whenever such case is necessary, if not by assigning these matters to the very centre of mental, emotional and psychological processes itself? If emotions and feelings, intellectual, cognitive, or volitional processes, and character attributes/personality traits are all '**SEIC-matters**', it is only logical that 'conscience-matters' necessarily become '*SEIC*-matters' too.

Umutima – 'Seat of Judgment'

Again, *umutima* cements its supremacy as the key psychological term by taking on, next to its 'triple-seat-functions', a further additional '***seat-function***', namely: the 'seat of judgment'. And it is *mu mutima* where 'judging' is executed. By this is meant that it is in the *SEIC* that moderation, censorship is executed; the thoughts, the actions (behaviour), the words, all are subject to monitoring and moderating processes. The collection of linguistic phrases provided here is but a sample and shall suffice to show the monitoring and moderating processes in the *SEIC* as well as being at times the interlocutor itself.

Linguistic Evidence – *Umutima* as 'Conscience'

umutima wandi taunseebanya: 'my *SEIC* has not shamed, despised me', meaning: I have nothing to blame myself for, my conscience is clear.

umutima mu nda: 'heart inside the abdominal region' (the heart of the innermost), meaning: to be conscientious, nothing to reproach myself with.

kampingu wa mutima: the judge of the *SEIC*.

ukupingula mu mutima: 'judging in the *SEIC*, to weigh issues' – to align oneself with norms and values, meaning: "to comply with one's conscience."

pa mulandu wakuti umutima obe uteku: 'on account of your soft *SEIC*' – because of having been touched, alarmed in the *SEIC*, meaning: because of your troubled conscience.

ukuilengulo mutima: 'to search oneself in the *SEIC*, to spy out one's own *SEIC*', meaning: to check motives, to examine one's conscience.

ukuiwamya umutima: 'self-beautification' of the *SEIC*, 'cleaning out of the heart', meaning: to undergo self-examination.

ukuisokolola kwa mutima: 'self-revelation' of the *SEIC*, 'self-disclosure' of the *SEIC*, meaning: to unburden, relieve the conscience.

umutima uwasanguluka: a pure *SEIC*, to be cleansed (acquitted) of guilt, be rid of taboos, meaning: a purified, cleared conscience.

umutima watetekelwa: SEIC of trusting, to be relied on – sticking to principles, holding to convictions, e.g. following one's conscience

camushinina mu mutima: conviction in the *SEIC*, meaning: being convicted in the heart of something e.g. the conscience has convicted.

ubulungani mu mutima: shameless 'promiscuity' in the *SEIC'*, meaning: totally without morals, morally decayed; without conscience.

mu mitima yabo batila abati: ico tucitile taciweme: in their hearts they said: what we did was not good; after reflecting, reasoning in their *SEICs* they realized the wrong they had done, meaning: their conscience smote them.

ukubuukuluke mu mutima: to break out again, appear again in the *SEIC*, meaning: to feel uneasy about something, something surfaced, a feeling in the heart; have pangs of conscience; also to change mind.

ukulakalaka no mutima: to be ill at ease with the *SEIC*, meaning: to have a troubled mind, not at peace with oneself, e.g. have a bad conscience.

'Conscience' – An Anthropological Theory

The overwhelming linguistic evidence establishes the Bemba word *umutima* as the solid base for it to be the prominent and outstanding anthropological key term. Part of this evidence confirms that '**conscience-matters' are indeed '*SEIC*-matters'**, and being '*SEIC*-matters', this 'thing' conscience consequently develops alongside the formation of the *SEIC*.

Enculturation and Language Acquisition

When a human being enters the world of other human beings, the child is exposed to and immersed into vital learning experiences. The new member enters a specific cultural environment whose governing principles and processes will be "fed" into the mental and emotional faculties, with the child also actively participating!, and internalisation of the same is achieved; not immediately – but a great deal happens during the first seven or eight years of childhood (see also Käser 2014b:101).

To be "fed" and to actively "wear"

To be "fed" culture and to "wear" culture, actively appropriating its elements, is what is termed as the process of enculturation (see Hiebert 1998:50; Kraft 1996:263). Contemporary anthropology has moved away from earlier conditioning and socialisation theories and understands "'the child' … to be an agent, actively engaged in constituting the ideas and practices that will inform its adult life" (Toren 2002:142). Of course, this does not mean that the child "can alone make meaning out of its experience. Rather, because humans are *biologically social* organisms, the process of making meaning is always mediated by relations with others" (:142).

Unmatched achievement

Similarly, language must be learned, which entails both: being taught and actively acquiring it. "Language acquisition refers to the process of attaining a specific variant of human language, such as English, Navajo, American Sign Language, or Korean" (Gleitman and Bloom 1999:434), and specific to this work, Bemba. The process of acquiring language is pretty intensive and rapid achievements are made. Gleitman and Bloom's (:434-435) observations on language acquisition can be summarised as follows:

- It "begins at birth, if not earlier. Children only a few days old can discriminate their own language from another, presumably through sensitivity to language-specific properties of prosody and phonetic patterning."
- "In the first several months of life, they discriminate among all known phonetic contrasts used in natural languages, but this ability diminishes over time such that by about 12 months, children distinguish only among the contrasts made in the language they are exposed to."
- "Between about the seventh and tenth month, infants begin reduplicative babbling, producing sounds such as "baba" and "gaga … Comprehension of a few words has been demonstrated as early as 9 months."
- "… first spoken words typically appear between 12 and 14 months."
- "At this initial stage, new words appear in speech at the rate of about two or three a week and are produced in isolation (that is, in "one-word sentences"). The rate of vocabulary growth increases and so does the character of the vocabulary, with verbs and adjectives being added and functional morphemes beginning to appear."
- "By the age of 3 years or before … children's utterances increase in length and complexity."
- "… close-to-adult proficiency is attained by the age of 4–5 years despite large differences in children's mentalities and motivations, the circumstances of their rearing, and the particular language to which they are exposed."

This striking achievement is unmatched. Gleitman and Bloom assert that

> "[n]either the natural communication systems of infrahumans nor the outcomes for apes specially tutored in aspects of spoken or signed systems approach in content or formal complexity the achievements of the most ordinary 3-year-old human" … and "children are the only things (living or nonliving) that are capable of this learning… " (:434).

Enculturation and Socialisation

Embedded in culture learning and language acquisition are the specifics of how to behave (one set of communication) and how to speak (use language – another set of communication) in a given cultural environment. This process requires steering and guidance "because children learning the cultural elements do not sort them carefully into the appropriate cultural matrix where the elements belong" (Käser 2014b:100). Also, this sorting process prioritises behaviour in the sense that culturally sanctioned behaviour takes precedence over some other possible behaviour. Through the process of enculturation children are socialised into the value system and the prevalent norms and they learn behaviour that is acceptable, from a cultural insider point of view, 'normal' behaviour.

> Norms are culturally determined patterns of thinking or sets of rules guiding human behaviour which are viewed in this way by the majority of those belonging to a culture; norms encourage by their observance what members would consider "correct", "decent" or "normal" behaviour. Norms are not necessarily rigid, since they allow deviations or have built-in tolerance for flexible application whenever the situation requires (:103).

Values are in a cultural sense

> … patterns of thought which develop what is considered worthwhile and worth striving for. Examples for values from Western cultures are prosperity, youthfulness, self-confidence, being slim and much more (:105).

Values are not absolute

Values differ and they may be treated as absolutes only in one specific cultural environment. Cultures clash because of conflicting values, that is, two sets of 'absolutes' may collide setting people up to oppose each other. If culture 'A' prioritises the intricate and sophisticated make-up of mechanical implements and therefore its need for maintenance for prolonged use, and culture 'B' prioritises its ceaseless use and constant availability neglecting maintenance (because it costs money and schedules ought to be observed), and since they are anyway not meant to last into eternity, people might find it rather difficult to operate and co-operate on the same plane. Some values are esteemed to be higher than others. "These are the *explicit* values … and include, in a Western setting, faithfulness, truthfulness, being slim etc." In contrast, "other values are cultivated less deliberately, and could therefore not be described so easily. These are the *implicit* values"; (Käser 2014b:106) (e.g. in a southern African context, if you lend something to another person s/he may 'borrow it for good'). Norms work in the same way; some are explicit, others are implicit.

Values create objectives

Because of regarding certain values as absolutes, we are prepared to fight or even suffer for them when a compromise seems not agreeable or feasible. In a less dramatic way, values can create great motivational power in stirring people to action. Hosting visitors and welcoming them into the home is a high value in Bemba society and on such occasions, people are stirred into action (especially the kitchen team getting busy to prepare food). "The fact that notions of value motivate us to action means that their impact is normative at the same time, e.g. they give a characteristic structure to our way of acting" (:106).

Values are hierarchical

Values are prioritised. In a Western setting "faithfulness has a higher value than being slim" (:106). In a southern African setting, being people oriented takes precedence over being time oriented. At times "values form complicated and substantial sub-systems" (:106). Again, within a southern African setting to follow protocol in recognising and properly greeting representatives of political or traditional authority in public space is mandatory and a set of values are attached to follow protocol. Taken to the extreme, to change or eradicate certain values, one would have to change or eradicate culture. The right to live a self-initiated and self-determined life, for example, as advocated by human rights, and the practice of Female Genital Mutilation (FGM), regarded as a fundamental value (and becoming normative at the same time) in certain cultures, where a self-determined life for girls, regarding this practice, is still out of the question for many, puts these value systems in diametrical opposition. To achieve self-determination in relation to FGM, culture change must occur.

Right and Wrong

Right and wrong are fundamentally tied into norms and values and their execution becomes an issue of ethics.[5] *Moral psychology* examines the main questions of ethics, such as what is "inherently valuable, what constitutes human well-being, and what justice and decency toward others demand" (Deigh 1999:561). Naturally, answers to these questions require broader examination of another set of themes, which Deigh (:561) specifies as:

- understanding of the primary motives of human behaviour,
- the sources of pleasure and pain in human life,
- the capacity humans have for voluntary action,
- and the nature of such psychological states and processes as desire, emotion, conscience, deliberation, choice, character or personality, and volition.

Studying these themes is principally to ask about the nature of the intellectual and emotional capacities of human beings, which supersedes that of animals, and that is why human beings qualify as moral agents. Moral agency is subject to moral assessment and that is why humans are morally responsible for their actions. But to be morally responsible requires capacity for understanding the moral quality of their actions and for being motivated to act accordingly. And what are the full capacities which qualify a person as moral agent? Modern ethics largely concentrates on the role and importance of reason in moral thought and moral motivation (Deigh 1999).

The Rationalist Philosophers – Kant and Friends

Deigh comments on the two schools of thought concerned with moral thought and moral motivation: One school says that reason alone, assuming its full and unimpaired development, is sufficient for moral agency; the other school takes a negative position. Kant, the rationalist reformer, and others in his trail, defend the former. Reason, they argue, works in a twofold way for human beings:

- instructing a person about the moral quality of one's actions
- but also producing motivation to act morally (:561)

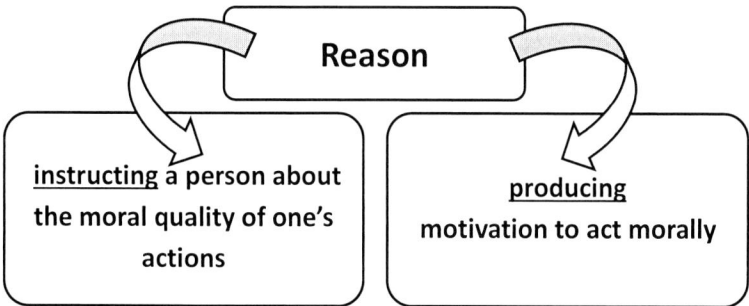

Figure 15: Twofold Way Reason Works for Human Beings

Motivation comes from two fundamental kinds of desire, rational and non-rational.

> Rational desires have their source in the operations of reason, nonrational in animal appetite and passion. Accordingly, moral motivation, on this position, is a species of rational desire, and reason not only produces such desire [figure left] but is also capable of investing it with enough strength to suppress the conflicting impulses of appetite and passion [figure right] (:561).

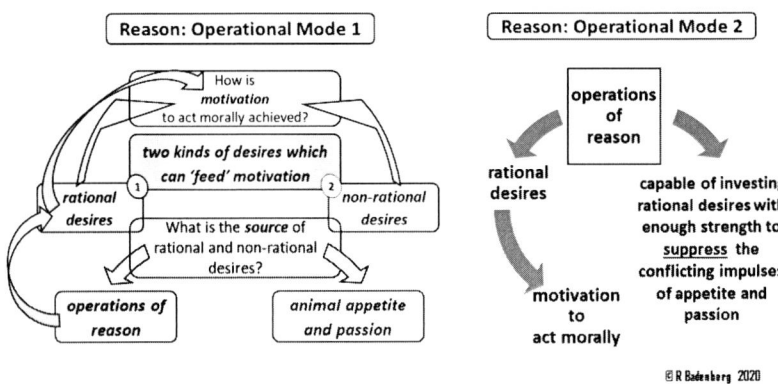

Figure 16: Two Operational Modes of Reason

For the rationalist, reason is supreme and "[m]oral agency in human beings thus consists in the governance of appetite and passion by reason, and the possession of reason is therefore alone ordinarily sufficient to make one responsible for one's actions" (:561).

The Empiricist Philosophers – Hume, Mill and Friends

The other school of thought is the empiricist philosophy quarters, for example, Hume and Mill who oppose the rationalist view in denying that "reason is ever the source of moral motivation and restrict its role in moral agency to instructing one about the moral quality of one's actions" (:561).

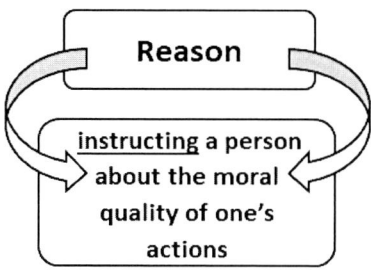

Figure 17: Reason – One-way Operational Mode Only

"On this view, all desires originate in animal appetite and passion, and reason works in the service of these desires to produce intelligent action" (:561); intelligent because the desires for objects are attained by well-aimed actions.

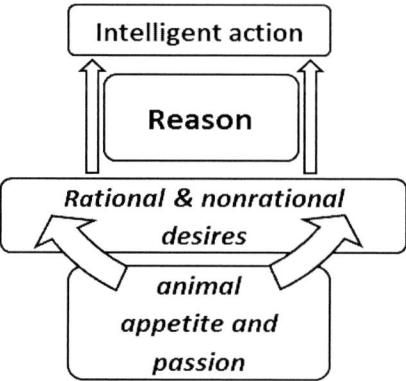

Figure 18: Reason in the Service of Desires

Consequently, moral motivation primarily focuses on the desire to act rightly and the aversion to act wrongly. These desires are not products of reason "but are instead acquired through some mechanical process of socialization by which their objects become associated with the objects of natural desires and aversions" (:561). Human beings act morally because of the cooperation among several forces, "including reason, but also including a desire to act rightly and an aversion to acting wrongly that originate in natural desires and aversions … and the acquisition of these desires and aversions is not guaranteed by the maturation of reason, the possession of reason is never alone sufficient to make one responsible for one's actions" (:561).

Learning the 'Dos and Don'ts'

What these two opposing views mean in relation to conscience is significant. Kant et. al, "make the independence and seeming authority of conscience the basis for attributing the phenomena of conscience, including their motivational force, to the operations of reason" (Deigh 1999:561).

What it also means, following Kant, is that reason is supreme, is innate in human beings and kind of exists supra-culturally. In relation to conscience, the Kantian school boldly asserts that "[c]onscience is not acquired. Every man, as a moral being, has it originally in himself as a relationship to himself" … and "[t]he reason, not the conscience, has to decide, whether an act is right or wrong" (Wiher 2004:49). But that is not the case. Reason is not supra-cultural (see A. MacIntyre 1988; L. Newbigin 1989), not something that exists outside cultural realities since reason is linked to language, ideas (cognitive foundations), norms and values, to knowledge that is learned, as all knowledge is culturally acquired (see Bosch 1991).

Toren (2002) argues that humans are biologically social. Hence, there is no need to uphold the distinction between biology and culture (Jahoda 2002) and go down neither the Kantian nor the Darwinian avenue. Rather, there is interrelationship between biology and culture, and being 'biologically social' calls for a closer look at socialisation as a thorough process, a primary force contributing to the formation of *SEIC* and this 'thing' conscience.

Käser (2014b) draws attention to a widespread misconception that "conscience is something given by nature to a person, a kind of organ which develops in a 'natural' way, independent of other people and influencing his social and cultural environment." (:110) But if culture "is the best milieu for understanding human beings" (Kapolyo 2005:117), then surely culture is also the environment where human beings become human beings in every aspect, which entails a great deal of learning. Every human society subjects its members to such a learning process and members "must learn how to conduct themselves in ways that are acceptable to their fellows. People articulate what must be learned as rules of conduct and lists of 'dos and don'ts'" (Goodenough 2003:2). Furthermore, people also learn to evaluate oneself and one's behaviour, and that of others, according to these cultural fundamentals. Ability to evaluate one's own behaviour and that of others is essential to living out culture, participating in its gifts, as well as recognising that it is essential to the perpetuation of culture.

With reference to the aforesaid, three opinions on conscience can be ruled out: 1) Reason is not supra-cultural, and reasoning follows within the logic of a particular cultural knowledge system. The basis of the phenomena of conscience cannot therefore be attributed to the operations of reason. 2) The distinction between biology and culture is an unnecessary and unfruitful one. Hence, 3) conscience is not given by nature, developing its capacity autonomously and independent of other people. The factual linguistic evidence in the Bemba context shows 'conscience-matters' to be genuinely '*SEIC*-matters', thus the 'thing' conscience develops alongside the ***formation of the SEIC*** and is part and parcel of the process of socialisation.

It was hinted earlier that conscience develops alongside the formation of *SEIC*. The "phenomenon of conscience has been examined by many different disciplines: philosophy, jurisprudence, theology, psychology, sociology, cultural anthropology and missiology" (Wiher 2003:30) and the question as to what conscience is, is beleaguered with an epistemological problem. The mechanisms by which conscience develops are equally widely discussed and cannot be pursued here in depth. I concentrate on what I consider essential elements for an ***anthropological theory*** of conscience, its development, and functions, especially important for cross-cultural purposes.

Culture and Conscience Orientation

Cultures have their own unique way of socialising their members. Cross-cultural studies confirm two basic strands of culture orientation differing fundamentally in how they set and mediate cultural goals: *Individualistic Cultures* vs. *Collectivistic Cultures* or *Guilt-oriented Cultures* vs. *Shame/Honour-oriented Cultures*. The designation 'Guilt-culture' vs. 'Shame-culture' ('Mead-Benedict Dichotomy', Wunderli 1990:18) is, however, too monolithic, too simplistic since no one culture is totally and exclusively one or the other. Rather, there is a prevalent orientation toward a cultural system which focuses primarily either on the individual or on the collective. Conscience orientation occurs within one or the other cultural orientation each with certain characteristic socialisation techniques and mechanisms, and consequently with differing outcomes.[6]

Proponents of recent socialisation studies (Hurrelmann 2006) define socialisation as

> The process by which the human organism, already fully biologically equipped, develops a socially capable personality, through interaction with the conditions of life. Socialisation is a lifelong adaptation to and involvement with one's natural capacities, including particularly the foundational physical and mental make-up of one's 'internal' reality, and the social and physical surroundings forming one's 'external' reality. (Hurrelmann 2006 in Werden 2013:185, translation from German DC).[7]

Werden (2013) adds two helpful, and in my opinion, quite important elements in the process, which she describes as

> … interaction with significant others and the act of appropriating their perspectives are decisive factors in the development of a self-reflexive und morally capable individual (:168; translation from German RB).[8]

The first important element is Werden's reference to the interaction with ***significant others*** and the second is the importance of the ***agency of the individual*** in appropriating their perspectives. Connected to these two elements is the factor of cultural goals which motivate the significant others to stage *their* interactions as significant others for the individual. Of similar interest is the question whether the number of significant others with whom a child interacts in the formative years of childhood matter.

Socialisation – culture specific

In his article on dual-income middle-class American families, McCollum (2002) pursues the issue "that couples find themselves pulled between divergent aims: meeting the demands of employers, on the one hand, and satisfying the needs of family, on the other" (:1). This tension is tied into certain perceptions, a primary (cultural) goal to be achieved, and directly affects child-rearing practices in middle-class American society.

As McCollum points out, child-rearing practices centre around the goal to instil in their children, in "subtle but systematic ways" that they should define themselves "by their innermost feelings, thoughts, and motives, and that their primary goal should be the establishment of an independent and unique self" (Rothbaum et al. 2000 in McCollum 2002:1). This systematic and persistent emphasis leads in the individual to a perception of self as a '"lonely navigator" who must eventually leave childhood attachments behind, and set out on a personal quest to cultivate innate potentials (Ikeda 1998:156 in McCollum 2002:1).

How do caregivers enable their children to define themselves by their innermost feelings, thoughts, and motives to eventually become an independent and unique self? From the findings of his study, McCollum presents following scenario. Being tied to work obligations and committed to family relationships at the same time places parents under tension, that is, on the one hand to utilize regular and prolonged periods of separation, and on the other hand, to promote and foster individuation of the child.

> "The sharp division that middle-class American caregivers create between isolated sleep and socially excited wakefulness is assumed by them to be a necessary and natural ordering of the infant's interpersonal world" (2002:3).

The child also experiences these competing aims as dynamic tension in as much as the 'rewards of the independence of the self' is countered by a growing desire for closeness and togetherness. From the age of two years, children are encouraged and stimulated to explore and discover their environment and with it raise the level of motivation to act in self-determined ways. This inevitably leads to a distancing between them and their significant others. Self-initiative and self-propelled activity attract rewards in terms of verbal praise of achievement by the parents/caregivers (active social exchange). For example, parents incorporate their children into tasks and chores, and after the task has been accomplished, entirely credit the child for its completion (:2).

McCollum observes:

1. outstanding were the patterns of interaction, that is, "how little physical contact middle-class caregivers have with their children."… "Caregivers hold infants infrequently and make frequent use of playpens and other equipment" (:3).
Reasons given were: a) "how important it is for the infants to have their own physical space" and b) "[a]s long as infants receive frequent bouts of visual and verbal stimuli, caregivers reason, they

are fine to spend long periods on their own sleeping or resting" (:3).
2. how often middle-class parents/caregivers engage with their "infants in repeated, intense forms of psychological connection," for example, "chatter in highly stylized ways with their infants, assured that they are communicating with them – emotionally if not linguistically" (:3).
Reasons given were: a) "they stress how they are trying to 'share' with their infants" and b) "imbue their infants with a sense of well-being" (:3).

As children mature, parents still insist on a stringent continuation of balancing "the competing goals of instilling separateness and cultivating closeness," and the "dominant cultural message that the caregivers … communicate to their children," says McCollum, "is that steady progress toward an individuated sense of self is essential for becoming a good and worthy person" (:5) but entails as flip-side: "progression toward autonomy – or separation from others" (:2). As the child grows older, the capacities for self-regulation and self-direction increase and

> … enable the child to meet this goal, increasingly demonstrate the characteristic that is considered the hallmark of emotional maturity in this society: namely, the ability to maintain emotional stability and self-esteem in the absence of external support and recognition (:5).

In addition, parents/caregivers also "insist that this healthy independence cannot be cultivated without a strong, ongoing interpersonal bond with important others, especially parents" (:5).

Résumé:
1. Child-rearing practices and modes of socialisation are culture specific (see also Mesman et. al. 2018, a recent study among the rural Gusii in Kenya).
2. They are based on certain cultural values, which aim to achieve a cultural goal, and are, through the process of socialisation, instilled into children, deeply informing their behaviour, their thought-patterns, and their emotional inner world.
3. Culture specific modes of socialisation also instil in a person a characteristic sense of self.

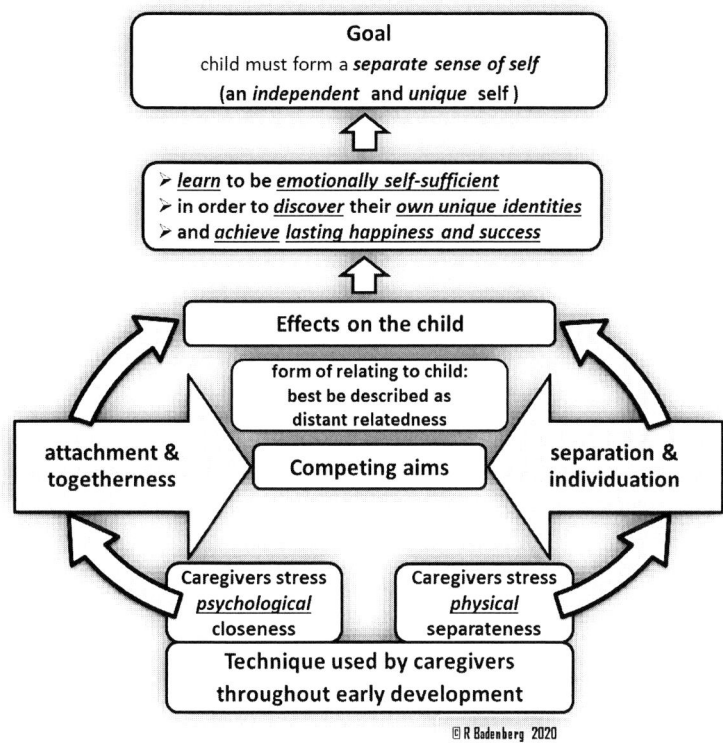

Figure 19: Middle-class American Child-rearing Techniques

In contrast to a highly individualizing socialisation process there are other, radically different approaches to socialise children into family, community, and society at large. McCollum, drawing on research by LeVine et. Al. (1994), draws attention to the fact that other cultures (like the rural Gusii in Kenya) stress different strategies:

- very close body contact with their infants all the times, day and night
- relatively little attention paid to the infant as an emotionally responsive being, in terms of eye contact, smile elicitation, and "vocal tones coded by Americans as forms of warmth and affection" (LeVine et al. 1994:255 in McCollum 2002:4).
- instead, caregivers strive in every way possible to soothe distress and calm excitement (:4).

Mesman et. al. question the level of supposed lack of sensitive care as proposed by LeVine et. al. who previously looked for markers such as "verbal interaction, warmth, and eye contact," which are, according to Mesman et. al., "not the defining features of sensitive caregiving" (Mesman 2018:7). However, they confirm that child-rearing practices with infants happen mostly "non-verbally in the form of (subtle) physical responsiveness by a variety of caregivers and seen to a high extent during infant feeding" (:1). Among the rural Gusii communities studied

> [a] general socialization goal of fostering optimal child development may include careful monitoring of infant needs and responsiveness to those needs, but also more harsh controlling strategies that teach the infant the behavioral boundaries that are important to maintain in a particular cultural community (:7)

Bemba child-rearing practices are certainly more in line with the studied Gusii communities in Kenya, which might by mere observation and lack of cultural insight appear as rather passive modes of caregiving (see section "*Umutima* – from *akatuutu* to *umuntu utuuntulu*").

The impact of cultural goals

What can certainly be deduced from this glimpse of cross-cultural material is a positive affirmation of the importance of cultural goals, which motivate the significant others to model and guide *their* interactions as significant others for the child. Also, the systematic way of instilling an individuated sense of self (middle-class America) may in a general way be indicative of Western cultures and allow for proposing that relatively *few significant others* (foremost parents) are part of this process. In contrast, collectivistic societies in general fall back on a ***greater number of significant others***, a variety of caregivers (e.g. Gusii and Bemba communities) or as Roland (2002) demonstrates with childrearing practices among Hindu extended families in Southeast Asia, all of whom reinforce and guide the socialisation of a child. A Japanese cultural setting looks at failure to treat others with proper respect and tactfulness as the worst possible behaviour (Wunderli 1990:78). For Japan, the cultural goal is to produce well-behaved and polite individuals. Other Asian cultures, too, emphasise the significance of the community, and parents use the group as reference for the children to check one's behaviour. The children model the attitude of their parents and "learn to fear possible negative opinions of others, particularly of those who are viewed as superior" (:110).

Naturally, differing socialisation techniques not only manage to produce well-adapted and well-functioning adults according to their specific cultural context, but they also affect the structure and dynamics of a person's emotional world. Two such powerful human emotions are guilt and shame and deserve a closer look.

Emotions – Guilt and Shame

June Gruber in her lecture on "Human Emotion: Shame and Guilt" (2013) elaborates on several relevant aspects of guilt and shame. She states that both emotions are socially painful and are part of the family of self-conscious or moral emotions. At birth humans do not yet have them at their disposal but acquire them with culture learning and they later form a powerful role in life. Gruber further explains on the characteristics of guilt and shame:

Characteristics of guilt:

The *Elicitor* (negative evaluation of a certain action) → causes certain *Behaviour* (negative emotion towards target) → *Consequence* (motivation to address problem).

Characteristics of shame:

The *Elicitor* (negative evaluation of self as a whole) → causes a certain *Behaviour* ('sense of smallness', hide from social group) → *Consequence* (less likely to take corrective action to address problem).

Gruber rightly points to important and significant cross-cultural differences in relation to shame.

Cross-cultural differences: Shame

Individualistic cultures	Collectivistic cultures
• self-identity separates from others • individual standards of norms	• self-identity cannot be separated from others • interpersonal standard of norms Role of Shame: • highly valued – esteemed as an emotion • hypercognized – plays a major role in daily life

| | • often leads to behavioural changes, motivated to fix group norm violation |

Figure 20: Cross-cultural Differences of Shame
Source: Gruber 2013

Of course, there is no one-cut cultural pattern on how shame plays out in the lived-in world even within the context of collectivistic or shame-oriented cultures. The role cultural specifics operate in the way emotions are elaborated is crucial. Nuckolls states that as human beings we are all born "with the same repertoire of basic emotions" (1996:64). But falling back on Gregory Bateson (*Naven* 1936) and his discussion on Iatmul "pride," Nuckolls concludes that "Iatmul 'pride'… is still pride as we know it, but to understand it is to take into account the *unique ways* (italics mine) in which it has been elaborated by Iatmul culture" (1996:64 in Badenberg 2008:241-242).

Matsumoto (1985) distinguishes two aspects of shame (*haji*) in Japanese society. He speaks of

> … *disgrace-haji* characterizing it as feeling vulnerable and weak toward others, connected with a negative self-evaluation and low self-esteem. It is associated with inconsistency or in congruency with the claimed social status and may result in losing face and humiliation. It also shames those belonging to the same group. It might result in committing suicide in order to restore lost honor. *Disgrace-haji* is regarded as social sanction, disrupting relationships and generating self-condemnation because of the wrong behavior. It is frequently employed as a sanction by the process of socialization (in Wunderli 1990:76).

A second aspect of shame Matsumoto calls *embarrassment-haji*. It arises when one experiences attention and exposure and makes a person feel uncomfortable and "sticking out" from the rest, "which is related to an uncertainty of relational distance (ma); a discrepancy between 'self' and 'other'" (Wunderli 1990:77). In contrast to *disgrace-haji*, Matsumoto asserts that *embarrassment-haji* has basically

> … no social sanctions, but only social functions: either as a starting point for developing new relationships, or to disrupt it. However, in a society where harmony and unity constitute the

core values, such 'discretion-shame' becomes a moral force sustaining personal and social order (in Wunderli :77).

Continuing with Gruber, guilt and shame share similarities but are also marked with differences. Gruber explains:

Guilt and Shame – Similarities:

- both are in the family of self-conscious or moral emotions
- associated with wrongdoing
- promote pro-social or altruistic behaviour
- they are experienced socially (self in the context of others)

Guilt arises on account of specific behaviour perceived by self and others perhaps as wrong. Shame, on the other hand, is not concerned with specific (wrong) behaviour but focuses on a global sense of self-evaluation that is negative, inherently flawed, wrong, or defective in some way. Nevertheless, the similarities between guilt and shame do not mean they are interchangeable, or one can be substituted for the other. Gruber draws out important differences between guilt and shame emotions.

Guilt and Shame – Salient differences:

Local vs. global focus

Guilt	Shame
• local behaviour: feeling bad about specific behaviour • "How could I have done *that*?" • there is something wrong with what I did	• global disposition: feeling bad about oneself • "How could *I* have done that?" • there is something wrong with me overall

Figure 21: Local vs. Global focus

Source: Gruber 2013

Potter-Efron situates shame in a shame/pride continuum and guilt in a guilt/moral pride continuum (1989:18,145f.).

> Shame issues involve [an individual's] identity, his whole self. In contrast, guilt refers to specific actual or contemplated behaviors of that individual. The shamed individual laments, 'How could *I* have done that?' while the guilty person asks, 'How

could I have done *that?'"* (1989:2 italics in original in Wiher 2004:71).

There are other differences between guilt and shame emotions and how both motivate people in terms of dealing with the effects of them. Two examples:

Motivation to amending vs. hiding behaviour

Guilt	Shame
• amending behaviour • motivation to address problem • apologize, undo, repair ("Face the music")	• hiding behaviour • motivation to hide problem • disappear or hide or escape from shame situation ("duck the heat")

Figure 22: Motivation to Amending vs. Hiding Behaviour
Source: Gruber 2013

Defensive vs. Non-defensive response

Guilt	Shame
• non-defensive response • more rational approach (discussing, acting) • manage anger constructively and proactively	• defensive response • more prone to blame others (way to escape the shame feeling) • prone to increased anger and aggressive behaviour

Figure 23: Defensive vs. Non-defensive Response
Source: Gruber 2013

Guilt-oriented vs. Shame-oriented Conscience

The existence of these two powerful human emotions is a universal given for all human cultures, albeit their expression and elaboration is culture specific. The cultural goals of the significant others guiding and determining their interactions with children in the formative years in their lives, with the child's active participation in this process, produce in the individual a certain sense of self as well as establishing a certain pattern of how to deal with the self-conscious emotions of guilt and shame. Lewis (1992) asserts that

> knowledge of standards, rules and goals, and the evaluation of behaviour in relation to these standards and to self becomes then the cause for self-conscious emotions, that is, shame (:85),

and is pretty much developed "toward the end of the third year (1992:48, 66, 94 in Wiher 2003:79).

And, as Wiher rightly emphasises: "It is obvious that one can only study conscience from one's own conscience orientation" (Wiher 2003:31) and people may be at odds with a differing one. Westerners may negate the importance of shame in their own cultures but Hilgers (1996) suggests:

> Shame – in digestible fractions – is the guardian of self and of self-limits; it is the feeling without which there is no personal development and no successful psychotherapy, no identity and no healthy search for autonomy. But it is also the feeling which causes regression, isolation, destruction, and violence, once out of control (:24 in Wiher 2003:84).

There is also agreement in the literature that the number of significant others who instil certain cultural goals, and with it, acceptable behaviour, matters. With reference to individualistic cultures it is important to note "that the parents themselves nearly exclusively constitute the significant others whose punishment is feared and whose principles become internalized" (Wunderli 1990:109). What this means for the development of conscience is that the "guilt-oriented conscience feels guilt as the significant other is introjected" (Wiher 2003:158). In other words, a child introjects the norm as well as the significant other who is so to say the embodiment of the norm. The type of conscience which develops in this kind of cultural environment is called *super-ego*.

Regarding collectivistic cultures the group is the prominent reference for behaviour and later for the social functioning of an individual. Consequently, shame features prominently in the affairs of daily life and a "shame-oriented conscience feels anxiety as expectation of abandonment, and shame only after the discovery of the violation" (Wiher 2003:158). The type of conscience which develops in this kind of cultural environment is called *ego-ideal*.

It was stressed earlier that only two aspects of an anthropological theory of conscience, its development and functions, especially important for cross-cultural purposes, will be considered in this work. Developmental factors of conscience were addressed showing that individualistic or guilt-oriented culture and collectivistic or shame/honour-oriented cultures, because of differing operating cultural goals, differing child-rearing techniques and the number of significant others, lead in their members to also acquire a culture specific conscience-orientation. If there is noticeable difference in the acquisition of a certain conscience-orientation – can it be expected that the functions of this 'thing' conscience are similarly diverse or is there an over-arching communality across cultural boundaries and cultural specifics? And, if 'yes', what are the salient features of the functions of conscience constituting an anthropological theory of conscience?

An Anthropological Theory of Conscience According to Käser

Consciences guide a person's *social behaviour* according to existing standards and values (Käser 2014b:111) – and there is no human culture on earth which is without them!

In aligning oneself with what is deemed right or wrong, good or bad, conscience fulfils important *social functions*. Without such categories and the need to adhere to them, "society cannot be maintained as a coherent structure" (:112). This is true universally! Käser terms this the "horizontal dimension of conscience" (:112).

In relation to behaviour that is deemed good or bad but falls under a higher jurisdiction (transcendental authority, deity, God), conscience takes on *religious functions"* ... Käser calls this "the vertical dimension of conscience" (:112). There are probably very few human cultures where this aspect is totally obsolete.

Conscience evokes the *moral laws* (:112) to bear upon an individual touching him or her emotionally, and also motivating him or her to carry out certain actions. Living out culture is to advocate for or promulgate a specific variant of moral laws. There is no human culture without moral laws!

<u>Universal communalities – affirmative</u>

The question whether there is an over-arching communality across cultural boundaries and cultural specifics of this 'thing' conscience can be answered in the affirmative. Therefore, we now need to specify the salient features of the functions of conscience constituting an anthropological theory of conscience.

<u>Universal functions – affirmative</u>

Despite the significant differences in how the moral emotions of guilt and shame are culturally elaborated, and therefore giving guidance to certain differing patterns of behaviours, the way deviating behaviour is monitored by a powerful inner sensor ('conscience)', has but one single *modus operanti*. That is to say, the single *modus operanti* is strictly referenced in terms of the functions of this inner apparatus and has universal validity.

Käser states: "In all human societies a grown adult's developed conscience has the following functions" (:114):

> 1) It **examines** actions, whether planned or already committed, to see if they harmonize with the norms of the society, group etc., or not. It is irrelevant whether an action or behaviour has already occurred or is only intended.
>
> 2.1) It **signals** compliance with these norms through a feeling of having done right or wrong. Actions and behaviour examined by conscience are revealed as good, proper or conforming to the norms. The feeling that results is popularly called "good conscience".
>
> 2.2) It **signals** non-compliance with these norms through the person feeling they are doing wrong, or that they have done wrong. Actions and behaviour examined by conscience are revealed as bad, improper or offending social norms. The resultant feeling is popularly called "bad conscience". This is held to be a **punishment**.
>
> 3) It **controls** the person through feelings of bad conscience and (generally) **prevents** offences against social norms by creating an expectation of punishment.

Figure 24: An Anthropological Theory of Conscience According to Käser
Source: Käser 2014b:114

'Conscience' – 'Vox Dei'?

Conscience is almost as tricky, if not problematic, a term to define as is the term culture (Kroeber and Kluckhohn 1952; Nuckolls 1996). What angle, perspective or definition gets it right? The omnipresence of this 'thing' among the cultures of the world can hardly be denied (although it is not that easily accepted either). The 'inner voice' as specific human experience that alarms people on account of intended or done actions, as spoken words or merely non-verbalised thoughts which 'miss the mark', is a universal phenomenon.

Differing Perspectives

A Darwinian perspective associates the formation of the 'inner voice' as a biological aspect of our evolutionary history as homo sapiens. A psychological, Freudian, perspective looks at the whole person as a psychic apparatus whereas others view humans as moral beings and posit a religious reason for the presence of the 'inner voice' and call it 'conscience', to some a divine vestige of some sort.

This section concentrates on a specific religious view, on Christian Theology which accommodates within its diverse and long history a similarly diverse range of opinions on this subject. The recent heightened interest in this field presents itself in new course-subjects with new terminology, calling it *Elenctics* (Elenktik in German), for example, Klaus Müller's voluminous publication *'Das Gewissen in Kultur und Religion'* (2010) or Hannes Wiher's elenctical study of *'Shame and Guilt' in cross-cultural contexts* (2003). However, I will narrow the field to concentrate on the understanding of conscience as *vox dei* (God's voice), which seems an interesting enough topic for study.

Eckstein (1983), in his theological-exegetical investigation into the usage of the Greek word συνείδεσις (*suneidesis* - 'conscience'), lists 14 occurrences in the New Testament writings of the apostle Paul for the Ionian verbal noun ἡ συνείδεσις (*syneidesis* – the 'conscience') and one occurrence of the reflexive term σύνοιδα ἐμαυτῶ (*sunoida emautou*, to know, be conscious of myself). The noun participle τό συνειδός (*to suneidos*) of Attic origin, and a synonymous term, is totally absent from Paul's writings as are the contemporaneous paraphrases of conscience as "observer", "witness", "convictor", "solicitor" or "judge". In other words, Paul deviates significantly in his usage of 'conscience' from common contemporaneous usage, and therefore its meanings, of this term. Instead, he uses *syneidesis* always in an absolute sense!, meaning *authority* (:311).

The function of *syneidesis* in terms of 'testifying,' 'confirming,' is explicitly mentioned in two passages (Romans 9:1 and 2 Cor. 1:12). Elsewhere, each time the contexts in which the term is used describe the task and the meaning of *syneidesis* in its absolute sense, since Paul does not consider a deeper, precise description of it by employing other possible grammatical devices (e.g. qualifying adjectives) (:311).

Paul's Unique Usage of Syneidesis

Outstanding is Paul's nuanced but uniform usage of *syneidesis* as authority. In doing so he <u>excludes</u> the term's etymological root 'co-knowing' as well as its abstract designation consciousness as regards its rational, intellectual, moral meaning. Furthermore, Paul <u>excludes</u> the definition as pure affective and actual 'conscience' in a neutral as well as in a specifically negative sense "conscience-stricken" or "conscience pricks" (:312).

Using *syneidesis* exclusively as authority, Paul emphasises its function!, namely, to control, evaluate and conscientise one's own behaviour, and at times that of others, according to prescribed and recognized norms (:312).

Important Conclusions

As a result:

- *syneidesis* itself is neither a principal knowledge about good and evil, as moral decision-making ability and demand for or proneness to goodness, nor is it an ethical authority deciding on concrete acts of behaviour also coaxing one to perform such behaviour – in the specific sense of a scholastic understanding of Conscientia (:312).
- *syneidesis*, therefore, in its function as authority, does not prescribe behaviour, but evaluates behaviour according to prescribed norms. With this definition of *syneidesis,* the classificatory designation of 'conscientia antecedens' (the antecedent conscience) is categorically excluded (:312).
- *syneidesis* as a classificatory designation of 'conscientia consequens' is insofar given as its subordinate role in reference to conscious adherence to existing norms and appropriate behaviour is stressed (:312).
- *syneidesis* not only evaluates or judges actions completed in the past, but also monitors present actions, merely intended actions as well as decision-making processes. However, *syneidesis* itself is not the decision-maker per se deciding on the moral or religious appropriateness of an action, but evaluates and judges thoughts, words and actions to signal agreement with what is generally and concretely accepted as binding and good. This judgement over behaviour of people can result in deeming it positive as well as negative, meaning agreement with the norms will be affirmed whereas transgression of norms will be punished or sanctioned (:312-313).
- *syneidesis* is for Paul henceforth a neutral authority redeeming *syneidesis* from a lop-sided guilt-consciousness and its sole function as judge. In a positive way Paul appeals to his *syneidesis* as objective authority giving testimony to his integrity. Moreover, the positive judgment of Paul's understanding of *syneidesis* is

analytical as it confirms – from a human perspective – his integrity as grace-based integrity (:313).
- *syneidesis* as authority is not exclusively ascribed to religious people, Christians in particular, but Paul presupposes *syneidesis* as a neutral – evaluating, judging and affirming – authority for everyone (:313).

In light of Paul's usage of *syneidesis* as authority presupposed for non-Christians and Christians alike, Paul forestalls another vital misunderstanding:

- *ho syneidesis* is no specific theological, but rather an anthropological term, which consequently <u>excludes</u> the notion that *ho syneidesis* operates as *vox dei* [God's voice], as *spiritus sacer* [holy, sanctified spirit indwelling a person as observer and guardian] or as *semen divinum* [divine semen] (:313).
- *syneidesis* is therefore neither directly nor specifically partaking of the Divine or as such reckoned as being divine in origin. Consequently, *syneidesis* cannot be understood as the go-between or the recipient of divine revelation and proclamation (:314).
- *syneidesis* functions therefore in general terms as an objective and neutral anthropological inner authority. This does not change even after the event of a religious experience, such as conversion and justification, since in principle its functional mode is maintained but, because of its renewed state, performs now in line with new and accepted and internalised norms, which consequently leads to new and appropriate behaviour (:314).
- Finally, the relationship of a person to his or her own *syneidesis* – as the objectively and unavoidably evaluating, judging and affirming authority – is concretely one of responsibility, hence the phrase *dia ten syneidesin* can attain the meaning "because of responsibility", or "on account of responsibility" (:314).

Syneidesis – A Definition

In summary, considering these various aspects, the following definition of *syneidesis* emerges. Eckstein states that the *syneidesis* is for Paul a **neutral and objective anthropological inner authority within the person, which objectively evaluates and judges behaviour in line with given and prescribed norms and accordingly raises critical or affirmative awareness.** Due to the functional mode of this inner authority the nature of the relationship between *syneidesis* and self is necessarily one of responsibility (:314). The dimension of responsibility is then extended to responsibility before God (Romans 12:1) and the anthropological concept of *syneidesis* receives a theological dimension (Wiher 2003).

The perusal of Eckstein's exegetical work on *syneidesis*, its occurrence, usage and functions in Paul's writings in the New Testament, reveals surprising coherence with and affinity to Käser's anthropological theory of 'conscience'. The phenomenon of an inner voice, an inner authority with the functions of monitoring, evaluating and judging congruent or deviating past or present behaviour of individuals with existing cultural norms – however diverse and distinct they may be across space and time – is amazing and unifying at the same time.

'Conscience' – Requisite for Humanizing Humans

In his novel "The Ox-Bow Incident" (1940), filmed in 1943 starring Henry Fonda, Van Tilburg Clark takes issue with how culture, within a small community in the far West in particular, constructs justice. The dramatisation of 'constructed' justice ends catastrophically in the denial of justice for those who required it most.

"The Ox-Bow Incident"

Nevada 1885. Three supposed cattle rustlers, who also get linked up to the supposed murder of the previous owner of the cattle, are chased, apprehended, and with the action-hungry local Deputy Sheriff in situ, are sentenced to death by hanging. The verdict is, however, not unanimously shared and a minority oppose it, but in the end the majority prevails. No matter how persuasive the arguments by the accused and some sympathisers are in denying the charge, the majority become the law, assuming the roles of prosecutor, jury, and judge simultaneously. Granting each of the three accused a last wish, one of them writes a letter to his unsuspecting wife and gives it to someone of the party opposing the self-proclaimed executioners of the 'law'. After reading it, he entreats the lynch mob fervently not to go ahead and to listen to what the letter says, but the "prosecutor-jury-judge" gang is not inclined to change in the slightest. Eventually, the sentence is carried out – justice done! After their finished work, they set about returning home, when they 'run into the law' and the local Sheriff discloses to them the supposed murder of the cattle owner is a mere fantasy – no murder was committed! What about 'justice' done? What about justice now? With the letter, the man swinging on the hanging tree hanged in the 'name of justice' raises his voice once more ...

> Laws are a lot more than words you put in a book or judges, or lawyers, or sheriffs you hire to carry it out. It's everything people ever found out about justice and what's right and wrong. It's the very conscience of humanity.
>
> There can't be any such thing as civilization unless people have a conscience. Because if people touch God anywhere, where is it except through their conscience. And what is anybody's conscience except a little piece of conscience of all men who ever lived. ('The Ox-Bow Incident':1943 – Based on the novel by Walter Van Tilburg Clark, 1940).

"Interpreting Life"

> "Conscience is the perfect interpreter of life" (Karl Barth).

Umutima – From *akatuutu* to *umuntu utuuntulu*

The Formation of SEIC

In Bemba thought a human person (*umuntu*) is born with a heart but without a functioning *SEIC*. Moreover, to be a human person is a matter of 'becoming' one and the beginning of it is not the birth-event. A new-born baby is called *akatuutu* and carries following grammatical characteristics:

aka- is prepositional and of the diminutive class of words expressing smallness or fineness regarding size, shape (form, design) or quantity.

-tuutu is adjectival and carries the idea of whiteness (connoting purity) or transparency (connoting emptiness).

The stem -*tuutuu* is found in connection with the verb *ukubuuta*, meaning "white" and in a wider sense "empty", for example: *mwashala fye tuutuu mu butala,* meaning: what remains in the grain bin, it is nothing but white (in there) – completely empty.

Akatuutu – a tiny (little), pure, transparent (empty) 'thing'.

The birth-event is a mere biological event and ushers *akatuutu* into the community of the living but leaves it in limbo until that status is removed and the process of becoming *umuntu* can commence, which occurs in the naming-event when *akatuutu* is given a name. Until then *akatuutu's SEIC* is void, that is, a tiny, pure, transparent (empty) 'thing'; a mere set of dispositions in need of proper formation.

Kwinika ishina – Naming Ceremony

Name is identity. "One's name represents one's authority, reality, and character. One's name has an influence upon a person and upon those who know that person," says Lutahoire (1974:39-40) about Bantu people in Tanzania. In Bemba culture the same idea is expressed when people say that only with the reception of a name will one become a full-fledged human being. The birth-event must be completed by the name-event since human-identity is achieved by name-identity, which requires the *Kwinika ishina*, naming ceremony.

Prior to being named, *akatuutu* must first free itself from the umbilical cord (*umutoto naupona*), the physical evidence of its former attachment to the mother.

In former times the falling-off of the umbilical cord was celebrated by a ceremony called: *umulilo wa mwana* (fire of the child). Labrecque explains:

> Once the umbilical cord has fallen off, the fire in the hut is extinguished and both embers and ashes are thrown into the pit to the west, far from the village (*ku masamba* = to the west). Once again, the hut is whitewashed, and a new fire, the sacred fire of the child is kindled. This new fire must last until the ceremony called *ukupoka umwana* (to receive the child) or *ukutwala ku mpasa*.
>
> Women who are at a marriageable age, pregnant women, and women suckling their babies at the breast may not use this fire (*mwingilila mu mulilo wa mwana*). People warn the husband that he is strictly forbidden to commit adultery (*elacila umwana*, he should not overstep the child). The wife takes good care by throwing some medicines into the fire so that she will be sure that her husband will behave. Any husband guilty of violating this custom of *umulio wa mwana* would fall prey to dire evils, e.g. *ututema* (uncleanness) and *amasho* (a spell resulting from failure to perform the ritual purification). Once the man has confessed his guilt, and made the necessary compensation, he must take a

medicine made from the root of the citapatapa tree (1934/1982:62).

The ***naming of a child*** is not a matter of random choice but is guided and directed and involves careful consideration. Guidance and direction in choosing the right name come via dreams (*ifiloto*) and it is understood that these dreams are not mere dreams but rather contentful communication from the realm of the forebears.

Departed family members are still counted as family members. Their counsel and wishes, given in dreams, are essential when choosing a name, which comes from the family line (often a recently departed family member).

At the time of naming some members of the family (parents of the child *mayosenge* [paternal aunt], *banyinasenge* [maternal aunt], uncles from both sides, grandfather, grandmother, some members of the community (nearby neighbours who are mostly elderly women) are present. The paternal aunt or the grandmother would try to ascertain or affirm the name of the child and the most certain way of knowing is through dreams one or more family members had during the time of the pregnancy of the mother. 'Valid' dreams are dreams in which a departed family member appears – ideally repeatedly. In case there were two different 'valid' dreams of different family members, a compromise would be reached by naming the child with the two names of the family members who appeared in the dreams. After that, the elders would sit for a while drinking beer. The mother and the baby are released to go home.

The birth-name, the naval name (*ishina lya mutoto*) is of very great importance. Tanguy comments:

> A child's birth name is never forgotten. If one asks an old person his naval name, he will not hesitate to give it. Even though the person may have changed his name several times, the birth name always remains the true name (1983:31).

Naming a first-born child

The first-born child of a married couple is always called after a person from the father's family unless the father is not known. In such a situation a boy receives the name of the mother's father and a girl receives the name of the mother's mother. Traditionally, when a couple has its firstborn child, the father's family would provide a name. Usually the child's paternal grandfather (when a boy) or the child's paternal grandmother (when a girl) are eligible candidates. Both could either be still alive or be dead already. If neither grandfather nor grandmother qualifies, the sister of the father (paternal aunt) is next. If this also fails, the search shifts to the mother's line starting with her brother (maternal uncle of the child).

The second child receives its name from the mother's line. First the maternal grandfather (if a boy) or grandmother (if a girl) are considered. If not, then the maternal uncle (*banalume*) is next in line. Should it not be him then someone else from that family is chosen. However, this practice is no longer rigidly followed, and children are even named after their father or mother.

Naming twins

When twins are born, both babies receive the same name *Mpundu*. They could still be given another name to distinguish one from the other. The child immediately born after twins will always be called *Chola,* and the one following next *Chisala*. The father of twins is called *shimpundu* (father of *mpundu*) and the mother is called *nampundu* (mother of *mpundu*).

Name is identity – but in Bemba thought carries yet another extremely vital dimension. With the name the child is no longer *akatuutu* but a human being. Even more importantly, the naming involves simultaneously the attachment of *umupashi* – the 'transcendental human companion' – (Badenberg 2002) to the child. Suffice to say at this point *umupashi* is a 'spirit being' (a forebear, ancestor) with a human biography who accumulated his biographical data among the family and community of which 'it' was once part.

Aided Education – Human Effort and Transcendental Cooperation

The kind of relationship that is formed between the child and *umupashi* is a very personal and intimate one (e.g. *umupashi wandi* – my *umupashi*) and the parents, family, and even the wider community, expect positive 'returns' from this union. Expectations circle around the idea that educating a child as it grows older will eventually lead to humanness and befitting behaviour toward parents, family, community, and society at large. The socialization process by interacting with significant others might not suffice but rests in the belief that human efforts are being complemented by the cooperation rendered by the child's *umupashi*. Ideas of what kind of assistance *umupashi* is able to provide toward a child's upbringing clearly centre on depositing *imibeele* (character attributes/personality traits) into the heart (*mu mutima*) of the child. *Umupashi* is the decisive agent in affecting the transformation of a tiny, pure, little transparent (empty) 'thing' (*akatuutu*) into a human being (*umuntu* – human person). *Imibeele* stem from the forebear of the name of the child, a "transcendental heritage" (Badenberg 2002:70, 90-96), and are, so to speak, revitalized or made tangible again in another person – the 'human companion'. Thus, the formation of the child's *SEIC* is a process with dual input.

However, children under five or six years of age are hardly referenced with *imibeele*. People simply say: *efya baice baba*, meaning: "that is how children are" and with it much of the (bad) behaviour of a child is excused and tolerated.[9] Perhaps this educational philosophy is connected to the belief that as *umupashi* deposits *imibeele* into the heart of a child, the formation of *SEIC* will sort of take its course over time and, consequently, little active '*SEIC* formation'[10] on the human side is required. Positively stated, too much human interference might 'disturb' the child's *umupashi* in effectively bringing about the proper formation of the *SEIC* and could lead to unintended and undesired repercussions.

At the age of 9 or 10years parents and family members pay more attention to the ways of a child. This is the time when the child will be told about the history and particulars of its name and the person from whom the name was inherited. The child is also made aware of who its relatives are, what position they have, and where and how it has to fit in within family, community, clan and the larger societal structures.

Ideal vs. Reality – When Life Goes Wrong

No society experiences its ideological premises to exactly mirror lived reality. Bemba society is aware of the discrepancy between ideal and reality. Like everywhere else children are children and seem less concerned with the ideal when it comes to delve into the world around them in, at times, a quite unconventional enterprise. Concerns arise when age can no longer excuse or tolerate a child's recurring misbehaviour against communal laws and values. More concerns arise when measures of reprimand and discipline seem without effect on a child's behaviour because the perpetuation of certain misbehaviour may concretely lead to a 'bent' or 'crooked' *SEIC*. Such cannot be allowed and calls for intervention, for instance, when a child is found to be in danger of a 'bent' *SEIC* because of continual stealing despite unsuccessful reformatory measures on the part of the parents. Family elders gather to address *umupashi* of the child in *word* and *deed*.

According to the seriousness of the matter, the deed could involve the death of a chicken with its blood being poured onto the ground. In accompaniment of the *deed*, the following *words* might be said.

> *Twamipeele nkoko iyi pakuti mutubeeleleko uluse uyu mwana aleke ubupupu.* "We present to you [*umupashi*] this chicken seeking mercy and pleading with you to forgive us so that this child desists from theft in the future."

The concern that is felt over the child who is showing a tendency of developing bad habits (e.g. stealing) and nourishing bad character traits (*imibeele iibi*) is brought before *umupashi*. Human shortcomings need forgiving but in pleading for mercy there is a request for intervention which carries the expectation of potential change in the child's behaviour in future. A way of expressing this hope is when people say:

> *Umupashi ulelungamika imibeele ya mu mutima. Umupashi* (usually the name is also mentioned) is straightening out *imibeele* (character traits) in the heart (*SEIC*).

The metaphor of "straightening out" implies that something was "bent," or "crooked." The perception is that bad character traits (*imibeele iibi*) are due to a "bent" or "crooked" *SEIC*! Alternatively, one could also say:

> *Umupashi uleoloolola imibeele ya mu mutima* (*umupashi* straightens *imibeele* in the heart)

The verb *ukuololo* has interesting features:

- *-oloole nsalu* = to iron a cloth (emphasis on flattening, straightening)
- *-oloole shiwi* = fig. to tune one's voice
- *-oloolo mulandu* = to 'straighten a case', meaning: to explain a case thoroughly, to make the right decision in a case
- *-oloolo muntu* = to 'straighten a human person', meaning: to teach a man the right way of acting
- *ukuoloolola* = to speak 'straight', meaning: to tell the truth (*aoloolola icishinka* = that man speaks the truth)

A successful calling on and intervention by *umupashi* would mean noticeable positive changes in the child's way of life, or in other words, the 'straightening out' of negative *imibeele* sets the formation of *SEIC* back on the right track.

Excursus: Issues Pertaining to Name-giving

Birth of twins

In former times (Labrecque 1934, Tanguy 1940-ties) the birth of twins (*ukufyala bampundu*) caused quite a stirring in the village and required certain ceremonies to be performed and practices to be followed. The village was polluted, fires had to be extinguished with the ashes thrown to the west (*ku masamba*) and a special ritual had to be performed by the parents. For the midwife who accepted the difficult task of weaning the twins (up to four years) it meant she had to abstain from marital relations with her husband. The *sing'ang'a* had to instigate a ceremonial, long lasting dance which subjected the unhappy parents to much ridicule; they were given medicine (*mulombo*) with which to wash themselves. All other villagers were also in need of purifying themselves by washing their bodies with remedies to prevent the swelling up of their bodies. Subsequent to these ceremonies, the unfortunate parents went home and had to perform the marriage act in the presence of two witnesses; thereafter they lit a new fire (*ukushiiko mulilo upya*) in their hut, signalling to the rest of the village to do the same, thus ensuring complete purification of the village (1934/1982:71).

Taboos because of twins

Moreover, the birth of twins placed parents and relatives under strict taboos. They had to observe uniformity in their upbringing. Whatever was done or given to one had to be done or given to the other too. The parents were to abstain from sexual relations until the twins were weaned; relatives were made to rub their bodies with the *mulombo* medicine and refusal to do so could lead to falling ill with the body swelling up and trembling all over (1934/1982:72).

Death and succession of one twin

Naming twins was different too. All other children received ancestral names; twins were only called '*Mpundu*' (the twins) and were considered being 'apart' from others (1934/1982:72).

Death of one twin also involved taboos for the surviving twin and the execution of certain ceremonies. First, the deceased was buried between two anthills; the surviving twin had to take medicine in order to be freed from following the deceased twin to the grave. A deceased twin had to be replaced or succeeded [a custom to be described in more detail in chapter six] and the parents were to look for a child within their families to take up the place (and name!) of the dead twin. From now on they were regarded as twins and the successor was subjected to the same restrictions; s/he would have to follow suit with the twin in everything and this would carry on even into adolescence. However, the restrictions ceased with marriage (1934/1982:73).

The practice of appointing a successor allows the conclusion that twins (although devoid of an ancestral name) were nevertheless with *umupashi*. This notion was certainly there when I did research many decades later when it was confirmed that twins do indeed have the same *umupashi*! This provided for the rationale why they are remarkably close to each other (e.g. why they are always dressed in the same way or given the same type of things, etc.). I was told this kind of *umupashi* is quite "funny", because how else could one explain why, if one of the two is crying, the other one would also cry; if one behaves in a certain way, the other would also behave in the same way.

Two names

Occasionally persons receive two names. This happens when something is wrong, for instance, when a new-born baby is constantly crying after a name has already been given.[11] A substitute name would be chosen.

Another reason for two names is the death of a family member very close in time to the delivery of a baby by a member of the family. The name of the deceased will automatically be passed on to the baby as an additional second name. It is customary for the father to come to see the child after the umbilical cord has fallen off. Should he not be entirely happy with the name chosen already, he can add a second name. The child would then have two names and two *imipashi*.

The most prominent feature about a child with two proper names is his or her two *imipashi* who would render their help in protecting it from harm. In a situation where a child receives a second name, the first *umupashi* is approached and something like this would be said:

> *Mwifulwa soandso* (mentioning the first name of the person concerned) *twamupeela na banenu, muleumfwana* (do not be angry soandso we give you a friend, a companion; co-operate with one another).

This ritual secures co-operation between the two *imipashi* of the child.

Acquisition of a new name

An interesting situation arises when an adult person is entirely unhappy or dissatisfied with *umupashi* received at the first naming ceremony as a child. It is possible to acquire another, a new name but it means that the 'old' *umupashi* has to leave, 'quit service', as it were, so that the 'new' *umupashi* can come and take over. But occasions where people acquire a new name are exceedingly rare. In the case of such a 'change of *umupashi*', the person would turn to the family elders, saying it was they who gave him his name (of course implying it was their fault that they are in this present state). The family elders would have consultations among themselves and, positively agreeing to the request, would call for a gathering to perform a ritual. Something like this would be said:

> *Nga niwe we mupashi walelenga ukuti uyu aleiba twakutamfya. Twamupeele ishina ya mubiyo* (it is you *umupashi* who is causing this one to steal; we chase you away. We give him the name of your companion).

This ritual assures that the 'old' *umupashi* takes leave and the 'new' *umupashi* takes over. After the new name has been given, the family, especially the elders, will watch that person. If things change, they know the old *umupashi* has successfully been released if not to say 'chased'.

Namesakes in the same family

A further interesting question arises when members of the same family bear the same name. For instance, if there is a well-to-do and respected person in the family and that person has eight children, it is highly likely that all eight children will later name one of their own children after their grandfather. All these descendant children would inherit the same *umupashi*. However, *umupashi* could be spoiled (see chapter five) by one of the persons who is weak in co-operating with *umupashi*. If there is a problem (the person not co-operating with *umupashi*) people would say:

> *Aitoolela fye imisango tefyo bashikulu bakwe bali* (s/he has picked up, meaning: developed his/her own kind or way of life which is different from what his or her grandfather was like).

To people who spoil their *umupashi* it is said:

pa nsaka tapabula ciwelewele (the community is without a fool, meaning: in this community there should be a fool).

If one of the eight family members who inherited the same name were to 'spoil' his *umupashi,* it could also affect that person's relationships with the other namesakes because there is a danger that keeping close contact with this person could make the others behave in the same way and 'spoil' their *umupashi* in the same way. But it would not 'spoil' the *umupashi* of the others or the way *umupashi* works with the others. If one of the eight name-bearers does however 'spoil' his/her *umupashi* and this situation cannot be corrected, this name would not appear in this particular family again, though it could be continued by the other seven families.

The Goal of 'SEIC-Formation'

The brief sketch on the formation of *SEIC* brings to light interesting aspects of personhood constructed from elements of the cultural world of the Bemba. Without the concept of *SEIC*, the importance of *imibeele* (the quality of them!), the instrumental role of *umupashi* in depositing them into the *SEIC* of a child, and the proper formation of *SEIC,* a philosophy on Bemba personhood positively lacks its fundamental premise. Early childhood education in a modern sense (like goal-oriented active engagement and interaction of body, heart and mind to help form the personality of the child) certainly does contrast with the philosophy of child education among traditional Bemba communities. To underscore the point made: the expression *ukutampa imibeele*, that is, to 'start' (actively begin) *imibeele* is always bad news since, for example, in early childhood, such behaviour leads to nothing but a 'bent' or 'crooked' *SEIC* as alluded to earlier.

The proper formation of *SEIC* is a major concern with every child that joins the human family since without it one cannot grow into full adulthood and become a full and mature member of the community. Rites of passage mark transitional stages from 'what was' to 'what is now' often highlighting the biological changes a person has experienced coupled, of course, with expectations to now conduct oneself according to the newly acquired status in society. The formation of *SEIC* must keep pace with the biological changes of the body and the process of '*SEIC*-formation' ought to climax in becoming a fully matured member of the community.

Evidence of 'SEIC-Formation'

Evidence of proper '*SEIC*-formation' is to be a person who demonstrates living the cultural norms and values or in other words, who displays the set of *imibeele* formed in the person's *SEIC* and which now become tangible in appropriate living. Linguistically interesting is how tangibility of *imibeele* is perceived or expressed.

(1) *Ukumoneka*[12] *ne mibeele,* meaning: "to appear with *imibeele,* that is, to come to light, to become visible, to become known, to display measurable behaviour." The phrase conveys the meaning that something hidden comes to light or is brought into the open. *Imibeele* appear. They become known. A child appears with *imibeele;* they are true projections of a hidden "treasury".

(2) *Ukukuula*[13] *ne mibeele,* meaning: "to grow with *imibeele,* that is, to grow up, to become tall, to grow of age." This term puts emphasis on building up something. As a child grows up, more and more of the true nature or quality of its "wiring" comes to light. Special attention must be paid to the conjunction *ne* (with) in both examples. A person is *with imibeele* but never possesses or owns them.

(3) *Ukulanga*[14] *imibeele,* meaning: "to show *imibeele,* that is, to make visible what is covered or hidden."

Noteworthy is the idea that *imibeele* do not in any way imply a genetically conditioned load. These three examples clearly show the fundamental difference between Western and Bemba thinking. *Imibeele* are the sum of an asset, of a treasury, of an inheritance, which is not of biological or genetic origin, but come via transcendental agency, via *umupashi* the 'transcendental human companion', and which in the end decisively and ultimately determine the quality of the *SEIC*.

To emphasise the aforesaid: When the parents are pleased with the "appearance" or "growing with" *imibeele* of their youngster, they know now that *umupashi* is doing his work. They say:

> *Umupashi ulekuula imibeele ya mu mutima* (*umupashi* is growing *imibeele* in the heart)

Note the linguistic shift from *ukukuula ne mibeele* (to grow with *imibeele*) when referring to a person to *ukukuula imibeele* (to grow *imibeele*) when referring to *umupashi*!

When *imibeele* 'appear' frequently, that is when the child acts and behaves in the same way the forbear of the name was renowned for, then it is said:

> *Imibeele ya bafwile yaba mu mutima wa mwana* (*imibeele* of the late one, they are now in the heart of the child)

Both verbs, "growing with" and "appearing", though grammatically active verbs, attain in the context in which they are being used a primarily passive meaning. However, something happens in the *SEIC* of a person and that is attributed to activeness on the part of *umupashi*!

When Life Goes Well

The formation of *SEIC* could perhaps be rated more or less complete when a human person is referred to as *ukuba na mano* or *umuntu wa mano*, 'to be with wisdom, intelligence' or to be a 'human person of wisdom, intelligence', which certainly includes a listening attitude, manners, also patience, friendliness, willing to share, respectability, hardworking (though it frightens people because it makes you grow old), helping people with conflicts, being honest, forgiving, reliable.

Another way of expressing the same idea from the perspective of *imibeele* is to say: *aliba uwapwililika mu mibeele yakwe*, s/he is good/complete/perfect in his or her *imibeele*. In addition, such a person would exhibit emotional stability, that is, not easily flaring up in anger, displaying an outburst of dissatisfaction, showing impatience, and so forth, in other words, someone who is able to check emotions, retain composure when (emotionally) under stress. A person who demonstrates these qualities habitually or permanently is truly a mature person. Such a person has a commendable heart, a *SEIC* of quality: *umutima uusuma*. Such a *SEIC* contains **all positive qualities of character and capacities of the intellect, all good and agreeable mental emotions and dispositions; someone who possesses decency; who is always ready to help, always doing good, friendly and respectful to all those around him**.

Whole and Complete – Umuntu Utuuntulu

To traverse the rugged terrain of human living in health and with mature personality, embodying true humanness, physiology and psychology – body, heart and *SEIC* – require development and formation. When in addition such a person walks in harmony with *umupashi*, the 'transcendental human companion' he or she is indeed *umuntu utuuntulu*, a whole, complete human person, a state one can only enjoy while in the body since a corpse can never be -*tuuntulu* even if full and total anatomical completeness is ascertained.

Conclusion

The unintelligible notion that a relative absence of visible manifestations of cultural achievements, like bombastic and aesthetic architecture or impressive technological achievements of many ethnic groups, would reflect a primitive mind is fallacious. Minds which develop sophisticated language structures with rich, nuanced and elaborate vocabulary, an abundance of literary tropes like metaphors, metonyms, idioms, or euphemisms, to tackle the reality of the human condition, especially in terms of psychophysical associations (Warren-Rothlin 2005), move far beyond the 'primitive' label.

Umutima (heart) encompasses a truly complex set of concepts ranging from physiology (with interesting anatomical features!) to psychology. In fact, the extremely elaborated richness of this term requires moving away from ill-fitting designations like 'psyche' or 'soul' to adopting a much more comprehensive definition, albeit an acronym (*SEIC*). This acronym provides a tool with which to establish a detailed and comprehensive description of Bemba psychology and ideas on personhood. In fact, the psychophysical associations of the body part term *umutima* reveals the interconnection between body (*umubili*) and other crucial elements of Bemba personhood such as *imibeele* (permanent psychic dispositions) and *umupashi*, a theme followed up in more detail in the next chapter.

Endnotes: Chapter Four

[1] Something Greenstein attests to the heart (*leb*) in biblical Hebrew stating that "The heart is a very particular organ within the chest cavity" because "When the heart speaks, it functions as an organ of speech" (2020:209, 211).

[2] As a Bantu language, Bemba also has the outstanding feature of grouping nouns into Classes. CiBemba, so termed by the Bemba people, has nine Classes (see Appendix 2), most of them consisting of a stem and a prefix. See also Geo W. Sims, 1959:9.

[3] The Present Perfect Tense refers to an immediate past and is translated into English by "is/"are." It expresses: "from today and still going on" and denotes a present condition.

[4] Death is expressed idiomatically: "done with visiting this land."

[5] Don Richardson (1974) relays a horror scenario, for Western minds, in what was previously known as New Dutch Guinea then Irian Jaya. In the past, among one of the indigenous Sawi (Sawuy) tribal groups, the building up and grooming of a bond of friendship over time with a member of a neighbouring group with which the village had been entrenched in enmity over generations, revealed essential values. They would invite each other to feasts and festivities until such a day when the time of the ultimate coup is deemed ripe and the host savagely takes the 'friend's' life. The cleverer the camouflaged 'friendship' was instigated, culminating in the culling of the 'friend', the more praise and honour could be earned. The cruel betrayal and the heinous murder were deemed appropriate Sawi ethical behaviour. Cultural norms and values provide the rationale and motivational force to act in such a way.

[6] „Vorerst gilt es hier festzuhalten, dass innerhalb der vergleichenden Theorien zu Scham und Schuld deren kulturelle Spezifität, genauer: ihre Abhängigkeit von dem soziologischen Kriterium der Individualisierung versus der Kollektivorientierung eines kulturellen Kontextes zu wenig Berücksichtigung gefunden hat, sei es von den Vertretern des Konzepts der sozialen Scham, sei es von denjenigen, die den Zusammenhang von Scham und den eigenen Werten eines Individuums betonen und damit das Bild einer individuellen Scham vorgezeichnet haben" (Werden 2013:183).

[7] „den Prozess, in dessen Verlauf sich der mit einer biologischen Ausstattung versehene menschliche Organismus zu einer sozial handlungsfähigen Persönlichkeit bildet, die sich über den Lebenslauf hinweg in

Auseinandersetzung mit den Lebensbedingungen weiterentwickelt. Sozialisation ist die lebenslange Aneignung von und Auseinandersetzung mit den natürlichen Anlagen, insbesondere den körperlichen und psychischen Grundlagen, die für den Menschen die 'innere' Realität bilden, und der sozialen und physikalischen Umwelt, die für den Menschen die 'äußere' Realität bilden" (Hurrelmann 2006 in Werden 2013:185).

[8] „Dass Sozialisation, die Auseinandersetzung mit signifikanten Anderen und der Akt der Perspektivenübernahme entscheidend sind für die Entwicklung zu einem selbstreflexiven und moralfähigen Individuum, sei hier vorausgesetzt" (Werden 2013:168).

[9] This type of education appears to be widespread, being found in cultures as far removed from Africa as Papua New Guinea. Kasprus reports that a mother in the Middle Ramu River area in Northeast New Guinea returned a white person's remonstration on her boy holding a burning cigar between his fingers while he was suckling his mother's breast, with the remark: "leave him go, he is only a baby and he likes it" (1973:61).

[10] Perhaps the formation process could be labeled as 'formatting' similar to what happens to a digital storage device to make it useable.

[11] Wendland cites a similar example in a Chewa context, where a student explained: "For example, just last year before I came to school here, my older sister wanted to give her newly born child the name of our [maternal] grandfather. But this baby cried for two whole days which, according to our ancient beliefs, meant that a different spirit wished the child to be called by its name. That was the spirit of my late [maternal] uncle. So as soon as this name was given, the baby stopped crying. Now what does that mean?" (Wendland n.d.:6).

[12] *Ukumoneka*, Infinitive of the transitive verb. The meaning ranges from "being visible, to appear" to a more figurative usage, "to become manifest, to be known" (e.g. *mulandu wamoneka*, meaning: "the case is known by all").

[13] *Ukukuula*, Infinitive of the transitive and intransitive verb. Intransitively used, the verb conveys a range of meanings. In our context it refers to "growing, becoming tall, coming of age" in the sense of "showing maturity."

[14] *Ukulanga* - infinitive of the transitive verb, meaning: "to show (a thing, something, to give an example)."

Mupashi wa mubiyo: tawendelwa
Mupashi of your friend:
not travelling for you!

Chapter Five

Umupashi – More than 'Spirit', more than 'Soul'

What can be noticed when sifting through anthropological literature is the great inconsistency or even confusion regarding the usage and definitions of 'soul' or 'spirit'. Perhaps this is partly due to the enormous complexity of these terms and the contents with which they are loaded. At the same time, it is also true that very often an attempt is made to grasp traditional indigenous concepts with western (Euro-American) language terminology.

> In ethnological publications as well, there is a blurring of the concepts, which has its roots in the (Indo-European-affected) semantic structures. Thus Walter Hirschberg's dictionary of ethnology (Wörterbuch der Völkerkunde) contains the wording: 'of spirits of the dead (the souls of the deceased)' (1965:143), similarly also in Bleibtreu-Ehrenberg 1991:75-93. In comparing the semantic features of both terms, soul and spirit, it is apparent that in European-Western thinking they are both spirit-like beings. But it is not possible to define spirits in terms of souls nor vice versa (Käser 2014:47).

This is to no avail. Already Franz Boas (1943) advocated for seriousness in analysing ideas and concepts of a culture which to him meant it has to happen according to their own terminologies, not ours (in Fischer 2010:50). Later Kenneth Pike (1967) formulated this analytical perspective as *emic perspective*, which basically means to take up a perspective from within a system, for example, an ethno-linguistic perspective (:37ff in Fischer 2010:50). As a case in point take the Bemba word *umupashi*.

Umupashi – Definitions in the Relevant Literature

Barnes (1922) was of the opinion that *umupashi* cannot be associated with a living person (1922:41). He was, however, restrained in his observation in as far as he tried to establish the meaning of *umupashi* according to the English concept of "spirit" or the Greek term "*pneuma*." Moreover, his article on the subject is rather short to say the least. His information is too vague to arrive at conclusive ideas on the concept of *umupashi* – a fact which Hochegger (1965), in his overview of soul concepts in Africa considering data from 1881 to 1961, rightly bemoans (1965:319).

Audrey I. Richards worked in Bembaland as the first anthropologist in the early 1930s. In her book *Mother-Right among the Central Bantu* (1934/1970), she remarks and specifically acknowledges the "unusually complete" identification that takes place between the deceased person and his or her heir. Every Bemba must be succeeded at death. The heir takes, next to his name, status, and social obligation, his *umupashi*. "In this case the identification between the dead man and his heir seems to me unusually complete" (Richards 1970:269). Richards interpreted this unusually complete identification as interaction of *umupashi* and a living person to mean that the former becomes the *"guardian spirit"* of the latter (Richards 1982:28-29).

Tanguy (1954/1983) writes that in Bemba thought the composition of a human being is twofold: the body (*umubili*) and the spirit (*umweo*). At death, *umweo* leaves the body and is called *umupashi*. Tanguy calls the *imipashi* (pl. of *umupashi*) the *"ghosts of the dead"* (1983:106).

For Werner (1971), the worship of the *imipashi* forms the "most significant personal commitment among the Bemba" (1971:7). His definition of *umupashi*, "*tutelary spirit,*"[1] is in essence a guardian or protector (of a living human being), following Richards' line of thinking.

More in line with Tanguy's definition of *imipashi* is Oger's (1972) who speaks of them as the *"souls of the ordinary departed"* (1972:27), while pointing out that there are exceptions like the nature of death or the mental state of a person during his lifetime.

Maxwell's position (1983) on *imipashi* takes on a forceful human twist. Though they are *"ancestral spirits,"* they undoubtedly have a human matrix. "They were humans once and may be born human again" (1983:23). Despite the superior powers of *imipashi*, which are obvious to and acknowledged by the community, the Bemba extricate themselves from their innate powers by "religious finesse" (1983:23).

Carey (1986) agrees with Maxwell, referring to *imipashi* as *"ancestral spirits"* (1986:32). However, Carey is less elaborate on how the human mode comes into play, but is more concerned in commenting on the rituals for *imipashi* such as veneration (*kupaala*), ritual beer drinking after the funeral (*bwalwa bwa lupopo*), succession (*ubupyani*), and so on (see 1986:32-39).

Ipenburg (1992) only briefly touches on the subject in a reference to the Bible translation by Lubwa protestant missionaries into the vernacular Bemba. He claims the Bemba word *umupashi* is "a word that originally meant *an ancestor who had passed on* [italics mine]" (1992:23).

Hinfelaar (1994) takes a a more nuanced position insofar as he draws attention to a Bemba person's ultimate strife in life during his earthly days. For example, during the girl's initiation rites (*Cisungu*) emphasis is laid on teaching the neophytes that perfect transcendence is achieved through the acquisition of the opposite gender (1994:6). "One is created here on earth in order to become a *Mupashi Mukankala*, a rich and generous spirit/forebear" (1994:6). It is in this regard that *umupashi* is to be understood as a ""*twin-gender shade*," that grants life and health to the next generation" (1994:6).

The attempt to appropriate 'spirit', 'soul', 'ghost', 'shade', or 'tutelary spirit' in order to squeeze their semantic load into *umupashi,* and in doing so, compromising the emic dimensions of *umupashi* is far too ambiguous, vague, often quite unclear or even quite badly distorting. In fact, neither of the terms suffice for a comprehensive description of *umupashi*. What can be said, however, at this point is that *umupashi* represents an outstanding feature of Bemba anthropology in general and Bemba personhood in particular.

Umupashi – A Semantic Approach

The word *umupashi* is a Class two noun (Hoch n.d.:68; Sims 1959:9) with the prefixes *umu* (singular) and *imi* (plural) respectively, the stem *–pash,* and a suffixed *-i*.

'Iso-gloss' Argument

Werner (1971) showed that certain Bemba terms, which are distributed among other Bantu dialects, must be of common origin. He based his argument on the fact that within a limited area the "process of dialect differentiation can be reasonably outlined" (1971:8). This dialect differentiation can be achieved by investigating to what degree correspondence between basic vocabularies of the dialects in each area occurs. Werner then presented an isogloss marking the score of correspondence in relation to the Bemba dialect. The areas which show eighty-five percent or more correspondence are the immediate neighbouring dialects (1971:8).

As regards *–pashi*, there is a *limited* and *solid* distribution among Bantu dialects, that is, those immediately adjoining the Bemba main area. Only the most immediate neighbours of the Bemba make use of the term *–pashi* in their respective dialects, suggesting that it came into use "before the dialects within the isogloss began to separate" (1971:8). Against the background of limited and solid geographical distribution, *umupashi* also remains a unique feature of those Bemba dialects in which it ascends to prominence regarding certain phenomena pertaining to a human being.

Verb Stem Argument

One main characteristic of the Bemba language is the verb, of which there are three categories: verbs denoting action, verbs of state ('becoming', 'getting'), and verbs of movement (towards or away from) (Oger 1993:41). *All verb suffixes end with a vowel. Nouns frequently carry the stem of a verb*[2] prefixed with the proper Class prefix (see Appendix 2) and a vowel as suffix. The verb *ukupala*[3] is transitive as well as intransitive and carries at least four meanings. First, *to resemble, to look like*; second, *to scrape*; third, *to suit, to be suitable, proper,* and fourth, *to flow over*.[4] The transitive causative extension of *ukupala* is *ukupasha*, meaning: "to cause to resemble, to transmit hereditary traits, features, qualities (good or bad)."[5] The derivative noun of **ukupasha** is **ici-pasho** with the primary meaning: "likeness, resemblance (physical or moral)."[6]

The conclusion that *umupashi* is also a derivative noun of the transitive causative verb *ukupasha* is warranted. In light of the grammatical argument that nouns derived from verbs are suffixed with a vowel, as is the case with the noun derivation ***ici-pash-o****,* it is argued that in a similar instance ***umu-pash-i*** fits the grammatical requirement for a derivative noun.

Noun Class Argument

In addition, the fact that *ici* and *umu* are Class prefixes of their respective Classes (see Appendix 1) is noteworthy. *Ici* (*Ifi* plural) are prefixes of the fourth Class of nouns and are used in an indefinite sense or as the Class for "things" in general. *Umu* (*Imi* plural) are prefixes of the second Class of nouns which refer to prominent parts or major organs of the body, objects of daily life, and the names of many trees (Hoch n.d.:68-75). Both nouns, *icipasho* and *umupashi,* derive from the same transitive causative verb stem *-pash* suffixed with a vowel *-a* and *-i* respectively. The vowel suffix *-i* is not exceptional to nouns of Class two, for example: *umubili* (body), *umushishi* (hair), *umukoshi* (neck) and others.

As seen above, nouns of Class two include prominent parts or major organs of the body. It might not be by mere accident at all that *umupashi* is allocated to this class. To the contrary, I think, there is a definite connection to the body as shown earlier. The linguistic affiliation of *umupashi* to body parts and body organs, to the human body as a whole, is one to be noted and strongly lends support to the close tie that exists between *umupashi* and the body of a human person!

An abridged table on major body parts underscores the aforesaid:

umu-bili	body
umu-twe	head
umu-ona (*umona*)	nose
umu-pu	breath
umu-kolomino	neck
umu-tima	heart
umu-sana	loins, lab, womb
umu-pashi	***not*** a specific body part! but closely associated with the body!

Figure 25: Abridged Table of Noun Class Two (umu- sg.) – Body Parts

Twin-gender and Genderless

A question arises whether *umupashi* is gender specific, that is to say, is it *umupashi* 'he' or *umupashi* 'she'? Personal pronouns are gender specific, male or female. There is, however, no neuter in Bemba and therefore no *umupashi* 'it'. This would mean one has to refer to *umupashi* either as 'he' or 'she'. But since *umupashi* is definitively understood to be a 'personal being', but ***without*** any gender endowment (gender neutral), the personal pronoun does not really work either. There is recognisable ambiguity here but none that causes concern to Bemba speakers. It merely adds to the special character of this word as well as highlighting the special affinity the Bemba have with *umupashi*. Though gender does not apply to *umupashi*, people do attach a personal pronoun to *umupashi*, for example, *umupashi wandi wacimpela icimonwa ku tulo*, means 'my *umupashi* ['he' or 'she' but not 'it'!] gave me a vision while asleep.' The genderlessness of *umupashi* is also the reason why both boys and girls can receive the same name. One cannot distinguish the sex of a person by only the name. For example, *Chilufya*, *Mutale*, *Mulenga*, *Bwalya*, and *Mubanga* are typical Bemba names given to boys and girls alike but when needed, the adjective male (*umwaume*) or female (*umwanakashi*) is added.

Concluding Argument

In light of the semantic investigation into the term *umupashi*, it is reasonable to conclude that *umupashi*

- has a causative influence on becoming a human person as well as bringing about a resemblance of true qualities required of a human person
- is very strongly associated with the human body of a living person, but is not a part of the body[7]

This is in complete agreement with Audrey Richards who spoke of an unusually complete identification between *umupashi* and a living human person (1970:269). But where Richards stepped short and did not proceed in her inquiry, was before asking the next logical questions: What is the nature of the causative influence on a living person? What exactly is it that makes this identification with a living human person so unusually complete? And in what way is *umupashi* associated with the human body of a living person?

The first question was dealt with (not exhaustively but fundamentally) in the previous chapter identifying *umutima* (heart) as SEIC whose proper formation is not only achieved through the socialization process within family and communal living but more and decisively so through the attachment of *umupashi* to a new-born child the moment it is given its name. From thereon *umupashi* exercises causative influence on a living human person by imparting or depositing *imibeele* (character traits) inside the heart (*mu mutima*) of the child, setting SEIC-formation into motion.

Answers to the second and third question require further inquiry which will be opened with the next paragraph and continued in the following chapter.

Umupashi – 'Spirit Double' of a Living Person

To bring together more aspects of *umupashi* in relation to a living human person, I move from *umupashi* – the 'transcendental human companion' to *umupashi* as *'spirit double.'* The reason for proposing the definition of *umupashi* as the *'spirit double of a living person'* stems from research I did in the Kasama area where I lived and worked from 1989-1991 and from 1995 to 2003. I developed enough competency in CiBemba to work without interpreters and moved freely among many village communities. From 1991 to 1995 I lived in the Copperbelt, never really losing touch with Lubemba. The linguistic data I collected over many years revealed that the concept of *'spirit double'* is an essential and important addition to what other researchers, as discussed earlier, had previously brought to light. The concept of *'spirit double'* is thoroughly documented in Käser's dissertation (1977, 2016), a linguistic documentation of the concept of 'soul' among the islanders of Truk (today Chuuk), a tiny island in the Pacific Ocean belonging to the Federated States of Micronesia.

The Concept of 'Spirit Double'

In the Truk (Chuuk) language the term *ngúún* carries various characteristics. *Ngúún* is the shadow of an object when the outer shape of the object is at least recognizable. Also, the mirror image of an object or a person is called *ngúún*. A third aspect of *ngúún* is the notion that all things in this world, next to their material, physical existence, also exist in an immaterial, spiritual form. These two forms are so meticulously identical that one can easily be mistaken for the other (1977:119-121). The *ngúún* of a human person, however, outweighs the *ngúún* of the two other above-mentioned non-material contexts.

First, a human being possesses two *'spirit doubles'* at the same time: a benevolent *'spirit double'* (*ngúnúyééch*) and a malevolent *'spirit double'* (*ngúnúnngaw*) (1977:229). Second, the *'spirit double'* of a human being has features that are exclusively his. The *ngúnúyééch* (benevolent *'spirit double'*) of a person can be seen in a person's dreams but, while he is awake, can only be seen by persons who qualify as a medium or seer. Above all, a *ngúnúyééch* possesses human-like features such as body attributes, speech and senses. But most important of all, the *ngúnúyééch* possesses *SEIC*. In times of trouble, a *ngúnúyééch* moans, might be frightened or feel homesick. Its permanent psychic disposition is positive and the *ngúnúyééch* is endowed with exceptional intelligence. In short, a *ngúnúyééch* resembles his human counterpart in detail, is intelligent and friendly, has a positive permanent psychic disposition, and has strongly attached emotions toward the physical body of a person (1977:232-237, 290-91). *Ngúnúyééch* is no mere spirit but a spirit being, and it is such on account of a characteristic nature of *SEIC*. Furthermore, it is a spirit double on account of its resemblance to and close association with a human person.

Umupashi: 'Spirit Double' with two Prominent Characteristics

Käser's definition of *'spirit double'* is absolutely fitting for the Bemba context on two accounts:

Resemblance

Umupashi resembles the human companion in detail and may appear in human-like form in a dream or as apparition, but his existence does not require a body. No one can identify one's own *umupashi* in a dream as such but can identify another person's *umupashi*. For instance, a man sees in a dream a real person dressed in white; the features are clearly recognizable with the face exactly resembling the face of his wife. However, what he sees is not his wife though but the *umupashi* of his wife. Therefore, 'spirit double' is a very appropriate and exact designation of *umupashi*.

Ideal, Genius SEIC

Furthermore, *umupashi* is conceived to be a good, benevolent, and beneficiary being to the extent that only *imibeele iisuma* (permanent positive psychic dispositions) are attributed to his *SEIC*. This is an extremely important fact about *umupashi* as a spirit being: the presence of *SEIC*. Not any kind of *SEIC* but the ideal, genius *SEIC*. However, this ideal, genius *SEIC* is not immune to feelings and emotions. On the contrary, *umupashi* does undergo psychic changes like feelings of anger and discontent but in temporary ways only. Outstanding is also *umupashi's* ability to engage in intellectual processes like thinking (*ukutontonkanya*, "to think, to ponder,"), wanting *(ukufwaya)*, and remembering *(ukubukisha*, "to cause to come back to life," or "to remember,") (see Badenberg 2002:70-71).

To strengthen the argument of an ideal, genius *SEIC* as the quality marker of *umupashi* as a benevolent spirit being, it is noteworthy that certain psychological states **cannot!** be applied to *umupashi*:

Non-applicable umupashi SEIC Designations

umupashi naufulunganya	to cause chaos, to mess up things, confuse issues; to be in a state of confusion
umupashi naupeshiwa amaano	to be at wits end
umupashi naushika	deep in the sense of thinking deeply, to contemplate in order to come to a solution
umupashi nausongoloka	narrow in the sense of being totally absorbed by something or someone; to only think of one thing all the time
umupashi nausabuka	sparkle in the sense of coming up with fitting solution, ideas; to have fully grasped something
umupashi ulapeeleela	oscillate in the sense of being uncertain about the (positive) outcome of a certain problem, issue, if something is going to work
umupashi ulatetema	vibrating, trembling in the sense of losing inner equilibrium; trembling inwardly (because of threat); be quickly thrown off course
umupashi nauluba	lost in the sense of losing direction or being confused in one's thinking; "be lost" in relation to what is going on around one; (e.g. looking for a solution as regards a particular matter and being totally at a loss = the more you look, the more you are surrounded by mysteries.

umupashi uupilibukapilibuka bwangu	always in a state of change, meaning: to be continually changing one's opinion, intentions, plans; never able to come to a decision about something.
umupashi uupilibukapilibuka limo limo	slow change in the sense of being hard-hearted, stubborn; hard to convince, to change mind or opinion
umupashi uubutuka	runs, in the sense of being a coward; someone who runs away from responsibility or taking on challenges; then also: quickly and willingly execute tasks, not procrastinating
umupashi walitambalala	straight, flat, stretched out flat in the sense of not easily being weighed down with cares and worries, etc.; someone with poise; to be able to take on easy work or tasks only; of little intelligence
umupashi nawima	standing up, raises itself in the sense of having understood, comprehended something; to make sense out of the confusion surrounding a matter, to have woken up from the slumbers of ignorance, unawareness, etc., if necessary, through the help or advice of another, feeling 'to be on top of things.'
umupashi naukupukula	reveals in the sense of disclosing, communicating everything one knows or is able to do

Figure 26: Non-applicable Umupashi SEIC Designations

Excursus: *The Concept of 'Spirit Double' - African Cultures and Elsewhere*

In the wake of exploring new worlds, investigative explorers, missionaries, anthropologists, and others saw 'cultural worlds' to be an equally fascinating and interesting terrain to be studied. By the turn of the twentieth century the phenomenon of an entity, (soul, spirit, shade, etc.) associated with a human being aroused heightened interest, but also caused confusion. Designations like 'double' appeared in anthropological literature and Encyclopaedias (e.g. Crawley 1911). A century later anthropological literature still registers a relative absence of detailed ethno-linguistic studies on personhood covering notions of the body, concepts of the *SEIC* and the *spirit double* and calls for more, much more research. The following few references will only hint – and I stress hint – at the widespread phenomenon of local theories on *spirit double* among many cultures around the globe.

With reference to Africa, the concept of *spirit double*, as proposed in this monograph, is a field of research that has so far been rather neglected[8], not because it is difficult to find, but rather because of squeezing this kind of spirit being into a Western terminological corset. As a case in point I refer to the *Encyclopedia of African Religion* (2009) where Zetla K. Elvi labours in sketching African belief systems under the entry 'soul', squeezing vital characteristics of *spirit double* into this ambiguous English term. Interestingly, the term *spirit double* does find mention in the encyclopaedia – indeed twice - albeit under the entry 'placenta'. Nevertheless, this concept has not gone unnoticed, and African scholars like Metuh-Ikenga (1991a and 1991b) and Ogunboye (2000) have reinforced this area of cultural anthropology by documenting the thought-world of the Igbo and the Yoruba in West Africa. As Metuh-Ikenga puts it, "to understand Igbo religious beliefs as the Igbo understand them."[9]

The Yoruba and Igbo – West Africa

In Igbo context, "the *chi*...is a sort of 'spirit double' or guardian genius associated with the person from the moment of conception...but *eke* is believed to be an ancestral shade incarnate in each new baby. The baby takes after the *eke* in appearance and/or character" (Ogunboye with Lois Fuller 2000:77-78). From this description it can be deduced that the Igbo associate a human person with two spirit doubles without whose 'inputs' a human being lacks essential constitutive elements of identity. Yoruba thought conceives of *ori* as a guardian spirit of the person (2000:77-78).

The Lugbara (Uganda) and Nyakyusa (Tanzania) – East Africa

The Lugbara of Uganda also have the term *ori* and may be defined as "the being that survives the death of the body." *Orindi* (the essence of the spirit being *ori*), is the seat of the emotions, probably even qualifying for *SEIC*. If and to what extent there exists a commonality between the *ori* of Yoruba thought and the *ori* of the Lugbara could be a worthwhile subject of investigation, especially in the light of the geographical distance between both ethnic groups. The interplay between *ori* and *orindi* is not just a linguistic accident but has specific bearings on the concept of person in Lugbara thought (Middleton 1973:493-494).

Godfrey Wilson studied the Nyakyusa people in the Tukuyu region of south-west Tanganyika, now Tanzania, in the 1930s. He was greatly interested in death rituals and death "featured centrally in his ethnographic description and his analysis" (Kalusa and Vaughan 2013:67). In his field notes he noted the Nyakyusa's firm and "'lively' belief in the survival of the dead as 'shades' or ancestors, whose interventions in the realm of the living had to be both acknowledged and managed" (2013:68). The purification rites that followed the burial were meant to achieve protection of the bereaved "ensuring their continued fertility (and that of the land)" (2013:70). Burial of the corpse had to be done correctly for the spirit to separate from it properly.

> Then followed a dangerous process through which the 'shade' or spirit of the deceased was removed from the bodies of the surviving spouse and close relatives. Once this had been accomplished the transformed spirit could be welcomed back into the family. The family hearth and the marital bed (2013:70-71).

The removal of the spirit from the widow and close relatives required sexual intercourse with a male relative of the deceased. Not to do so would be asking for serious trouble and "causing harm through *carelessness* and disregard for ritual" but proper obligatory burial rites "did not, however, mark the end of intimacy with the spirits of the deceased" (2013:71).

Wilson was profoundly excited about how ambivalent his informants felt about "the continued involvement of the spirits in their daily lives" to a degree that even male and female procreational powers were dependent "on the support of the spirit of the founding ancestor Kyela." He learned "that 'the shade and the semen are brothers', that the shades produced sexual desire in men and menstruation in women" (2013:71).

The spirit (*unsyuka*), 'shade' Wilson called it, "were not only present in the lives of the living, but central to them" (2013:76).

It is a pity that Wilson, and so many others with him even in contemporary works, clearly see the centrality of a spirit being in people's lives, even recognizing their intentional and intelligent interaction with human persons infusing them with assumed personality, but relegate it in the same breath to the numina of a depersonalized 'shade.' There is indeed "a long tradition of anthropological scholarship that describes ancestors as 'shades' with a presence in the physical world" (Gordon 2012:2). However, to be the kind of spirit being the Nyakyusa, and certainly the Bemba as well as many more ethnic groups who share a similar theory across Africa, acknowledge it to be, it definetely needs personality; it needs *SEIC*! What this requires is a different research methodology to bring these elements of *spirit double* and *SEIC* together, one which I outlined in detail in an earlier publication (Badenberg 2014).

If one looks for 'shades' – then surely one only gets 'shades'! In my view that is not enough. The paragraph on the Benuaq of East-Kalimantan exemplifies the kind of research needed to be able to speak in much more precise and specific ways about a whole complex of phenomena pertaining to personhood.

The Chin Peoples – Myanmar

The Chin peoples of south-eastern Asia inhabit the highland region along the borderline between western Myanmar and north-eastern India. Their understanding of well-being and sickness is connected to the presence or absence of spirit beings. *Tha* is the word for 'spirit'; prefixed with *thi, thi-tha* it means a dead spirit whereas the prefix *mihing* in connection with *tha, mihing-tha,* means 'human spirit' (Pau 2009:5). *Tha* (*mihing-tha*) is very important in matters of sickness or wellness. A person is thought of as being associated with (*mihing*)-*tha* which can indwell the body but also leave it. *Tha's* presence or absence from the body directly impacts one's physical condition either positively (wellness) or negatively (sickness). A permanent absence from or failure of *tha* to return to the body is disastrous and will eventually lead to the death of the person (2009:6). Sing Khaw Khai states that "when one is going to die soon, his [sic] spirit tha goes to places where he has been before and to those whom he is more mindful of. The spirit wanders not only during sleep but also during his wakefulness" (1995:127 in Pau 2009:2-6).

The Benuaq of East-Kalimantan – Indonesia

In his monumental study of the Benuaq of East-Kalimantan (640 pages!), Oliver Venz (2012) also bemoans the fact that there exists in the literature on Southeast Asian peoples great inconsistency in, and often confusion about, how to translate indigenous words or designating certain phenomena regarding their concept of personhood with multi-layered Euro-American terms, for example, the Benuaq word *juus*. Western scholars speak of *juus* commonly as "soul", "life soul", "spirit of the living person", "spirit", "supernatural agency", "vital force", "vital essence", "life force", "animate principle" or "invisible aspect", which hardly represents or matches the thought-pattern of the Benuaq (:187-188). Venz's interest in researching the Benuaq concept of personhood from an ethno-linguistic perspective unearths rich and detailed material which I will summarise here.

The Benuaq believe that a living person (*senarikng*) has three important constituent components: *unuk* (body), *juus* (which he convincingly defines as spirit double and dream ego – a theme I will follow up on later) and *asakng* (the *SEIC*) (:231).

To speak of *juus* as mere life-force or non-personal power misses the mark. *Juus* is regarded as a personal, individual being [the essential criterion is, of course, the presence of *SEIC*, as Venz attests (:267)]. The association of body (*unuk*) and *juus* is a fundamental requirement for the functioning of all autonomic, emotional, affective, and rational functions of a human person, meaning, it is the requisite for a healthy and conscious life (:231).

Juus has the ability to separate from the body or can be separated from it and can, however, during these phases of autonomous behaviour, on account of its nature and appearance, be experienced. The disassociation of *juus* from *unuk* during sleep, in which *juus* assumes appearance as the non-corporeal double of the person, is exempt from human influence. The fact that *juus* is identical in form to its human counterpart and counted as the person's double, leads to defining *juus* as **spirit double**. In addition, it also assumes the function of **dream ego** since both participate in the dream event (:231).

Apart from disassociation during sleep, *juus* can, in principle, be separated from its body, though such more or less "willingly" staged separation episodes are strictly reserved for a specific group of people, namely, the religious experts. Their dream egos require during their non-corporeal travel episodes special protection, as is the case immediately after successful re-association with the body at the end of the ritual. All other causes of disassociation of *juus* from the human body, like frightening it or taking it prisoner, are undesirable events. Also, all cases of temporal disassociations of *juus* from the human body are for the whole person at least dangerous, may lead to health implications or, on account of permanent separation, even lead to death. The event of experienced disassociation of *juus* from the human body necessitates immediate re-association procedures of both components through ritual (:231-232).

Juus is associated with the group of beings which are categorized as non-corporeal "(*esaaq yaq aweeq unuk*)" and invisible "(*esaaq yaq beaau ditaatn*)", however, *juus* is not formless but thought of as gestalt "(*umakng*)" (:232). Under normal circumstances *juus* is attached to a person as a kind of immaterial image, a double edition of that person. The concept of 'double' is further strengthened in the correspondence between *juus* and the mirror or shadow image (*inu*). The designation of *juus* as 'spirit double' is therefore fully justified, even more so as the Benuaq themselves speak of *juus* "as (the) Second (of us)" (:232).

Furthermore, *juus* is not only the term designating the spirit double of a human person, but also designates the spirit double of animals, plants and lifeless objects although *juus* in relation to humans, animals and plants rather assumes 'animating' quality and in relation to lifeless objects secures quality of 'vitality' (:232).

A final attribute of *juus* as the spirit double of a human person emphasizes its prophetic function since *juus* has the gift of foretelling approaching sickness, illness, or imminent death (:232).

The Israelites – Ancient Near East

In a recent study Richard Steiner (2015) presents impressive new evidence about the nature of the Hebrew term *nefesh*, traditionally broadly translated 'soul' (notwithstanding the fact that the term carries a wide range of connotations). New linguistic evidence (e.g. Ezek 13:18-21 and the Katumuwa Inscriptions) leads Steiner to speak of *nefesh* as 'disembodied spirit' while the person is still alive and with specific characteristics. Due to restrictions on space, only a very concise summary will be considered here (2015:124-127).

- נפש [*nefesh*] - is different from a חיים [*hayim - life*] (Ps 103:2–4; Job 10:1)
- נפש [*nefesh*] - has a spatial location (Jer 38:16; Ps 116:7)
- נפש [*nefesh*] - resides inside the body (2 Sam 1:9; 1 Kgs 17:22) in the blood of the flesh (Lev 17:11) when its owner is conscious
- נפש [*nefesh*] - when its owner is conscious, it is not part of the body (Isa 10:18; Job 2:5–6)
- נפש [*nefesh*] - can be punished by preventing it from joining its kinsmen in the afterlife (Gen 17:14; Lev 19:8; Num 9:13; etc.)
- נפש [*nefesh*] - during sleep, it could disengage from the body and wander about - become a disembodied *nefesh* – a **'dream-soul'** (the pl. of 'dream-soul' is נפשים [*nefeshim*])
- trapped inside the empty pillow casings (Ezek 13:17–21), the **dream-souls** would turn into **bird-souls** פרחות [*parachot*] 'souls-to-fly', awaiting the imminent demise of their owners, unless the latter agreed to ransom them
- נפש [*nefesh*] - although a part of the *person* (Gen 37:21; Deut 19:6, 11; etc.; cf. Gen 3:15; Ps 3:8; etc.), is not a part of the *body*. As a result, it has considerable freedom of movement.

Fascinating is that *nefesh* as 'disembodied spirit' genuinely qualifies as 'spirit double'. As such it is closely attached to the body - with a specific spatial location (blood) - but is **not** part of it. *Nefesh* as 'dream-soul' designates in anthropological jargon as spirit double of elevated status, ergo 'dream-ego' with a life on its own (disengaging from the body during sleep and wandering about). It therefore is absolutely critical to perceive of *nefesh* as possessing *SEIC* (something Steiner not explicitly states but its existence could be inferred from "circumstantial evidence, i.e., from the many verbs collocated with *nephesh* [sic]"… "since the verbs are always predicated of the *nephesh* [sic], never of some part of it")[10] and that harm done to *nefesh*, trapping it in pillow cases, turning it into a 'bird-soul', is in consequence a transformation of its *SEIC!*, altering its nature or quality in such a way, that functionality of the body cannot not be upheld, ergo a healthy and conscious life is severely threatened, and if not ransomed, will lead to a person's imminent demise.

Fascinating is also that with Steiner's linguistic study the presence of the concept of 'spirit double', and with it that of 'dream ego', is undoubtedly anchored deeply in ancient knowledge systems and thus reaches out from the past far across space and time.

Umupashi – 'Spirit Double' with Two Prominent Tasks: Protector and Guardian

Earlier it was seen that *umupashi's* attachment to a human person centres around *SEIC*-formation in the formative years of early childhood. But in addition, it is necessary to emphasise that *umupashi* also takes care of the body of his human companion over the whole span of life.

Protecting the Body

Human life includes the experience of disrupted well-being, of physical ailment, sickness, and even life-threatening illnesses. Medicine (*umuti*) and medical specialists (*bashing'ang'a*) have their place in curing physical afflictions. But in Bemba thought *umupashi* is (1) a powerful ally in keeping and enjoying physical well-being and (2) his closeness to the body as well as a harmonious walk with his human companion is thought to **uphold the functionality of the body!**

Beneficent Spirit Action – Umupashi the Body-protector

Physical and mental health issues are often connected to forceful and effective outside interference by spirit forces. The loss of physical health, and with it reduced functionality of the body!, is disastrous and the need for body protection is obvious. So is the need for a body-protector! One of *umupashi's* prominent tasks is to be that body-protector. Physical well-being, bodily health, and high energy levels attest more to the capability and presence of one's body-protector then it does to quality nutritional input to the body.

However, not all people are recognised to have *umupashi* as 'spirit double, e.g. mad persons: *ishilu* and *icipuba*) and therefore lack a powerful body-protector. As hinted earlier, grave danger looms over a person who is targeted by *bamuloshi*, those who practice *ubuloshi* (destructive magic). A successful attack could lead to misfortune, sickness, even to the death of a person. It is the task of a person's *umupashi* to prevent such incidences. *Umupashi* guards a person all the time. When asleep, *umupashi* is actively moving near and far to fend off possible danger from witchcraft. Space and time are no restrictions since *umupashi* is able to be present in many places at the same time.

On the other hand, body protection can be withdrawn for reasons of careless living, neglect or offending one's *umupashi*. Certain sicknesses are indicative of *umupashi's* withdrawal: *Impepo* (fever), *umutwe* (headache), *mu cifuba* (chest pain). When these things occur, people say:

> *umupashi naumukumya naumuletela impepo/ umutwe/ mu cifuba* (*umupashi* has touched him or her, he brought him or her fever/ headache/ chest pain).

This kind of "touch" cannot be felt as such but the effect of it in manifested illness can.

Safeguarding the SEIC

The pivotal role of *umupashi* in the education of a child and the proper formation of its *SEIC* has already been discussed earlier. Of course, the formative years of *SEIC* during childhood, though extremely important, do not terminate *umupashi's* task with his human companion. Not only does *SEIC*-formation matter, but also that the *SEIC* is kept in shape, that is, its acquired and established qualities must be 'maintained'. In real terms it means keeping the *SEIC* in line with cultural norms and values by demonstrating culturally acceptable behaviour, which also means to live in harmony with *umupashi*. Viewed from *umupashi's* perspective it means guarding the *SEIC* of a person so that one may live and maintain a good and acceptable lifestyle. This is no minor issue for a person as s/he is indeed able to 'spoil' his/her *umupashi* by the acts one commits or the way of living one has adopted.

Fatal Human Action – The Possibility of Destroying Umupashi

Right living, accepting and following cultural norms and values, is the path to keeping the balance in life. But balance can be lost – even to a disastrous degree!

Self-induced Destruction

How a person lives matters. How a person lives out humanness matters not only in relation to other human beings but deeply and significantly to one's own welfare. A permanent negligent lifestyle is considered to eventually lead to *ukonaula umupashi*, destruction of *umupashi*! As with other things in life, there is a beginning which develops into a tendency and as it continues, gradually edges into a habit, a state of being, and in a worst-case scenario, the irreversibility of it.

The destruction of *umupashi* is a process of progressively spoiling *umupashi* until its bitter end. If, for example, drinking is going from bad to worse, it is said: *naaya aleonaula umupashi* (s/he is in the process of spoiling his/her *umupashi*). The fact of leading oneself to addictive drinking has now, apart from the harmful physical effects this may have on the body and health, led to *naonaula umupashi,* a definitive process of damaging, ruining, and yes, destroying *umupashi*. The certainty of the effect of this process is *naonaika umupashi* (s/he has now spoiled, rendered useless, destroyed *umupashi*), and the irreversibility of it means: *nomba umupashi naonaikilila fye,* "now s/he has absolutely, completely spoiled, rendered useless, destroyed his/her *umupashi.*"

Analytically, two processes take effect: (1) permanently damaging the quality of **one's own *SEIC***, and (2) simultaneously the destruction of *umupashi,* which in fact is a **complete destruction of *umupahsi's SEIC*!** Such a person is now *aaba ne ciwa* – 's/he is with a bad spirit', meaning with a fallen spirit (*iciwa* from the verb *ukuwa* – 'to fall'), which is literally indicative of the total change the *SEIC* has undergone. *Umupashi* is now no longer the benevolent 'spirit double' but has turned into *iciwa,* nowadays popularly referred to as *icibanda,* a malevolent spirit being, and for that matter, a malevolent 'spirit double' because of the nature of his altered *SEIC*!

People who are regarded as having gone down this road are definitely witchdoctors (*bamuloshi*) or mad people (*mashilu*). Another consequence of their fate is the inevitable loss of their name to the potential repertoire of names available to future generations within their families and clans. They will be forgotten as their names vanish with the corpse, in time totally obliterated from the memory of the living. This is also true of barren women (*ng'umba*), impotent men (*bucibola*), lepers (*bafibashi*), and persons who committed suicide (*ukwiipayo mwine*). Their exclusion from human society means total exclusion for they also have definitely forfeited their benefit to future generations.

Foreign-induced Destruction

Societal equilibrium hinges on successful, good, honest, reciprocal relationships among members of society. Human experience, however, deviates from this rationally desired reality of harmony on account of powerful mental and emotional forces released onto the lives of people. Jealousy is one such power, a negative mental and emotional force which can wreak havoc on communities. It is one of the driving forces keeping witchcraft (*ubuloshi*) activities alive, which in turn instils a great sense of fear in people since the danger of becoming a target of witchcraft attacks is ever present.

The most effective way to harm a person for reasons of jealousy (*mufimbila*, lit. a condition of swelling [of the *SEIC*]) or revenge is to engage the service of a 'sorcerer' (*muuloshi*). His specialised knowledge about **ubwanga** – witchcraft implements, the things used by him to carry out his work, is often the preferred way to inflict harm in a secret way and thereby releasing this negative mental and emotional force. The ultimate strike, of course, is to take life.

When death occurs in a family and there is suspicion about the circumstances of how a person died (not 'normal' but abnormal or 'untimely' death) (Käser 2014a:200) it can and will not just be accepted. For sure, this is accredited to the work of *muuloshi* and the family takes strong interest in finding out who the culprit is. Now, if *muuloshi* gets wind of this suspicion and fears to be identified, he would most certainly go and seek advice or help from a "professional confiner" (a specialist practitioner in the group of *shing'ang'a*) to 'confine' *umupashi* of the deceased person in order not to run the risk of being attacked himself by *umupashi* of the late, who, in order to revenge the death of the body of his human companion, will seek his own justice. Especially murderers, *ifipondo* (killers by knife, poison, etc.) and *abaloshi* ('sorcerers') are in need of assistance from the "professional confiner" in order to 'confine' (*ukukupikila* from *ukupika* v.t.): 1) to cover, to put a lid or cover on; 2) to shut, close) *umupashi* of the victim who died a death worth avenging by *umupashi* of the deceased.

"Professional confiners" operate in utmost secrecy; they are a kind of secret society and common people hardly know of, and even less so, know them. Their repertoire of 'confining' *umupashi* of a living person requires special rituals, so powerful that the confiner can 'trap' *umupashi* and 'confine' him to a certain place.[11] The longer the 'confinement' is successful, the more devastating the effects since now *umupashi* is separated from his human companion, unable to render protection of the body, upholding its functionality as well as guard against evil-minded spirit forces. The result is clear: the person will succumb to sickness and will often die very quickly.

An interesting story was told to me which happened in 1993 while I lived in the area.

> There was a certain Mr. S. who lived in a village in the vicinity of Kasama. He had a dream that he was beaten up by a mob of children and a few adults. When he woke up in the morning, he was very sick (not able to get up). The following morning, he died.
>
> My friend and informant saw him the very morning after he had had the dream. Now before Mr. S. died, he also told others his dream, saying that the leader of the mob was his own late son, who had earlier died mysteriously in the Lukupa river. This is what had happened to him:
>
> One day the son went out fishing; after some time, he and his friends lit a fire to warm themselves up. Suddenly the son got up, jumped into the water headlong where it was extremely shallow, breaking his spinal cord and neck. His friends rushed and retrieved him, but they could not render him any help. He lay motionless on the ground, and after being taken home, he remained in this state for about a month at his home and died.

When the people present heard that his late son was the mob-leader, they knew why he had this dream. The content of the dream is what the late son's *umupashi* did to the father. People inferred from the dream that there was no doubt that Mr. S. had instigated his own son's death through *ubuloshi* (witchcraft, magic)! In turn, his late son's *umupashi* revenged this terrible death by 'beating him up', *umupashi naumuma*!, also acquiring assistance by calling other *imipashi*. That is why he was so sick, failed to get up and only a day later died. To be 'beaten up' by *umupashi/imipashi* almost certainly means a minimal chance of survival and inevitable death ensues.

Persons who die abnormally (impotence, barrenness, suicide, etc.) or untimely (accident, illness, etc.) cannot pass on their name and cannot pass on to the realm of the ancestors. The tragedy is obvious.

A word about *muuloshi* ('sorcerer'): his malevolent 'spirit double' (*iciwa* aka *icibanda*) has a serious *SEIC* deficiency, that is, he is a cunning double who is said to be *icibanda cawayanguka*, meaning by indwelling *muuloshi* he can make him to appear a friendly, likeable person to the community around him in order to cover up and hide his real identity (*SEIC*)!

Muuloshi's 'success' in carrying out his evil work is foremost a successful 'elimination' of another person's *umupashi* by powerful rituals leading to 'imprisonment' or 'confinement'. For this reason, communities are often without peaceful and fear-free times, experiencing disturbed and upset communal harmony, also affecting the societal equilibrium at large.

Excursus: 'Improving' one's own Umupashi

A person is not only able to 'spoil' or even 'completely destroy' his or her *umupashi* but one can also 'improve' one's *umupashi*. In instances where the previous bearer of the name was a very hard-working person, which is the reason why he is remembered, but at the same time was a polygamist, the current bearer of the name is not obliged to follow suit in this regard. If the current bearer of the name, however, displays other noble *imibeele* such as generosity, humility and other similar qualities, then s/he has effectively improved his or her *umupashi*.

It appears that there is remarkable flexibility in the relationship between *umupashi* and his 'human companion', allowing for different outcomes. The 'improving' of *umupashi* seems to me a particular kind of flexibility in the sense that it would not mean to really 'add' a particular *umubeele* (trait) to *umupashi*, but rather a kind of triggering that kind of *umubeele* in *umupashi's SEIC*, which lay dormant, through proper living of the 'human companion'. Perhaps one could employ the metaphor of synchronization to describe the interdependence involved in 'constructing' a *SEIC* that is 'honourable' while in the body and 'durable' once the material, corporeal abode has resigned itself to the earth.

It also appears that there is a measure of ambiguity between the person and *umupashi* insofar as, on the one hand, it is one of *umupashi's* primary tasks with a living person to shape, format that person's *imibeele* in order to form a quality *SEIC* and, at the other hand, if this 'project' does not turn out so well, people will blame *umupashi* for the absence of *imibeele* congruent with cultural norms and values.

Sickness – Body and Spirit

In Western concepts the terminology used when sickness strikes (in a very broad sense, e.g. infections, malaria and many others) would be in the realm of 'body and bacteria'. But other cultural knowledge systems seem less concerned with the microscopic perspective and instead opt, for reasons of staying within their own coherent logical worldview structures, to posit different 'pairing partners' and find 'body and spirit' equally reasonable, real and true.

Elsewhere I have written on the dialectic relationship between culture and personality with reference to sickness and healing in the Bemba context (Badenberg 2008). I wrote

> The Bemba concept of illness is significantly different from Western scientific models of illness.[12] The latter are built on precepts of a materialistic view of illness, healing and health, whereas the Bemba concept is mainly based on a transcendental spiritual view of illness, healing and health.[13] Consequently, to the Bemba, illnesses and their causes are subject to different patterns of categorization. Of course, the groups of sickness categories are not clean-cut entities, nor are they always rigorously followed. However, the group categories do exist (:73).

A concise outline of some sickness categories should be helpful here.

Diseases Caused by Violation of Traditional Laws: Amalwele ya Makowesha

In chapter three I alluded to bodily well-being, good health resulting more from a close association of body and *umupashi* than from healthy living and balanced nutrition. Also, of further consideration is the adherence to traditional laws centring around sex and fire, which tie into the perceptions and categories of cause and effect of certain kinds of sickness and illness. They are referred to as *amalwele ya makowesha* (sicknesses of contamination). Among them are *Ulunse* leading to *Cifimba*[14] (acute malnutrition): *Kwashiorkor*, *Ulunse* leading to *Ukondoloka*[15] (Acute Malnutrition): *Merasmus* and *Imililo/Amakowesha* leading to *Cifimba* (Acute Malnutrition): *Kwashiorkor*.

Ulunse

A very general description of *ulunse* is the perception that early resumption of sexual intercourse after delivery leading to early pregnancy will cause *ulunse* in the infant.[16] At the first sign of a pregnancy during breastfeeding, the child is abruptly weaned. The abrupt weaning causes psychological[17] and physical problems in the child. The rationale is that the breastfeeding child is "sucking the blood of the fetus in the womb." People say: *alionekela* meaning, "he/she (the child) has sucked the blood of the fetus."

The fetus is thought of as consisting of blood. Since the blood circulates in the body, it also reaches the breast of the mother and is thus sucked through breast-feeding, which contaminates the milk and causes the breast-fed child to fall sick. Therefore, the child is weaned immediately. A recurring sickness of the weaned child, e.g., diarrhea, is known as *alilwala ulunse* meaning, "he/she has the sickness of *ulunse*.

Imililo/Amakowesha

There are all kinds of taboos connected to biology, sex and fire with contaminating effects if not observed. I will select two scenarios:

1. Intra-marital sex makes a person "hot, warm" (*icikabilila*). The child cannot be touched and fed before the bodies involved in the sex act have cooled down, or the hands have been washed. If this rule is not followed, the child may become *amakowesha* (that is, enter the state of contamination when fed) which leads to *Cifimba* (*kwashiorkor*) and eventually to death.

2. Extra-marital sex of either the wife or the husband makes her or him a potential threat to the health of the child. This can happen when such a person *touches the cooking*$_L$ or *the fireplace*, or *feeds the child*$_L$ or *holds the child* without having bathed or cleansed himself with herbs beforehand; the child may suffer from *amakowesha*. The state of "contamination" can cause the child to experience weight loss, loss of appetite, *ukondoloka* (wasting), fragility (*ukunyomboloka*),[18] chronic cough, or chronic diarrhoea, all of which lead to *Cifimba* (*kwashiorkor*) and eventually to death.

Diseases Caused by Witchcraft (Ubuloshi): Amalwele ya Kulowekwa

Icuulu

The word *Icuulu* designating this sickness is derived from the anthill (also called *cuulu*). There are some three points of reference: (1) *cuulu* (pl. *fyuulu*), is a symbol of endurance. The anthill is known for its solidity and sturdiness; (2) *cuulu* is also a swear word and may also symbolize death;[19] and (3) *cuulu*, the anthill, stands out from its environment because of its conical shape. These three characteristics accompany a person who is *ukulwala icuulu*, "to suffer from" or "to be sick with *icuulu*." *Icuulu* is a swelling (at times rather big) on the body and resembles the shape of an anthill. The spot where *icuulu* manifests itself is usually extremely hard and often forms a solid lump.

However, indications are that this sickness takes a long time to ultimately cause the death of a person. Someone suffering from *icuulu* may initially feel pain in their whole body, but later experience pain at one particular part of the body. *Icuulu* is not locally bound to only one place, but may shift to other parts of the body, e.g., from the leg to the arm, from the leg to the abdomen and so forth. Importantly, when *icuulu* manifests itself as abdominal swelling, a person is faced with imminent death; the manifestation of *icuulu* in the stomach is a harbinger of death. Often *icuulu* is ascribed to witchcraft attacks (Badenberg 2008:82ff).

Ulusuku

Another sickness that is attributed to the effects of witchcraft is *ulusuku*. The predominant symptom of *ulusuku* is an inflated stomach. The belly of a person grows unexplainably big even though the intake of food is normal and fairly moderate. When a woman suffers from this sickness, one might assume she is pregnant. *Ulusuku* sickness can affect all people.

The word *ulusuku* is derived from the intransitive verb *ukusuka* meaning, "to be bad, to turn sour." *Ukusuka* means (1) an egg which has not developed into a chick. The egg is without yolk but contains whitish water or fluid. *Ilini nalisuka,* "the egg is bad, has turned sour, the egg inside has become watery." (2) *Ukusuka* is also used on Mwango fruits, for example, *Mwango naisuka*, "the fleshy part of the Mwango has become watery." Furthermore, the verb *ukusuka* (3) appears in the context of milk, *uyu mukaka nausuka,* "the milk has turned sour." The abnormally big belly is due to great amounts of water or whitish fluid inside the stomach, like the whitish fluid in the analogy of the egg without a yolk.

There are instances when *ulusuku* is perceived as a normal sickness. In such cases, the belly is not extraordinarily big and is treated by people in the community or by medical personnel in clinics or hospitals. However, if a person's belly appears to be unusually and extraordinarily big, the sickness is diagnosed as *ulusuku lwa kulowekwa,* meaning: *ulusuku* due to bewitchment.

Intifu

The *Intifu* sickness is diagnosed if the following two symptoms are present: (1) *ukubyola,* "to belch" and (2) *ukutifula,* "persistent hiccups." It is understood that *ukubyola* and *ukutikula* are both natural body functions that occur after eating. However, regular hiccups in short intervals with no signs of improvement, and side-pains (*utubali*) over a prolonged period of time even at night and during sleep are eventually related to *Intifu*. *Intifu* and *ubuloshi* (witchcraft) are interrelated. A common perception about this sickness is that it is untreatable by medical persons. Dillon-Malone comments that "the illnesses more specifically identified with the African psychiatrist are commonly known as "African diseases" as distinct from those which, it is believed, can be cured by western-type medicines. Wizardry falls into the former category" (1988:1160). The option of seeking medical advice and/or treatment from the hospital is almost ruled out.

Diseases Caused by Spirit Beings: Amalwele ya Mipashi

Umusamfu

Umusamfu is known to be a sudden, unexpected sickness. The description I was given emphasized the suddenness with which *umusamfu* takes hold of a person. In young children from the ages of one to five years, fever is also a symptom. The feverish condition causes shivers and nervous agitation. Also, at times, the whole body stiffens and *ifulo* (foaming from the mouth) appears. *Ifulo* is a sign of *umusamfu*, which only occurs in children. *Umusamfu* is predominantly found among infants and usually occurs only once. It can be cured as discussed below. Usually *umusamfu* is not preceded by a history of illness. Such sudden sicknesses are related to *imipashi*, ancestral familial spirits who employ sicknesses like *umusamfu* to declare interest or express their dissatisfaction with family or communal affairs by targeting an individual person. Technically speaking, *umusamfu* are fits or epileptic episodes. When *umusamfu* strikes a person, the suddenness and severity of the attack may leave a person unconscious. But usually the person recovers after a short time.

Sudden, unexpected sickness (fits) followed by a quick death are often diagnosed as *umusamfu*. A repetition of *umusamfu* is called *cipumputu*, "kind of fits, which also affects adults." Fits leave a person unconscious for a short time. When the fit is over, the person returns to a normal state. Some people explain the unconsciousness as a disruption between *umupashi* (spirit double) and the person. Reoccurring *cipumputu* is perceived as an unstable or weak relationship between a person and his spirit double. The names of persons suffering from *cipumputu* are will no longer be passed on in the family lineage.[20] During the lifetime of persons who are prone to *cipumputu*, they are referred to as *alikwata icipumputu*, "he/she has fits/epilepsy," or *alilwala icipumputu*, "he/she has the sickness of fits/epilepsy," and are not given responsibility within the community. In most cases such persons have to rely on the help of their families.

"Spirit Sickness": Ubulwele bwa Ngulu

Ubulwele bwa ngulu is distinguished from sicknesses that are caused by *imipashi* (familial spirit doubles) such as *umusamfu* as outlined in the section above. "Spirit sickness" occupies a very special place within the array of sicknesses known to the Bemba with two characteristics: (1) It is not considered to be an ordinary ailment, and (2) it is not an illness that is caused by bewitching (*ubulwele bwa kulowekwa*).[21]

Ubulwele bwa ngulu is considered to be a mysterious illness, *ubulwele ubushilondolweke,* meaning, (1) "an affliction that cannot be explained;" an illness that is mysterious by its suddenness and its effects on the person. (2) "Something" has seized a person who had been enjoying good health and who was neither mentally deranged nor epileptic. This something – "it" – wanders in the body, disturbs the mind, and affects the behaviour of a person (see Oger 1972a:3).

Sicknesses related to *ngulu* spirits can be expressed in two different ways: (1) *ngulu naimukumya* (*ngulu* has/have touched him), or (2) *ngulu shilemucusha* (*ngulu* cause/causes him suffering). Symptoms of *ubulwele bwa ngulu* can be treated. However, the range of medicine available is rather limited and mainly confined to *impemba* (white clay), which is given to the patient in small portions to eat. At times, patients may also ask for drums to be beaten, maybe for only five minutes, to which they dance. After the dance is finished, the fever (or whatever the symptom was) is gone, and the person is fine again.

Sickness Attributed to one's own Umupashi

The thought that one's own spirit double who is so strongly associated with the body of his 'human companion' should bring harm and impaired functionality to the body seems bizarre. Earlier this situation has already been addressed, and so it will suffice to briefly outline its rationale again.

When a person **offends** his or her *umupashi* a reaction on the part of the latter could cause *impepo, umutwe or mu cifuba*. When this happens, people say:

> *umupashi naumukumya naumuletela impepo/ umutwe/ mu cifuba*
> (*umupashi* has "touched" him, he brought him fever, headache, chest pain)

This kind of "touch" cannot be felt as such, but its result as manifested sickness will be felt.

When a person **offends** the *umupashi* of another person (e.g. killing the person through witchcraft), the late person's *umupashi* may take revenge (see story of Mr. S.). People will say after a dream in which they dreamed they were beaten by someone unknown to them and after waking up and feeling severe pain:

> *umupashi naumuma mu mubili* (*umupashi* has "hit" the body)

In the event of death within hours, people will say: *umupashi naumuma*!

Umupashi – 'Spirit Double' as 'Dream Ego'

> In western ethnopsychology the ultimate responsibility for the dream is understood to lie within the mind of the dreamer. Despite the apparent alterity of dream experience, it is seen as an expression of the individual's unconscious desires and drives (Groark 2010:101).

Obviously, there is then but one kind of dream for which the dreamer takes sole responsibility. "But what happens," Groark asks, "when local theories posit more than one self (or rather, an extension of one's self) as the subject of the dream?" (2010:101). And how about the Malagassy villagers when they emphasise that dreams occur "when other people [especially ancestors] enter you and thought *through* you in order to achieve their ends"? (Bloch 2015:294).

So far is has been shown that the concept of *umupashi* is multi-faceted, the 'spirit double' carrying out two prominent tasks: protection of the body and safeguarding the *SEIC*. There is a third facet of *umupashi* of a living person.

While the choosing of the name of a child is a family affair it is even more so an affair for *umupashi* of a forebear. Dreams are the channel of communicating *umupashi's* wish to attach himself to the new family member, which is acknowledged in giving the child the forebear's name. Dreams are instrumental in becoming a human being and dreams remain instrumental in the pursuit of life. Mandunu remarks: "The dream-world is real for

Africans and is given the same attention as the affairs of daily life (1992:47). Dreams provide reasons for action,[22] they influence considerations in the process of decision-making and they function as an explanatory template when life needs answers.[23] Bemba society, like many others in Africa (Mbiti 1997) – and around the world – attaches great importance to dreams. They come in two categories.[24]

Dreams and Dreams

A first observation is an interesting linguistic finding. It is not possible to say: *umutima naulota icilota*, meaning: "the heart (*SEIC*) has dreamed a dream." But one can say: *ifiloto fya matontonkanya*, meaning: "the dreams of the thoughts." For instance, *icintu nga uletontonkanyapo kuti wacilota*, meaning: "a thing, if you think and think about it, you can dream about it." Such dreams, however, are mostly irrelevant because they are the product and projection of one's own wishes and aspirations. Dreams of this nature come and go; they have no bearing on acting or giving guidance in evaluating considerations in the decision-making process.

'Double' Episodes

A second category of dreams is *ifiloto fya ku mupashi*, meaning: "the dreams from *umupashi*." As seen earlier, they have "quality" because *iciloto ca ku mupashi cilakwata ubupilibulo*, meaning: "dreams from *umupashi*, they always have a turning to, pointing to, that is, they have a meaning." They come with quality assurance as they are clear in the sense that one can remember every detail, but most importantly they come true. Often, they point to the future, being a sign of something ahead (*ukusobola ifikacitika nangu ifilecitika*), for instance, what sex a child to be born will be. One can hear statements like: *nacilota ndeloba imilonge*, meaning: "I dreamed I was fishing *imilonge*" (species of Bubble Fish). The message is clear: there will be a child, and it will be a boy. There is also an equivalent phrase regarding the sex of a girl.

Of significance is when people say *umupashi wandi wacimpeela iciloto,* my *umupashi* has given me (last night) a dream. Groark's question brought to the discussion earlier proves more than relevant. Certainly, Bemba local theory posits <u>two</u> personal beings who participate in the dream episode: the person and his *umupashi*! This idea is worth emphasising as the speaker is able to switch from passive mode, *umupashi* has given me, to active mode *nacilota iciloto,* I dreamed a dream, without confusing the issue. And to drive this point even further: **the contents of the dream are the experiences and encounters of *umupashi* when wandering about (*ukwendauka*) while the person is asleep.** A dream is *umupashi's* gift to its human companion to let the person in on his activities.

Also, such dreams are a window into the future and because they originate with *umupashi*, present and future, immanence and transcendence fuse into one whole reality, reality *per se*. They very often become a motivational force to act. In cultural anthropological terms, *umupashi* is a 'spirit double' but with special status: **'*dream-ego*'** (see Käser 2014a:161; 2014b:190, 197).

Venz defines the characteristics of the term dream-ego as the temporary absence from the body of a living person and the final separation from it when death occurs. Dreams are the encounters and experiences of this being and its presence, the indwelling of the body, is a precondition for consciousness and life (2012:37).

Messaging Episodes

While *umupashi* is able to let his human companion in on his adventures and endeavours, he can also act as messenger between members of the same family. Instances of great importance to the family are relayed through a dream given by *umupashi* to a certain person. The same dream would also be given to another family member. When people meet for discussions and relate to one another the dreams they have had, the two individuals who dreamed the same dream are identified. They would say: *umupashi wacenda* (*umupashi* was travelling). The understanding is that *imipashi* (plural of *umupashi*) of the same family line recognise each other as belonging to the same family. Good communication, cooperation, and mutual understanding among them is easily achieved and the same message can reach two different persons. The family and the 'dreamers' now have total assurance of the direction they should take. Since the guidance of *imipashi* is guaranteed, relief and comfort can settle again in the family.

An unsettling situation arises through a long absence of *umupashi* from a person. *Umupashi,* being a 'responsible guy', only seeking the good of his human companion, is not always rewarded in reciprocal manner. Humans are humans; they are liable to 'breach of contract' for which *umupashi* has but one remedy – to withdraw from protecting the body and safeguarding the *SEIC* for disciplinary measures.

Dream of Dreams

Being absent, *umupashi* cannot warn his human companion of looming dangers, especially those which are caused by sorcery. Manifestations of bad dreams or nightmares are thought to be a sure sign that *umupashi* is not in close vicinity to an individual. Dreams about cows, fierce dogs, snakes (python or puff adder) are counted as attacks of sorcery, for *muuloshi* favours these animals because he prefers to use parts of them in releasing his magical powers onto people. Absence of *umupashi* also means a person is cut off from access to transcendental knowledge so essential for one's journey through life.

Umupashi – The 'Being that Survives the Death of the Body'

The human body is a temporal institution. No matter how long or how short physical existence lasts, the moment of material, biological finality is to come. Every society on earth experiences this reality as an unavoidable fact of living the human life. But not every society embraces the same philosophy on life and consequently the same philosophy on when the body encounters the end of life. Western societies, in general, hold to a philosophy which defines death to be the ultimate terminal point. Life is all there is. Death marks the finality of existence. Full stop.

However, this is quite a minority viewpoint among the broad cultural heritage in contemporary societies around the world. In fact, most cultures not only think otherwise but they define death to be only the terminal point of the physical body.

The ethno-linguistic investigation on personhood in Bemba thought has shown that the concept of *umupashi* is multi-faceted, ranging from 'transcendental human companion' to 'spirit double', who carries out two prominent tasks: protection of the body and safeguarding the *SEIC*, and to 'spirit double' of exclusive status: dream ego. Not surprisingly, and as can be expected, there is yet another facet of *umupashi* of a living person.

We have seen that among the Bemba there exist rather complex ideas on becoming a human being, and more importantly so, on becoming a human person. Biology plays a subordinate role in both aspects whereas *umupashi* is thought to be instrumental both in giving human identity and in ascertaining *SEIC*-quality.

Old age is due to a strong *umupashi*. Though he cannot prevent the death of the body as such, *umupashi* can strengthen a person effectively to grow old. But death due to sickness is attributed to the failure of *umupashi* to render effective protection. *Umupashi* itself does not age; he is as strong in the body of old age as was the case when becoming attached to his human companion at the name-giving ceremony in early childhood. Of old people who still ride their bicycle it is said:

> *balikwata umupashi wa maka nangu line bakotele* (s/he has got *umupashi* of power/strength even though s/he is old)

The logic of subordinate biology also applies to the moment when the body has totally ceased to maintain the function of its members. The death of the body is not the end of being because **umupashi is the 'being that survives the death of the body' and perpetuates the personality of the deceased**.[25] Stated differently, the cessation of biological processes, first and foremost that of the heart, turns the body (*umubili*) into a corpse (*ici-tumbi*) (*umubili* now regressed into a mere 'thing' - *ici-tumbi*) yet the 'core', that which uniquely defines the identity and individuality of a human person, the *SEIC*, traverses the threshold of death. The anatomical heart (*umutima*) gives up on life but an intact, fully matured 'acquired heart' – *umutima* as *SEIC*, cannot be touched by biological death.

Conclusion

The attempt to grasp traditional indigenous 'soul' or 'spirit' concepts with western (Euro-American) language terminology is often a futile attempt and bars not only the anthropological research community from intelligently talking with one another, but also hindering a better communication with members of a community who embody these concepts. To simply speak of 'souls', 'spirits' or 'shades' leaves a wealth of other significant ideas connected to these phenomena untouched and therefore deforms or neglects rich cultural heritage by which people organize and anchor their lives.

Of course, ideas change and beliefs experience alteration. With this in view it is granted that the concept of *umupashi* as the 'spirit double' of a living person encompassing an array of other interlocking elements (e.g. 'dream ego') – and other important ones to which attention will be drawn in the following chapter – may not exercise intellectual and emotional appeal to the same degree in every detail for every Bemba in contemporary society.[26] However, deep-seated assumptions on the nature of the cosmos and the human person are pretty solid blocks withstanding the winds of change and their abrasive dust for a long time. Despite the dynamics that operate in culture and the variations of people's personal views on this subject, the validity and the relevance of what this chapter has unearthed on the subject of *umupashi* is not diminished. Finally, I mainly consider Bemba rural village communities, which tend to be far more traditional and conservative as opposed to Bemba communities of metropolitan background.

Endnotes: Chapter Five

[1] I am not satisfied with the term "tutelary spirit" in relation to *umupashi*, because, as Schoffeleers remarks, the term carries a wide range of meanings. He says, "Tutelary spirits appear to be of a great variety. There are snake deities, High Gods, prophet-like figures, deceased chiefs, priests and other persons of fame" (1999:11).

[2] There are three different kinds of nouns. The common noun, the proper noun, and the derivative noun (a noun which derives from another noun, adjective, verb or adverb). Compare Hoch n.d.: 44.

[3] Not to be confused with *ukupaala*, meaning: (1) "to invoke the ancestors," (2) "to bless," (3) "to blow out," (4) "to start growing." (White Fathers, *Dictionary* 1991: s.v. "-paala").

[4] White Fathers, *Dictionary*, s.v. "-pala."

[5] White Fathers, *Dictionary*, s.v. "-pasha."

[6] White Fathers, *Dictionary*, s.v. "cipasho." As an example: *uyu mwana namwishibile cipasho, apala wishi uo naishiba*, lit., "this child, I know him by his resemblance, he resembles, looks like his father whom I know."

[7] Richard C. Steiner (2015) has made an interesting case for the ancient Hebrew concept of *nefesh*, traditionally viewed as a disembodied soul only after the death of the body, to be critically reviewed. He asserts that *nefesh* can be (temporarily) located outside the human body while a person is still alive. Also, "the נפש [*nefesh*], although a part of the *person* … is not a part of the *body* … . As a result, it has considerable freedom of movement" (2015:125).

[8] "Until recently, Western scholars have failed to appreciate the extent to which African religions are founded upon a systematic anthropology and ethics," says Ray (in Metuh-Ikenga 1991:51).

[9] Quoted in "BookNotes for Africa: Notes on Recent Africa-related Publications of Potential Interest for Theological Educators and Libraries in Africa." Theological College of Central Africa (TCCA), Zambia and Harare Theological College, Zimbabwe, no. 4 (October 1997):1-21, 11. The Book review is signed with the letters LKF (the full name could not be traced).

[10] Private correspondence with Prof. Steiner on 8 October, 2020.

[11] Similar beliefs exist among the Kaonde and Lunda people of Zambia. The spirit double of a person can be deposited for safety in some external

object (antelope's horn, crab's shell). If the container is stolen/destroyed, the person will die within the year.

[12] Western medicine looks at the symptoms (of a sickness) and separates body and mind. Eastern and African medicine look at the whole body. Dr. Robert Abel, ophthalmologist, in a radio interview on "Talk to America," a program of *Voice of America* broadcast on Sunday, April 2, 2000.

[13] Compare also LeBacq [1998]:18.

[14] *Cifimba* is derived from the intransitive verb *ukufimba*, meaning "to swell, to be swollen." *The White Fathers Bemba-English Dictionary*, (1991) s.v. "-*fimba*."

[15] *Ukondoloka* is an intransitive verb meaning: "to be emaciated, to be wasted."

[16] Frank LeBacq, interview by author, Kasama, Zambia, January 20, 2000. Dr. LeBacq was Technical Advisor Health/ District Medical Officer of Kasama District from June 1994 to June 2000.

[17] Ritchie attempted to theorize on the emotional effects of nursing (breastfeeding) and weaning on African children at length. His basic line of thinking was that the different modes of nursing and weaning practised by the mothers of European babies and African babies will have a lasting effect on individuals of either culture for lifetime. (I use the term culture here in a very general way). Ritchie's theory alleges that an infant subjected to a regulated measure of feeding intervals triggers in him or her anger and hatred (aroused by a momentary parting from the mother and her breast felt as a severe privation) as well as love and gladness (aroused by the return of the mother and her breast and felt as a condition of utmost pleasure). "This regularity of nursing establishes a keen time-sense," says Ritchie. The interrupted intervals of feeding cause the infant to learn to reconcile the "pain of privation" with the "joy of indulgence" giving compensation for having to wait. Therefore, Ritchie writes "the past provides a precedent for the future, and the child learns to wait with purpose." On the other hand, a child that enjoys the mother's breast at any given time and moment, as is the case in African cultures, keeps the child in the present. It instils in him or her the notion that the present is a state of perfect pleasure, or at least pleasure can be obtained at will if only demands for it are articulated.

This state of timeless pleasure impacts the consciousness of the suckling greatly as the duration of the nursing period, the time the infant has access to the mother's breast, extends at least from one year up to two years and even beyond (1968:9-19). Abrupt weaning, as is the case when *ulunse* prompts the mother's decisive action, constitutes the painful ending of the child's hitherto fully conscious pleasure. The magnitude of the emotional upheaval this situation creates (having to cope with a forced separation from a fully conscious pleasure and the ambivalence of hate and love towards the mother) is enormous. The situation is further aggravated by erratic food patterns (caused by poverty and/or the reaction of refusal toward the introduction of "new" or alternative eating habits as it means venturing out into the unknown) prevalent in so many village communities within Kasama District. The brutal reality of now regulated, though irregular, feeding patterns which are dependent on a great number of variables (water, firewood, type of food available, workload of women, access to primary health care facilities etc.) and the stereotypical diet according to months and seasons, greatly contribute to

malnutrition in children under five. For statistics on malnutrition in children under five in Kasama District see Nangawe et. al. 1997. The psychological impact of abrupt weaning must not be taken lightly. There are strong emotional reactions to which the child is subjected. Mothers literally scare away their babies from the breast by applying hot pepper on the nipple, or wearing frightening objects underneath their brassieres, etc. (Nangawe et. al. 1998a:28).

[18] *Ukunyomboloka* is an intransitive verb meaning "to be tall and slender, slim, lanky." It also means "to be emaciated." *The White Fathers*, Dictionary, (1991), s.v. "*-nyomboloka*."

[19] When taking an oath, the expression *ku cuulu*! can be heard. Compare *The White Fathers Bemba-English Dictionary* (1991) s.v. "*-cuulu*." In a sample case of *Mutumwa Nchimi* diagnosis, the anthill was associated with a shining light that was moving towards a house at night. The majority of the family members occupying the house were struck with sicknesses and at one time the husband said that both he and his wife were going to die if the sicknesses continued. The shining light supposedly emanating from the anthill was the harbinger of ill-fate, continued sickness, and eventually death. For a complete account of the Sample Case see Dillon-Malone (1988:1170-1172).

[20] This is the ideal and largely common practice. However, there might be exceptions, for example, when an ancestor was renowned for exceptional skills, displayed outstanding character attributes, or was praised for certain achievements during his lifetime.

[21] *Ukulowa* (active infinitive), meaning "to bewitch." *Ukulowekwa* (passive infinitive), meaning "to be bewitched."

[22] "In African life dreams play a central role" (Mbiti 1997:511-522, 511).

[23] African cultures give ancestors high esteem. "Ancestors are believed to offer advice through dreams, visions, or ghostly visitations" (Cook 1985:35-47, 35).

[24] Among the *Akamba* there also exist two categories of dreams, good and bad (Gehman 1990:157).

[25] Musonda says of the Bisa, a Bemba speaking people: "*umutima* survives after death and the *umupashi* continues to have it. If an individual had a good *umutima* then his or her *umupashi* would have a good *umutima* too" (1996:126).

[26] In the quest for understanding human culture, the history of studying culture and cultural themes has experienced a great many different approaches and opinions like, for example, the Durkheimian view. For Obeyesekere, Durkheim's early view of culture ("culture exists independent of and before the individual" (1984:111) led anthropologists to belief that "shared culture must produce shared behavior - or, to be more exact, behavioral regularity" (1984:111). A view Obeyesekere calls a "horrendous fallacy" (1984:111).

He further says that "collectively held knowledge may vary with individuals and groups within a larger society (1984:111). The emphasis clearly is on "the same degree per se." The concept of *umupashi* as the "spirit double" of a living person is knowledge held by members of Bemba culture. This knowledge is, however, held collectively as well as individually. "Collectively held knowledge" is the smelter from which individuals draw the substances to form and construct individual ideas/concepts, which in turn will eventually be infused into the smelter again and become part of the "collectively held knowledge" as the individual ideas/concepts circulate and permeate society again.

Uo mwenda nankwe: ni mfwa mbiyo
the one with whom you travel: death, your companion

Chapter Six

Mfwa – More than 'Giving up the Ghost'

Death: 'Gateway' to Perpetuity – *Umweo Wamuyayaya*

A Bemba Myth

> When God created the first human beings, man and woman, he also made two perfumed bags. One was brilliantly designed with many coloured beads, each one more beautiful than its neighbour. It was a more attractive thing than many other pieces of cloth. The other bag was made from the bark of the "mutaba" tree. It was simple, unattractive, without a special design and with no beads. One day God called Mushili, (the name of the first man, which means earth).
>
> He told Mushili to come with his wife as he had something to show him. On their arrival, God showed them the two bags, saying: "You see these bags. Both are scented. One contains life and the other death. Choose which ever you want."
>
> The woman's attention was drawn immediately to the very colourful bag. And that was her choice! Without consulting her husband, she seized the beautiful bag, which she so coveted, and said to her husband: "Come, follow me." As soon as they reached their home, burning with curiosity, the woman opened the bag. To her great horror, an evil spirit (iciwa) jumped out. Shortly after the birth of her first child, the woman died. So, death entered into the world. It strikes everybody. No one is forgotten (Tanguy 1983:55).

'Gone' – But only 'Gone Away'

Biological death is unavoidable, universal, and with its occurrence, leaves a gap within the ranks of family and the community at large. Bemba philosophy posits to its members that though a person is gone, s/he has only 'gone away', transitioned from one mode of existence to an otherworldly mode of existence. Life in essence is marked by a string of transitioning processes – *rites de passage* (e.g. name-giving ceremony, initiation rites, marriage, and others) but death has a transitional quality on its own merit. All other transitory stages concern a human being in reference to maturity in body and personality and are, therefore, conditioned by space and time. Death is an exception. Ojiwang says: "Death is … introducing a person into the world of the spirit" (1996:44). To be even more precise in reference to the Bemba: death is the gateway to <u>becoming</u> a spirit being, of which there are two categories: *imipashi* (good, benevolent spirit beings) and *ifiwa* (evil or bad spirit beings), meaning, that they have become evil and harmful (Kapolyo n.d.; Lumbwe 2009).

Aging is Natural – Death is Not

The aging of the body is natural, death is not. Tanguy writes in the 1950s that

> Death is never considered to be natural: There is always an underlying cause, except when a person dies a good and peaceful death. Then people say: 'aaifwile fye', he just passed away, like a candle that has been extinguished, or 'aafwa imfwa Lesa', the life which God had given him is finished. This is usually said of old people. In such a case no one comes under suspicion, no evocation of spirits is needed (1983:55; Labrecque 1934/1982:67).

This presumption is still a strongly held view among many Bemba communities across Lubemba. The good and peaceful ('normal') death is one kind among many others; just one way of other ways of experiencing death with serious to profoundly serious implications. The abnormal or 'untimely' deaths are by far the most common reasons for death. Tanguy lists and explains several abnormal or 'untimely' deaths (1983:55-57).

One Death – But Many Different Kinds

I will shortlist them and occasionally add some explanation:
- mysterious death (*afwe cimuku*, or *cimfilimfili*)

- accidental death (*ubusanso*)
- death through illness
- death through lightning (*incuba*)

  whoever dies through lightning is cursed. To find the culprit a ritual hunt is arranged. "When the accused is a dead person … the family of the accused must invoke (*ukupepa*) the dead relative to appease him (*ukupaala*) and to beg him to cease bringing affliction on people" (1954/1983:55).
- death brought on by beer
- death through indigestion
- death from unknown causes (*ubulwele ubushilondolweke*)
- epidemics (*icikuko*)
- several deaths during one lunar month in the same village
- several deaths in the house
- death resulting from a curse

  In such a case the accused is already known. "But a ritual hunt will make known the bad spirit which took hold of him and caused him to curse. The person who made the curse is summoned to the chief's tribunal and made to pay a fine. The relatives of the dead person will refuse henceforth to have anything to do with this person, for in their eyes he is a murderer" (1954/1983:56).
- suicide

  In former days one reason for a male person to commit suicide was because of impotency. People would say: "*Te mwaume wine wine, aba cibola, malyombo*" (he is not a true man, he is impotent) (Labrecque 1934/1982:75). Nowadays all cases of suicide are considered as acts of spite, an immensely powerful way to take revenge. Sometimes people do this in order to seek justice because of perceived unbearable injustice done to them. They know through suicide their *umupashi* will turn into *iciwa* and thus torment and "wreak vengeance upon the living" (Lumbwe 2009:95).

Taking Care of the Dying Body – *ukonga*

The following is what I encountered and what was shared with me some twenty years ago, but procedures might meanwhile have changed in various ways.

When the death of the body is near, two immediate family members come close to the dying person. They close the eyes and the mouth (*ku kupisha -*

the teeth must not show). The fingers, hands, arms, and legs are stretched. Thereafter they say: *umuntu waonga* (*ukonga*, meaning: "to arrange a corpse for burial)." Then they tie a cloth around the head to keep the mouth tightly closed.

The above account may already contain changed elements because Lumbwe writes of *ukonga* performed in former times:

> …initially the attendants would ensure that the eyes and mouth were closed. Thereafter the corpse would be placed in the traditional posture for burial, which was done as follows: the arms were folded in a position that brings the closed fists under the chin, the legs doubled up with knees touching the abdomen, while the heels of the feet touch against the lower part of the thighs – a posture known as ukufuka umubili (folding up of the body – a posture similar to that of a foetus in the womb) (2009:96).

Ukonga is performed whether the deceased person was a man, a woman, or a child.

Taking Care of a Dead Body – *ukushika*

Apart from *ukonga* other main burial rites are observed which are *ichilindi* (hole) and *ukubika iloba muchilindi* (filling the grave with soil/earth). The corpse (*icitumbi*) is given its final resting place in burial (*ukushika*). Lumbwe provides a brief explanation of both rites.

Ichilindi: Lumbwe states: "… the corpse would be laid with head facing the east, a thing that is done in the hope that the deceased person's soul would rise with the sun" (2009:96) but also to remind everyone of *ku kabanga e kwatulile ifikolwe*, from the east our ancestors had their origin. Continuing with Lumbwe

> … the deceased's bracelet and necklace would be broken and thrown into the grave to ensure that the body is confined to the grave. Furthermore, the relatives would also be expected to shower the grave with offerings such as polished shells (impande) and white beads (ubulungu ubwabuta) to honour the deceased (2009:96).

Ukubika iloba muchilindi: After lowering of the corpse in to the grave and before filling it with soil "the relatives of the deceased would throw in some earth by kneeling at the edge of the grave and pushing some earth with their elbows" (2009:97). Select grave diggers then fill in the soil until it is completely filled. In former times "articles such as bracelets, necklaces, inongo (clay pot) and other small kitchen utensils would be placed all over the grave" adding that "the utensils placed all over the grave to be of any use to the deceased … (the dead do things in opposite ways to the living) …, they would be destroyed by piercing or cracking them before placing them on the grave" (2009:97). The burial rite ends here, and people start leaving the cemetery.

Death of People in Authority

The death of people in authority necessitates special funeral rites and burial arrangements across space and time, as archaeological data around the world confirm. There are, of course, great differences among contemporary as well as ancient societies in how status and authority are honoured in death and for the afterlife. The Bemba in Zambia have no history of elaborate building structures (e.g. pyramids, burial mounds) or mausoleums for their honoured dead yet there is obvious distinction between 'royal' and 'common' people in life as well as in death.

Pre-independence Days

> When a person of authority dies, no tears are shed as for 'ordinary people' (ababapi), but instead, the drums are beaten in a special way. This is how it is done: the drum is beaten hard with two drumsticks (mishimpo) together, then it is beaten lightly in a prolonged roll (imishika). This drumming will last several hours. The 'cilukaluka' dance is performed throughout the village. After this, offerings of beer and food are put at the door of the deceased's hut. The aim of all these ceremonies is twofold: to honour the dead person, and to beg him to be good to the villagers who remain. According to people's belief, the spirit of the deceased lives and survives after death and can exercise a good or evil influence on the living. It can even come to life again. The spirit of the deceased remains in the hut throughout the day, and it is pleased with the tokens of respect which are offered to it in the way of drumming, dancing, and of course, it can eat and drink at ease of the food which has been brought to the house. Naturally, commoners will not receive such great tokens of respect (Labrecque 1934/1982:83).

Post-independence Days: Death of a Chief's son

Here, I have consulted my own notes, parts of unpublished research material from the mid-1990's.[1]

Mr. C. Mwamba, the late headman of Chafwa Village, died on 30 May 1995. He was the son of the late Chief Mwamba who had died some four years prior to him.

Mr. C. became headman in the late 1980's and was appointed by his father, the then Senior Chief Mwamba, because within the Chafwa village community two families were fighting for the headmanship. The late Mr. C. Mwamba was around 40 years of age and had been suffering from an illness for some 5-6 years.

On 2 June, burial was arranged at *Sunkutu*. This place lies west of Kasama, near a stream called *Milenga Mukalamba*. The cemetery itself is called *Sunkutu* (the place where all sons of Bemba Chiefs and even sub-Chiefs are buried).

Procedure of Burial

From Chafwa village the body is taken to Mwika village where the headman awaits their arrival. Entry to the village is barred by sort of a roadblock put up by the headman and his people. Payment of money (a handsome amount it is) is expected to be made at the spot. In former times payments were made in the form of animals - goats, sheep or in material goods (e.g. blankets). The relatives of the late person will have to shoulders these expenses after which they are given permission to proceed to a place called *pa nsakwe*. There they will find the *Insakwe* (kind of shelter - branches are bent to meet at the top. Size about two meters by two meters) where they spend a night. The leader of the procession is called *Muchilingwa*, not a relative of the late person, and he is responsible for taking care of bodies of late chiefs and sons of chiefs.

One of *Muchilingwa's* chief duties inside the *Insakwe* is guarding the body. If necessary, others will assist him - special people chosen by him who are not relatives of the dead person. Upon arrival of the funeral procession a cow is killed, some of its blood is taken to smear the place of the head and the feet of the corpse. The cow must be donated either by the present Chief or the relatives. Slaughtering is done by the *Muchilingwa* himself and the meat is eaten during the night. Some of it is given to the headman of Mwika village. Come next morning, they proceed to *Sunkutu* which is a couple of hours away. On arrival of the funerary procession all those who have come here for the very first time are to stand separately at the entrance. The *Muchilingwa* then cuts off a branch of a certain tree with which he strikes the standing persons lightly. This is meant to guarantee their safe departure after the burial ceremony at Sunkutu. After this *Muchilingwa* performs some rituals, calling on the spirits (*imipashi*) of those who are already buried here to accept the spirit (*umupashi*) of the deceased.

The grave was dug by men from Mwika village prior to the burial. No payment is made. But they may get a share of the meat of the slaughtered cow or the headman of Mwika gives them some money which he was given as the procession was about to enter his village. Most of the speech is done by the *Muchilingwa*. In this instance a church choir was also requested by the relatives to sing at the burial. From the departure from the village where the late headman died to the burial grounds at Sunkutu, the body was carried in a coffin. While lowering into the grave, the choir sings until the grave is filled with soil and a small mound on top is formed. More speeches, even reading of Scriptures, follow. After concluding the ceremony *Muchilingwa* dismisses the people and makes sure everybody is leaving Sunkutu. The people are now free to go home.

The relatives, too, return home and gather in the village at the funeral house. The *Muchilingwa* has also joined the gathering and announces the kind and amount of payment he is to receive for his services rendered. This could be two of the best blankets, a new hoe, soap, a white sheet of material (*umwala*) etc., etc. *Muchilingwa* makes sure that when he leaves to go home, he will take with him every item of his payment. The relatives will undertake every effort to see that all which was demanded is at hand right away. To anger the *Muchilingwa* could be a costly and fearsome matter.

The gathering at the funeral house will last for several days. It is now the duty of the village committee to choose a suitable successor to the late headman. This procedure of selecting can take as long as a year. If they fail to find somebody, the case is then referred to the chief who then will appoint somebody headman, preferably one of his own relatives, or one of his sons or daughters. Neither the village committee nor the villagers can revoke this appointment even if a woman is appointed to be the headwoman of the village.

The Death of Chitimukulu – 'Keeping the King Divine'

The Bemba political system has at its very top Chitimukulu, their Paramount chief. His political significance is, however, less attributed to his outstanding administrative aptitude than to the beliefs in his supernatural powers. The same is true with other major chiefs of Lubemba.

Audrey Richards, in her 1968 Henry Myers Lecture at the Royal Anthropological Institute, entitled her lecture 'Keeping the King Divine'. In it she argued that "his 'supernatural power' was the only real power he had" (Kalusa and Vaughan 2013:50) – and which he was left with after colonial rule ended his political sovereignty at the end of the 19th century (1899). Though hierarchical in nature, Bemba political powers were, even prior to British rule (and still are), caught in "structural opposition between the Chief and his councillors" and "the frequent and prolonged succession disputes at the death of Chitimukulu (and of two or three other major chiefs)" (:49) was another contested area. As Paramount chief he is "the ritual head of the people" (:50). Chieftainship was his through a long line of ancestors and ancestresses and – through his councillors – is in possession of their relics and in guardianship of these most sacred relics of the Bemba (:50).

While the life of Chitimukulu is a balancing act to uphold cosmic order and stability for all of Lubemba and its people through a set of vital rituals ("symbolic mechanisms"), so is his death nothing short of being an outright "'disaster'", as Richards put it (:51). Disaster because now the land was "said to have 'gone cold', … "to have 'broken into pieces;'" (:51) it "entered into a kind of 'state of emergency'" (:53).

The disaster was indeed a 'total disaster.' According to Richards and Vitebsky, central

> 'seems to be a loss of contact and control over the land:access to the spirits of the land is blocked, since only a living Chief has this access. Hence there is a suspension during the interregnum of all regular rites related to the land. The land has become inaccessible, *kuloba'* (in Kalusa and Vaughan 2013:54).

The one-year period of interregnum – it lasted from the announcement of Chitimukulu's death until the ascension of his successor – adds to the disastrous situation, "institutionalized through a complex and very lengthy death ritual that involved the embalming of the dead chief's body" (:49) and (up to the beginning of the 20th century) human sacrifice.

> The body of the Chitimukulu was placed under the control of a set of officals known as *bafingo* or undertakers, including embalmers and pall-bearers. The Chief's body was taken to the hut of his head-wife and placed on a raised platform, wrapped

in a cloth. Over the following year or so the body was regularly bathed in a specially prepared embalming fluid, until completely desiccated (and likened to a 'seed'). Eventually the body was transported in a procession from the Chitmukulu's headquarters, across the river Chambeshi, to the burial ground at Mwalulue, which housed all the relics of previous Chitimukulus (and other chiefs of the ruling clan) and was presided over by the Shimwalule (2013:55).

Death and burial rites of Bemba Chiefs reach back to the time when they still perceived of themselves as Luba who had left their country of origin in search of new lands. Oral traditions recount the death and burial of their first Chitimukulu at Mwalulue.

Burial arrangements for ChitiMukulu [Chiti the Great] – the first Chitimukulu

The Body of *ChitiMukulu* [Chiti the Great] *Fwamwamba UmuLuba* (Rude basket made of leaves) (Mushindo 1977:2), the first Chitimukulu, was preserved complete apart from the intestines, which were buried in his hut at Citaba Camp while still engaged in their migratory journey begun in the sixteenth century. From the beginning, *NkoleMukulu Umwimbilwa Mapembwe* (One who had trenches dug against him) (1977:2), the immediate younger brother, *Kapamba* (*Mukulu*) *Mubanshi* (1977:2) the youngest of the three brothers, some nieces and nephews, and councillors were searching for a burial ground where they could take care of the tomb and worship the chief at the end of each year (1977:22). The search turned out to take quite long, penetrating ever deeper into foreign terrains of the northern plateau.

> From Kaunga, Nkole moved to the Mikunku stream where he built a camp, Mapunga (misfortune); and from there he went on to the Katonga river and built a booth called *Muungu wambuto, ni Lesa abiika*, that is to say, "The squash is for seed: God kept it laid aside for that purpose," on discoverig that his only surviving [younger] brother [Kapamba] was a leper and he remained alone responsible for the future of his people (1977:23).

When *NkoleMukulu* finally located a suitable place for burying his brother, he discovered the land belonged to a woman named Chimbala who was without a husband (1977:23). He asked her if she was prepared to cleanse the men who buried *ChitiMukulu* after the funeral to which she replied that she

> had no husband and a cleansing food had to be prepared by a married woman after coitus, she was not in a position to make the necessary preparation for the ceremony (1977:23).

However, *NkoleMukulu* wished Chimbala to look after the burial ground "and told her to let her slave do the duty of a husband, so that she might cleanse the men who buried the chief" (1977:24). In the course of making arrangements for his brother *ChitiMukulu* to be buried, *NkoleMukulu* himself died (mysteriously). Eventually *ChitiMukulu's* grave was dug, his body placed in there, head facing toward the east, and gifts put beside the body ("Indian shells, ivory, earthernwares, white and coloured clothes and houshold utensils") thought to be useful in the other world. The night after burial of *ChitiMukulu*, Chimbala fulfilled her promised duty with her slave Kabotwe and in the morning prepared the required thick porridge for cleansing those who buried the chief as they had contact with his body. *NkoleMukulu* was buried in the following year at the same time, in the same way (1977:25-26).

Moving on to the twentieth century: The Chief's burial ground at Mwalule is taken care of by the custodian, the Shimwalule, who is assisted by three women who are no longer of child-bearing age. They are wives of dead chiefs, or more exactly, the 'wives of the relics' (*bamukabenye*) and for this reason it is forbidden for them to have sexual intercourse. Breaching this taboo would be regarded as adultery and would in consequence bring all kinds of calamities over the people. No exception but one!

> After the burial of a chief at Mwalulue, one of these women has to sleep with Shimwalule in order to purify the country. After their intercourse a new fire is kindled in the village of Shimwalule himself and his house is white-washed (Tanguy 1983:111).

The ritualized sexual act clears the land from the contamination brought over it by the death of the Chitimukulu. The work of the three women is to honour the royal spirits. It is through them that Chitimukulu offers libations and sacrifices to the ancestors. These women worship in Shimwalule's village in front of the house of the relics (*babenye*) and not in the grove. For this work, they are remunerated (1954/1983:111).

Death and burial rituals develop over time especially against the backdrop of a migratory history resting on a set of cultural practices, with roots in worldview structures from the old land, which will experience modifications as people settle in the new land, also producing modified worldview structures.

The death of subsequent Chitimukulus needs a closer look for more than what has been sketched out above. Of special interest to this work is the nature of his death – not natural!

Kalusa and Vaughan provide a kind of summary of the complexity of events sorrounding the Chief's death. This is based on Richards' collection of ethnographic material collected in the 1930s and 1950s. Richards provides evidence

> that the Bemba had strangled their dying chiefs, fearful that if they were left to breath their last naturally, they would breath out the *mipashi* or spirits of the land (Kalusa and Vaughan 2013:51).

But later she seems to contradict herself by saying

> …the paramount chief derives his power from the spirits of the dead predecessors and must not be allowed to die with these spirits still in his body. Throttling a senoir chief (this not only applied to the Chitimukulu, but also to other senior chiefs of the 'Crocodile' Clan) kept the spirits safe in the chief's body, which was then embalmed and preserved as a 'relic' (2013:51).

Alhough Kalusa and Vaughan detect this apparent contradiction, they rate it as "perhaps indicative of how difficult she (and others) found it to pin down Bemba beliefs on this subject" (2013:82). Maybe – maybe not.

Regicide – some questions

The fact that the Chitimukulu was "strangled by senior councillors before he breathed his last, with a view to keeping the spirits of the ancestors inside the body" (2013:54). Richards herself, in a letter to Edmund Leach in 1982, desribes in detail procedures of regicide of senior chiefs showing that even the "colonial authorities, she implied, turned a blind eye to regicide" (Kalusa and Vaughan 2013:52).

It is also true that the Chief, and other major chiefs, embody more than one *umupashi* while alive. The Chitimukulu in particular embodies an accumulation of *imipashi* of previous Chitimukulus. In fact, even in Richards' time, the then Chitimukulu could rely on a long line of predecessors and with it an assembly of *imipashi* indwelling his body, among them, of course, *umupashi* of the very first Chitimukulu, founder of the *Beena Ng'andu* dynasty.

Why is there such a strong emphasis on strangling the Chitimukulu and keeping his assembly of *imipashi* inside the body when otherwise this is unthinkable and elaborate rituals assure proper detachment of *umupashi* from the body of his 'human companion' – as will be shown later?

Why absolutely desiccating, a complete drying out of the body, for, so to say, 'safekeeping' of *imipashi*?

Why is a body prepared in such a way explicitly deemed to be the proper storage chamber for all royal *imipashi*?

Regicide – some considerations

Perhaps there is a slight but meaningful difference, apart from the physical implications, between dying by breathing his last, thus breathing out the *imipashi* in a slow process, and throttling, which ends life much more abruptly and catches *imipashi* sort of by 'surprise' confining them inside the body.

In other words, *imipashi* are prevented from being set free by exhaling – sort of disallowing disorderly non-ritualized exiting – to roam about at will while a successor to Chieftainship is still a long way off. The long interregnum makes the land inaccessible, *kuloba*, and you cannot have, on top of it all, *imipashi* of the highest order being let loose on rampaging bouts, possibly also wreaking havoc on all Lubemba communities, bringing sickness and disease. There is common agreement that *umupashi* of a chief (and were it only one *umupashi* – which is not the case) is regarded as having a higher status than that of ordinary members of Bemba society.

The traditional form of 'embalming' by desiccating the body, so very different "from the other forms of embalming (practised in present-day Zambia as elsewhere), which aim to slow down decomposition and create an appearance of wholeness" reduces the body "to a 'seed'-like substance," (Kalusa and Vaughan 2013:83, endnote 28), and may be explained on grounds of essential, critical worldview elements.

Perhaps this 'seed'-like substance of the body symbolizes the desiccated body as seed (Ground Peas, Beans, Sorghum, Millet and others), with the hardened outer shell (skin), shielding the core with its preserving, conserving 'germinating power' over a long period of time.

Perhaps the 'seed'-like substance, taken as seed-metaphor, is the very kind of 'environment' which best safeguards, or even guarantees safeguarding against 'loss' or roaming about of the *imipashi* until such moment when through enactment of proper rituals, they break conservation as the new Chitimukulu ascends to power taking with him the very *imipashi* of his predecessors now taking up residence again in his own body.

Perhaps the 'seed-metaphor' has roots as far back as when *NkoleMukulu*, in search of a burial ground for his late brother *ChitiMukulu*, and upon discovering that his younger brother Kapamba is a leper, called the booth at the Katonga river *Muungu wambuto, ni Lesa abiika*, "the squash is for seed: God kept it laid aside for that purpose," meaning **he** is that seed (*imbuto*). And it is he who is now solely responsible for the future of his people. A very interesting metaphorically decorated statement about Divine election!

The seed-metaphor als surfaces in Emilio Chishimba Mulolani's theology as head of his Mutima Church, established as an African Independent Church in Zambia in 1958 (Burlington 2004:115). Emilio is of Bemba ethnicity and his mother is a "decendent of a paramount chief, Chitimukulu Chinchinta, a historical figure (Roberts 1973)" (Burlington 1998:77).

Emilio's incredibly complex and complicated theology is radically different from mainstream Christian theologies as well as being hugely different from traditional notions of personhood, for example, rejecting "the notion of indwelling ancestral spirits" (Burlington 2004:147).

Nevertheless, the seed-metaphor is central to his concept of Trinity, "especially its second person, the Seed-Heart (*Lulelya*) or Child (*Mwana*) of God the Ancestor (*Lesa Chikolwe*) (Chishimba 1997b:4 in Burlington 2008:8)" and " is responsible for nurturing human souls, sustaining them through the experience of embodiment and suffering and moving them toward their eternal destiny in the heavenly realm" (Chishimba 1996:4, 1995:1 in Burlington 2008:8-9).

All I am saying is that Bemba foundational assumptions on the order and costituent elements and powers of their cultural universe allows their members to call up these worldview structures, encase them in metaphors (each culture has its favourite ones – like the one under discussion) to be deployed for various purposes in order to achieve cultural, political or theological goals.

Returning to the seed-metaphor applied to the desiccated body of Chitimukulu, the normal process of decay of the body would certainly call for a cutting-point, a final detachment of *imipashi* from the body of the late Chitimukulu. But since burial rites, which assure detachment from the body and safe passage to the spirit world, cannot be officiated until after the interregnum is over, *imipashi* have to be kept safe in the desiccated body until indwelling of the new body is ritually enacted.

In other words, the safe and smooth transitioning of *imipashi* from the late Chitimukulu to the new Chitimukulu, endowing him with the very 'supernatural powers' for which he is renowned to possess, is absolutely vital, indeed it is critical for land and people, since the "life and death of Chitimukulu was [and is] connected to the life and death of every subject" (Kalusa and Vaughan 2013:51). With the purification of the land – and only because of it! – the land is no longer inaccessible, *'kuloba'*; a new cycle of life, both for agricultural and cultural/social activities, can resume.

A safe and smooth transitioning process of *imipashi* from one Chitimukulu to the next Chitimukulu is indeed vital, even critical for 'Keeping the King Divine'.

This also explains, in a way, the "complex attitude of admiration and fear which the Mubemba [Bemba person] has for his chief – an attitude which cuts across ties of personal loyalty and kinship sentiment" (Richards 1936:1).

To put it pointedly: Do not mess with Chitimukulu as it would mean to mess with his *imipashi*! Total disaster for those who dared! Total disaster for the land – for it will not be spared!

Death of Common or Ordinary People (Ababapi)

In pre-independence days death was greatly dreaded and was infused with cruel consequences for husband and wife alike.

Dreaded Death – It is Bad for Widowers

Labrecque, writing in the 1930-ties, gives following account:

> Neither widow nor widower has any part to play in the funeral ceremonies because in most cases they are considered the cause of the death of their partner in marriage. Sometimes the

widower is bound and flogged, all the property of his wife such as ornaments, clothes, hoes etc. are taken by the deceased's relatives. Happy indeed is the man who, as a result of the incantations, is not accused of sorcery or of being possessed by a bad spirit, for then the reprisals would be really terrible.

Dreaded Death – It is Worse for Widows

The lot of the widow is no better. She is beaten, bound and scoffed at. All her husband's possessions such as grain bins with food go to the parents of the deceased. She is reduced to begging (ukupula) until her destiny is known by revealing the degree of her culpability for the death of her husband. But what is worse, this 'muka-mfwilwa (widow) is placed under an interdict. 'She is haunted by the death in her body' (aba ne mfwa mu nda). As long as she is haunted by the death of her husband she cannot re-marry. To marry while under interdict would result in the death of the new spouse. So people say of such a person: 'E cilwa buko iciisa ulubansa nga lwabuta' (this is to fight the in-law who comes in a crowd). This applies also to the widower. Both must drive away death (Labrecque 1934/1982:87-88).

The departure of a person from the community of the living on account of the death of the body involves a multitude of important, even critical matters which require attention and action. On the one hand there are the more mundane tasks (e.g. informing relatives, food and drinks for funeral gathering, coffin, grave-digging and so forth) to be organized and executed. On the other hand, there are the ritual-based activities – I call them the 'critical obligations' tapping deep into worldview structures.

Ubupyani – Succession and Inheritance

Bemba culture has a complex system of rituals at death, immediately after death, at burial, the funeral gathering, and even thereafter. The most prominent feature is to succeed *(ukupyana)* a dead person regardless of age and sex. **Every person who dies must be succeeded by a living person**,[2] though the mode of succession differs according to age, sex and marital status. For instance, the death of a married male person requires his replacement, that is, he is being succeeded by another male person (*ukupyanika umwaume uwaupa*). Succession also includes inheriting: the heir takes, next to his name, his status, and social obligation, his *umupashi*. Richards regarded this intricate set of inheritance features as something she labelled as an unusually complete identification between the dead man and his heir (1970:269).

> Succession and inheritance matters are deliberated at isambo/isambwe lyamfwa (family gathering after burial of the deceased relative). At this gathering, if the deceased was married, both families (that of the deceased and that of his/her in-laws) are expected to be represented as the clan of the deceased claims its rights (Lumbwe 2009:97).

Ukupyana – Ritualised Removal of Death (kutamfye mfwa)

Ubupyani (succession and inheritance) is to undertake *ukupyana* – to drive away death (*kutamfye mfwa*), and in case the late person was married, to make it possible to remarry. As can be expected, those two features are highly ritualized.

To give a full account of all particularities and aspects of death and the pertaining rituals for all people according to their rank and status is beyond my reach. What I can do is provide in descriptive form major and essential aspects of death and associated ritual practices. Two aspects deserve mentioning and explaining: (1) death must be driven away (*ukutamfye mfwa*); (2) succession and inheritance (*ubupyani*) – including distribution of belongings – must be done.

Lumbwe summarizes that:

> Succession (*ukupyana*) does not occur in the same way after every death. Depending upon the circumstances and the agreement reached by the clan, the following options may be considered. In the case of shimfwilwa (widower), impyani (successor) for his wife must be her sister or a close family member from her clan. There are no restrictions and therefore the family may choose a married woman or maiden (umushimbe) as a successor; in the case of a mukamfwilwa (widow), the clan may choose a married man or a bachelor (nkungulume) as a successor (2009:98).

<u>Death of a wife</u>

> To drive away the death of his wife who haunts him, the husband must seek to have clandestine marriage relations for two

days with a sister or niece of his dead wife. The ceremony differs according to the state of the woman who agrees to sleep with him, whether she is married or not (Labrecque 1934/1982:88).

If the women chosen is unmarried:

> The ceremony lasts two days and it takes place in the village. After the widower has done the marriage act for the first time with the young woman, she puts two 'utwinga' (little pots) on the fire. They are filled with water and remedies (roots from the mubwilili). One of the 'utwinga' is called 'kalubi' (fetish) and the other 'icikota' (the big woman). The water from the 'kalubi' is thrown on the road along which the funeral procession passed. (Aitila amenshi mwi'shinda lya mucishi = she throws the water on the route to the grave). On the second day the widower and the young woman together place the 'akapalwilo' (marriage pot) on the fire, and together remove it from the fire when the water is hot in order to wash themselves. This is the definite bond of marriage. "Amupa, e myupile mu kupyanina, e mipyanine amupa no kupa (He marries her, this this is the way of marrying in the ritual to remove death) (Labrecque 1934/1982:88).

If there is no unmarried woman:

> It sometimes happens that a widower does not find a relative of his dead wife with whom he can free himself from the 'death'. So, he appeals to any widow to help him. If her relatives agree, she is given to him in marriage. (Bamupa cishishi = he marries this next of kin in order to throw away the spirit and death). With her, he first of all goes through the ceremony of 'ukutamfye mfwa'. They then say: "E wamupokela mfwa" (she has taken death away from him); "E wamutamfishe mfwa" (she has cleared death away from him); E wamupokela umupashi" (she has liberated him from the spirit of the deceased) (Labrecque 1934/1982:88).

A more recent account of what happens at the death of a wife:
- she has to be succeeded
- the first stage of *ubupyani* (*ukunwa amenshi*) is performed.
- the family looks for a woman who is not married: a 'cleared' widow or a divorced woman. The woman is brought to the man and they will then be married husband and wife. Children of both

unions become now the responsibility of the man. (However, it can often happen that many a times children who join the family are on the disadvantaged side and are being neglected).
- If no such woman is found, they now look for a virgin girl from among the family. In this case normal wedding procedures take place, or he just takes her home. Such a marriage is regarded as a strong *ukupyana ing'anda*.
- If the death of the deceased was related to an illness (such as HIV/AIDS) the man is made to wear white beads (*ukukaka akalungu*) and no sexual relationship is required.

Death of a husband

Obviously, cultures change over time and with it some practices are either discontinued or modified. Labrecque's account from the 1930s mentions items in the ceremony which are no longer relevant to modern life.

> The widow (mukamfilwa, uwafwilwa mulume = whose husband has died):First of all there is the ceremony or 'ukunwa amenshi' (to drink water) which consists in giving the bows and arrows belonging to the dead husband to a new nephew or grandnephew who is destined to replace his uncle by taking his name and performing his functions (e kutola amata, e kupyana amata, e kufumye mifitalila ya mubiye = this is to take arrows, this is to inherit arrows, to take away bad things from one's neighbour). Another way of putting this is: "E kubule mishingo (amata) ya munankwe" (this is to inherit the possessions and wife of the dead man (1934/1982:89).

Ukupyana – Ritualized Succession and Inheritance

The Bemba inheritance custom is a credo which says that – under normal circumstances – no person just leaves this world anyhow. Everyone needs to be succeeded and the 'human gap' must be closed.

Succession of a child, unmarried person, old person – ukunwa amenshi

A child is commonly succeeded by the grandfather or grandmother still alive who then becomes *impyani*, a successor. *Impyani* takes on *umupashi* of the child (*asenda mupashi wa mwana*, meaning: "he/she carries away *umupashi* of the child.")[3]

Unmarried or old persons (who cannot re-marry) are also succeeded. This appropriation happens at the first stage of succession *(ubupyani)* and is called *ukunwa amenshi* (to drink water). The ceremony takes place after the burial within a relatively short period of time (about the time it takes to brew enough beer for the public to honour its participation and sympathy in remembrance of the late person. Some beer is reserved for the family members in a small calabash).

Every person who dies (unless mad, leper, wizard or *bamwabi* etc.) must be succeeded *(ukupyanwa)* by a living person. At the death of a person, the family would look for a suitable candidate to become *impyani*. Preference is given to persons who are younger than the deceased and who are from the father's family line. If no person is found, the search continues with the mother's line. Considered are only those who are younger than the mother of the late person. Preference is given to the mother's brother *(bayama)* who must be younger than her. An adult or even a child from his family can become *impyani*. *Impyani* must not yet have grandchildren of his own. Should there be in either family line an expecting mother, no search for *impyani* is necessary, since the child to be born automatically succeeds *(ukupyana)* the late person, who might be of any age.

The father's line and the mother's line are considered as *ing'anda inono* as opposed to *ing'anda ikalamba*, the house/family in which the death occurred. A member of *ing'anda ikalamba* cannot succeed a deceased person from *ing'anda ikalamba*.

Drinking Water – the ukunwa amenshi ceremony

The family members put the small calabash with beer *(umufungo)* in the midst of them and discuss who of the family can succeed *(ukunwa amenshi)* the deceased. When the right person is found, the calabash is removed, and the person *(uwakunwa amenshi)* is put in the middle instead.

The father of the late person (if he is also dead, the younger brother of the father) would take some water in his mouth and spray it on the chest *(pa cifuba)* and on the back *(pa numa)* of *impyani*. This is called *ukupaala* (to bless), for example:

> *ulekuula fye ulelosha impumi mu mulu ube fye ngo mutaba* (just grow, directing your face to heaven, just be like a baobab tree = just grow without any problems)

The ceremony is called *ukupyanika* (to appoint successor) and is meant to unite both *imipashi* (*umupashi* of the deceased and *umupashi* of the successor), so that *impyani* can inherit the name of the deceased. Both names are now "active", that is, they come into use. The union of both *imipashi* does not necessarily mean an addition of strength, abilities or improve the successor though his second *umupashi* is to provide additional protection from harm, especially from acts of sorcery. The rationale is that an adult person already has his own ways; his personality has already individual character traits. He is already with his own *imibeele*. His personality has already come to maturity. That is why a baby to be born soon will automatically receive the name of that late person in order to revitalize the personality of the forebear. A person who has succeeded once and becomes again the only candidate to qualify as successor in the event of another death, can be allowed to succeed a second time. After that, no more. This second succession is restricted to a family of whom he has not succeeded anyone. It must be from another family.

Kapolyo (2005) offers following description of *ukunwa amenshi*:

Inheriting a name!

> After the death of a man or woman, the relatives gather to appoint the person who will inherit the deceased. It is important to establish that inheritance in this case has little to do with receiving bequests and everything to do with 'becoming' in a mysterious way the person who has died. Symbolically the family through the ceremony invite back the departed and renew contact with him or her (Mbiti 1969:152). At the appointed time, a younger relative will be nominated. Sometimes the deceased might have nominated the person he desired.

> In matrilineal ethnic groups, [like the Bemba], the line of inheritance goes through a man's sister and their children, his uterine nephews and nieces (Richards 1950:222). This is perhaps what makes the sisters of a man so special and important. They bear him the boys who will take his name after his death.

Inheriting people not wealth!

> The ritual is chaired by a leading member of the family and all involved are asked to sit in a circle and the nominee is asked to sit in the middle of the circle. The subject is given water to drink

> [therefore this part of *ubupyani* is called *ukunwa amenshi* – to drink water; R.B.] and token chattels [belongings] from the wardrobe of the deceased. He or she may also be given some implements that defined the major activity of the deceased. For example, he may be given a gun if the deceased had been a hunter, a hoe for a farmer and so on. Then words are uttered inviting back the deceased to take up residence in the body of the nominee. Notice that people inherit people not wealth.

Inheriting status and position of the deceased!

> From that moment on the candidate in effect becomes the departed. All who had relationships with the departed transfer those to the candidate so that they relate to him or her in the same way they would have related to the departed. A man whose daughter has inherited his grandmother will always treat her with the same love and respect as he would his departed forebear. This person will henceforth be the representative of the departed among the living. The living/dead are immanent, i.e. co-existent with each other, and involved among their people in this way. As the ritual of inheritance unfolds, comments are invited from everyone who wishes to speak. The speakers address the nominee in words that make it clear that they are addressing the departed. The nominee has effectively *become* the dead person.

> The children of the departed will regard the nominee in effect, and defer to him, as if he were their real father. Boys inherit their maternal uncle and girls inherit their maternal aunts" (2005:135-137).

The person performing the ritual is the only one who can give blessings (*amapalo*) to *uwakunwa amenshi*. The other persons present put some money on a plate and say some words of encouragement and take their seat again. This is also called: *ukushikula*.[4] After that, the distribution of all the possessions of the deceased is done (*ukusalanganya imishingo*). *Imishingo* are always kept by an old woman of the family until this moment arrives. The distribution of items is carried out by *uwakwakanya imishango*, the person selected to distribute. Even the widow has no say in who gets what. The distribution of items concludes the ceremony and people go home.

Succession of a married man – *ukutamfye mfwa*

The death of a husband means that the widow is under obligation to undergo a second ritual (*ukutamfye mfwa*) after a minimum of one year and maximum up to two years have elapsed. The family of the deceased now looks for a suitable male candidate (*impyani*), to succeed the late husband. *Impyani* must be younger than the deceased and come from the lower house (a man from the late father's family line. If no one is found it shifts to the late mother's family line) and again to the uncle of the late (brother of his mother) or the aunt (sister of the father).

Final discussions are reserved to a very few family members in order to keep the identity of the candidate secret. The completion of the second stage of succession demands sexual intercourse of *impyani* and the widow. The execution of the rite is done privately and only a few family members are informed when and where it is being performed. The following day an announcement is made introducing the new husband of the widow to the public and the new father to the children, if there were any, and *ukushikula* is performed again. In this way *impyani* has fulfilled *ukupyana nganda*, the succession of the house of the late husband. If *impyani* is already married, he must obtain approval from his wife prior to the sexual union with the widow. Should she withhold approval he cannot be a rightful *impyani*.

However, it happens that some men force their way without the consent of their wives, this is called: *alekaka umupashi* (he is tying *umupashi* of the late husband to the house of the widow). Such a kind of succession would be counted as illegal and *umupashi* of the deceased would also see it the same way and turn himself[5] into *cibanda* (*umupashi naualuka cibanda* = *umupashi* has changed into *cibanda*) and would from now on torment those living in the house of the late person. As a further consequence it also means divorce from his first wife and he will then have to stay with the widow, who will become his wife.

In the case of *impyani* obtaining consent from his wife to have sexual relation with the widow, it would mean she simultaneously makes her husband a polygamist – and the legal father of the widow's children. He is now bound to his first wife through marriage and to his second wife through succession.

There is, however, the alternative of *ukubulako fye umupashi*, meaning: "to take away *umupashi*." Hereby *impyani* executes *ubupyani* (succession) through sexual intercourse with the widow but relationship ends here, and he stays with his first wife.

The widow is not obligated to become the wife of her brother-in-law, especially if he is married already as this would mean she enters a polygamous marriage. Susan Sakala comments:

> The relative of the deceased goes to the bedroom with the widow and has sex with her. The relatives come in the morning to perform something similar to the wedding ceremony. They say: 'Our family comes from there and is very hard-working…' But only if both come out of the house. If the man does not want to take over, he doesn't come out of the house. Man and woman discuss before they go out. When the men are forced by their relatives to inherit the wife of their brother to keep up respect, then they will not come out. Even the woman can stay in the house if she does not want to marry. Often the widow secretly tells one of the brothers who wants to inherit her that he should be the one, not the others. Then she will not refuse. The widow can also come out earlier, furious. Then the inheritance does not take place. You have to go through some steps, herbs and oils before you come out, you cannot just run out by yourself, the elders are calling you (in Offe 2010:77-78).

Widowhood – restrictive living

For widows, death of their husbands is still an exceedingly difficult situation. In a quite recent work, Offe (2010) highlights the particular circumstances widowhood involves, especially during the mourning period where a widow has to follow certain restrictions for the purpose of sharing the sorrow of her late husband:

- during the first week, until burial takes place, sleeping on the floor on hard ground
- the widow is not allowed to wash und put on new clothes
- she cannot prepare food or come near the fireplace of the family
- the most important restriction is to absolutely abstain from sexual intercourse
- she is not allowed to cut or braid her hair – as a deterrent for men – and to shave body hair
- she has to wear a headscarf (*umupango*) which is not tied at the back of the head but allows others full view of her uncut and unstyled hair. This is necessary until her status of being a widow has ended. [A widower ties it around his upper left arm. *Umupango*

indicates that a widow or widower has not yet undergone *ubupyani*].

- she is in a state of 'uncleanness' and it has to be ritually removed (*ubutafika*, cleansing, 'white-colouring'). This takes place about a year after the death of the husband in the house of the parents of the deceased.
- Cleansing is achieved through sexual intercourse with a younger classificatory brother of the deceased (brothers are, next to other sons of the mother of the deceased, all sons of sisters to the mother [sons of maternal aunts], that is, parallel cousins of the husband). This brother inherits the widow and her widowhood is removed (Offe 2010:75-76).

The execution of *ubupyani* is vital because there is fear that the widow or the widower can get mad or even die if s/he marries before *ubupyani* has been performed. Madness (*ubushilu*) due to such illegal union (sexual intercourse) before *ubupyani* is performed, cannot be cured. The cause for such misfortune is attributed to *umupashi*.

> *Umupashi uwawafwa taufuma mu ng'anda nga tabalapyanika* (*umupashi* of the one who died does not leave the house if they don't do succession)

The completion of the ceremony frees the widow or widower from the death of his or her partner in marriage.

Ukupyana – Ritualized Liberation from the Deceased (*ukupokela umupashi*)

Until the onslaught of the HIV/AIDS pandemic sexual intercourse was the ultimate way to *kutamfye mfwa* (to drive away death) or put differently to *kupokela umupashi* – to liberate from the *umupashi* of the deceased. The union of husband and wife in blood, sex and spirit is so binding that it "endures through death itself." (Maxwell 1983:32) The purpose of sexual intercourse in the "succession rite" (*ukupyana*) is "to chase away death" (*ukutamfye mfwa*) from the clan of the survivor. In turn it liberates *umupashi* from the dead body and brings him back (*ukubwesha umupashi*) to the clan of the deceased. To show neglect by not performing this ceremony would mean for the surviving spouse to "remain too hot a medium to remarry" (Maxwell 1983:32 quoted from Labrecque 1934/1982:68-69).

Not to follow the cultural path, for example, to have sexual relations or enter into marriage with a widow or widower whose late partner has not yet been succeeded (*tabalapyanikwa*), invites serious trouble. *Umupashi* of the deceased would be wedged, as it were, between the lovers and due to jealousy, would not tolerate this, turn into *icibanda* (Offe 2010:80) and two things might happen: a) either *umupashi* causes the man and the woman to go mad (*ukufulunganya* – to cause chaos, to mess up, confuse [their *SEICs*] or b) he causes their deaths (through this kind of madness). Someone courting a widow or widower whose late partner has not yet been succeeded might receive warnings from *umupashi*, danger signals like seeing snakes around the house when s/he comes visiting or give him/her frightening dreams of snakes, be drowned in the river, and so forth.

Modernizing Ubupyani – three options

Contemporary Bemba society allows for three options of *ubupyani*:

- *ukupyana ing'anda:* (a rightfully married *impyani* obtains approval of the first wife to perform ritual sexual intercourse with the widow, inherits her and marries the widow.
- *ukubulako fye umupashi*: (approval of the first wife to perform *ubupyani* by having sexual relation with the widow but relationship ends here, and he stays with his first wife. He does not become a polygamist.
- *ukukaka akalungu* (common these days): if the death of the late husband was related to an illness (such as HIV/AIDS) or if among the family members no suitable *impyani* is found, *ukukaka akalungu* is performed.

Ukukaka akalungu are white beads strung on a thin cotton threat and tied around the wrist of either arm. Since the cotton is not strong it can break easily and is interpreted as completion of *ubupyani* (*ubupyani nabusumina*) (the easy breaking of the threat is ascribed to *umupashi* who signals his approval in this way).

What is so special about *ubulungu* (white beads)?:

- they drive away evil spirits (*ifibanda/ ifiwi*)
- they clear *umupashi* of a deceased person
- they bring luck, e.g. when hunting luck is absent for a while, the hunters get some white beads, construct *ulufuba* (a small spirit shrine) and call on the *imipashi* of the family to provide meat. Then

- they throw the *ubulungu* in all four directions, say some words and go hunting
- they drive away illness

Chileshe states for the Kamena area (some 40km north of Kasama, the provincial administrative town), that people often attribute illnesses and deaths related to tuberculosis and HIV/AIDS "to witchcraft (*ubuloshi*). On the other hand, some people seem to have a good idea that the disease is transmitted sexually because the once popular practice of wife inheritance (*ukupyana*) seems to be in decline" (Chileshe 2005:112).

'Taking care' of Umupashi

Offe (2010), in her work on widowhood of Bemba women, speaks of the liminal phase a widow must undergo. But in fact, as she rightly points out, the widow is not the only affected party who undergoes a liminal phase. Between the death of a married man and the ritual cleansing of the widow, both the deceased and the widow have no fixed status.

Liminal Phase – Deceased, Widow and Relatives

The *deceased and the widow are suspended, as it were, in this liminal phase* until after the cleansing ritual has been performed and the widow is again able to take up social status and social obligations as a married woman (:82).

Huntington and Metcalf comment:

> Kin are contaminated by death because they partake in death. Each severed relationship leaves a living person that much reduced: a social and psychological amputee. Of all relatives, the widow is the most disfigured. Like the dead man, she must undergo a liminal phase during which her identity is readjusted (Huntington, Metcalf 1991:82).

Her social status needs reconfiguring after the death of her late husband because through his death her relationships with her family, the family of her in-laws, and the community at large will have to be redefined. In other words, the *surviving family members also undergo a liminal phase* since the loss of a member leaves a gap behind and with it a reconstituting of a net of relationships is necessary (Offe 2010:82)

Liminal Phase – *Umupashi* too!

But one other party of those who are thrown into a liminal phase by the deceased husband is often not appropriately considered. Offe hints at it by saying that the deceased stays, 'lives' with the spouse as spirit during her liminal phase up until its cessation through the ritual cleansing of the widow enabling him to now become a matrilineal ancestor (2010:82). To clarify the matter: the deceased is the *umupashi* of the deceased who is undergoing a liminal phase too! Ergo, there are several affected parties thrown into a liminal phase caused by the death of the body of a human person, of which *umupashi* is not the least affected! On the contrary!

The other parties affected by the death of the person can share their sufferings with each other and after ritual observance regain normal social status and with the passing of time the initial hurting the loss of a husband, a family member has caused, will gradually ebb away. The moment of death ends physical life but more importantly is the moment when *umupashi* separates from the body (*umupashi wapatulukula ku mubili*, meaning: *umupashi* has separated from the body). The point of exit of *umupashi* is not specifically referenced but people say that *umupashi* could leave together with *umweo*, an immaterial spiritual substance meaning: "breath" and also "life", through the nose and mouth. A corpse is without *umupashi* (*umubili washala fye eka*, meaning: the body alone remains behind); life has ended (*ukuleka umweo*, meaning: to stop life, to breathe one's last, to die; life has stopped). Death is pronounced immediately after breathing has stopped.

Liminal Phase – '*Umupashi* Perspective'

The nature of *umupashi's* liminal phase is equally a period of 'suffering'. Let us look at it from this perspective, a '*umupashi* perspective', if I may say so.

Death of the body effects separation of *umupashi* from the body of his, perhaps long-time, 'human companion'. This is not an easily achieved process because *umupashi* does not – cannot! – just disappear into the transcendental realm. So, he keeps close to human beings; enjoys human company even more so when tokens of respect are extended to him like drumming, dancing, and, of course, food and drink, which he can enjoy (Labrecque 1934/1982:83).

Sometimes the death of his 'human companion' may partly be attributed to a moment of carelessness, a moment of absence on the part of *umupashi* leaving his 'human companion' vulnerable to other forces. The terrible result (death) brings much sorrow even remorse to *umupashi* and his *SEIC* is tormented with emotional pain.

Similarly, *umupashi* may suffer emotional pain merely because a long-time harmonious relationship with his 'human companion' has sadly ended by a good and peaceful death, the death of the body he so long protected and cared for.

Then there is the fact that the body is subjected to a process of decay which is extremely unpleasant, pushing *umupashi* constantly but forcefully away and, with the burial of the corpse, marking the final cutting-point from his 'human companion'.

This period of the liminal phase of *umupashi* is putting a strain on his *SEIC*, destabilizing his emotional equilibrium for which he was formerly renowned. Having had to let go of his 'human companion', *umupashi* now seeks 'refuge' with the widow in the same house until *ubupyani* is completed. During this period *umupashi* acts as a guardian to the woman also taking responsibility to guard the house.

Lumbwe asserts:

> The Bemba believe that if a person dies, something of the dead person remains in the living, and if the soul (umupashi) returns, it is most likely that it would choose the former partner. This way the clan of the deceased has to remove all spiritual and human connections that might still remain (2004:39).

It is now all the clearer why the widow is to undergo the cleansing ritual because this is still widely perceived to be the 'king's highway', the one and only way to end the liminal phase for both of them! and with it, enable both of them to regain status!

Both need to be separated from each other but not anyhow! And not anywhere! The cleansing ritual is performed in the house, the bedroom, of the widow. Ritualised sexual intercourse with *impyani* severs all emotional ties to her and *umupashi* disassociates from her and associates himself from now on with *impyani*.

In any case, whether through sexual relation or *ukukaka akalungu* (stringing up of white beads worn around the wrist of either arm), ritualized liberation from the *umupashi* of the deceased (*ukupokela umupashi*) must be executed. To extricate oneself from this duty is to attempt the impossible!

This is fact for yet another reason. The clan of the deceased husband will certainly lay claim to the *umupashi* of their deceased family member for him to become an honourable ancestor and to be of future 'service' to them. Without ritualized liberation of *umupashi* such future beneficent contribution to their clan and lineage cannot be enacted (see also Offe 2010:79)

Destiny: Becoming an Honoured Ancestor – *Mupashi Mukankala*

Survival after death "is an axiom of life." (Willoughby 1970:2) One would certainly not commit oneself too far in saying that this is an axiom widely shared, and to a certain degree in similar form, across the entire African continent. Just as one does not go unprepared to the King's court so it is with African cultures which do not just escort their members to the very last door of physical existence and leave them, so to say, unprepared and empty-handed in the spiritual realm. This threshold is meant to be crossed over and African cultural knowledge systems provision their members for the afterlife so that they do not meet their destiny unprepared.

Clothed in Ritual and Closed by Ritual

The Bemba worldview on this matter comes to light in the burial rites of their aristocracy as well as those for commoners, in the way that surviving family members take leave of their departed members. Everything is clothed in ritual and everything gets closed by ritual. One does not just dig a hole and commit the corpse to the earth. This must be done properly since there is concern for the 'being that survives the death of the body'. There is concern for *umupashi*, his well-being beyond the threshold of death. That is why items put in the grave are not merely intended for decorative purposes. Lumbwe writes that they are meant

> to shower the grave with offerings such as polished shells (impande) and white beads (ubulungu ubwabuta) to honour the deceased. This gesture would also give the deceased the means to buy fire when he/she reached God (Lesa) (2009:96).

Fire figures extremely importantly in the Bemba worldview. Richards (1956/1982) speaks of sex and fire as the "*idée maîtresse* behind most of the ritual behaviour of the Bemba" (1982:30). Maxwell (1983) sees water, blood, sex, fire and life as "root metaphors" of Bemba culture as they "set in motion their most sacred values" (1983:28).

Fire heats the water in the nuptial pot (*akanweno*), the possession of the wife. The washing of hands with warm water from the pot after the conjugal act (*ukucite cupo*) washes off the condition of hotness from the body of husband and wife.

Fire heats the water in the '*akapalwilo*' (marriage pot) required for the widower and the unmarried woman after the sexual act to wash themselves. This is the definitive bond of marriage and ritually removes the death of the late wife of the widower.

An uncleansed widow cannot prepare food or come near the fireplace of the family.

Fire cooks the food for husband and children and menstruating women are to stay clear of it; they are not in the position to touch the studs of the fireplace where cooking is done.

Fire signals a new status for the baby after the umbilical cord has fallen off with the kindling of the new fire, the sacred fire of the child.

A new fire is lit in the whole village after pollution has been purged from it.

Economic rites or the installation of a new Regent is always followed "by the lighting of new fires at the capital" (Kalusa and Vaughan 2013:50).

And fire as something which one needs to have at final destination points at continuation of vital and sacred rites in order to lead a normal and proper afterlife. Wilson, researching among the neighbouring Nyakyusa/Ngonde ethnic groups in the Tukuyu region of Tanzania

> seemed to indicate that 'afterlife' was primarily a social rather than a spatial concept. It was less a place than a community of spirits that had a marked tendency toward mobility, visiting the living in their dreams, tormenting those who had neglected their duties or who had infringed taboos, and, more positively, ensuring health, fertility and the continuation of life (Kalusa and Vaughan 2013:77).

Moving to India, a similar notion can be found. The Kols of India seem to also perceive of the afterlife as primarily a social rather than a spatial concept.

> The corpse is placed on the ground immediately after death so that the soul can find its way to the home of the dead beneath the earth. The body is washed and painted yellow to chase away the evil spirits who try to stop the soul on its journey. It is then placed on a pyre, together with rice and the tools of the

deceased. Rice cakes and silver coins for the journey to the nether world are placed in the mouth of the corpse. After cremation the men gather the bones and take them to hang in a pot in the house of the dead. Rice is thrown along the way so that the deceased, should he or she return in spite of all precautions, will have something to eat and will not harm anyone. After a time, the deceased is "married" to the spirits in the lower world with singing, dancing, and feasting. Finally, the bones are buried in a field (Hiebert 1998:180).

One Needs Means to Reach

Along with the offering of items placed in the grave there is the idea that the journey of *umupashi* in the world beyond is not an 'easy-going, 'carefree ride'. One needs means to reach. Not only that. Because

> if this precautionary measure was not taken, the deceased's soul [*umupashi* R.B.] would not know where to go and end up roaming about (Lumbwe 2009:97) .

Final destiny of *umupashi* is not easily secured nor can it be assumed as an automatic given once a human person has breathed out his/her last breath. As much as one can get lost in this world, *umupashi* can get lost in the other. The idea that a departed *umupashi* would be ending up roaming about is bad news indeed, since for this 'roaming about' is not taking place in the 'nowhere region' of the lands beyond, but definitely in the immediate vicinity of human habitat! The idea of *imipashi* who linger around the communities as 'living dead' having their malevolent dealings with living family members, and the community at large, is very much dreaded. For *umupashi* to be sent on his journey in the lands beyond without necessary means, would oblige him to seek retribution for such of negligence. What else is he supposed to do other than to lash out at ungrateful, uncaring people among whom he lived embodied in his 'human companion'? Not on rare occasions does this perspective on life and death instil great and an ever-present fear into the hearts of people across the communities in Lubemba. Again, drawing on Wilson and his research among the neighbouring Nyakyusa/Ngonde, he also "stressed the *fear* aroused by death among the Nyakyusa." (in Kalusa and Vaughan 2013:69) and the necessity of complying with rituals at death (2013:71).

'Rich and Generous'

But what is the other end of the spectrum like? What is the good end in the afterlife? Hinfelaar puts it rather nicely:

> One is created here on earth in order to become a *Mupashi Mukankala*, a rich and generous spirit/forebear (1994:6).

This grand philosophy requires a coherent worldview; an integrated concept of how the world is structured and of the human person who embodies this concept, acting it out on centre stage by normal daily communal living and within the ritualized cycle of life.

'Reincarnation?'

From the Bemba perspective of 'life' and the axiom of survival after death, the 'afterlife', the issue of 'reincarnation' is prone to arise. In my view, this term is ill-fitted for describing the revitalization of the "incorporeal dimension" (Klass 1995) of *umupashi,* as it may include the notion of fate and the inescapability of a person's destiny. This is not the case, at least not in the Bemba context.

A person in his or her lifetime is indeed capable of effectively breaking the cycle of perpetuity ('multiple corporeal incarnations') through careless living. A definite result and boundary can be established before the end of one's days. No vagueness here and no promise of weighing of the 'good deeds' vs. 'bad deeds' on a divine scale after earthly life has been concluded. The lifestyle and *imibeele* of a person correspond in a reciprocal manner. Bad morals and permanent negligence to adhere to communal norms and values not only affect a person's own *SEIC*, but also qualitatively alters the *SEIC* of one's *umupashi* to such a degree that the benevolent 'spirit double' (*umupashi*) turns into a malevolent 'spirit double' (*icibanda*) during lifetime. Such a person forfeits his or her potential of 'reincarnating' again in the world of the living but most definitely the potential of becoming a *"Mupashi Mukankala"*, a rich and generous forebear, ergo ancestor with means and potential. In the event of that person's death while in this unreformed state, the name will be erased from the potential repertoire of family names. No revitalization, no reincarnation!

It must also be emphasized that when talking of reincarnation in reference to the Bemba understanding of *umupashi* as spirit being, one has to bear in mind that two different biographies of two human beings, whose lives take place in differing time and space settings, come into play, and there will by no means be a total merging of the two in order to fuse into becoming just one. Thus, reincarnation in this (classical) sense is out.

To be clear – not *abantu* - human persons, that is, corporeal beings in perishable bodies, are 'recycled', but *SEICs* of *abantu* are; not any *SEICs*, but quality *SEICs*, marked quality (*imibeele iisuma*) that is. The recycling of a *SEIC* initially furnished with 'transcendental heritage' is, however, not an automatic given. *Umuntu* and *umupashi* together format the *SEIC* on the stage of communal living where Bemba norms and values moderate a person's life-style, and if it goes well, will then constitute the *SEIC* with which *umupashi* continues after the death of the body of his 'human companion'. Cycle completed! – Cycle opened!

Following is my attempt to graphically illustrate first a 'Linear-Life-Companionship' between *umupashi* and his 'human companion' and second the *Umupashi* 'Life-Cycle'.

Umuntu-Umupashi 'Linear Life Companionship'

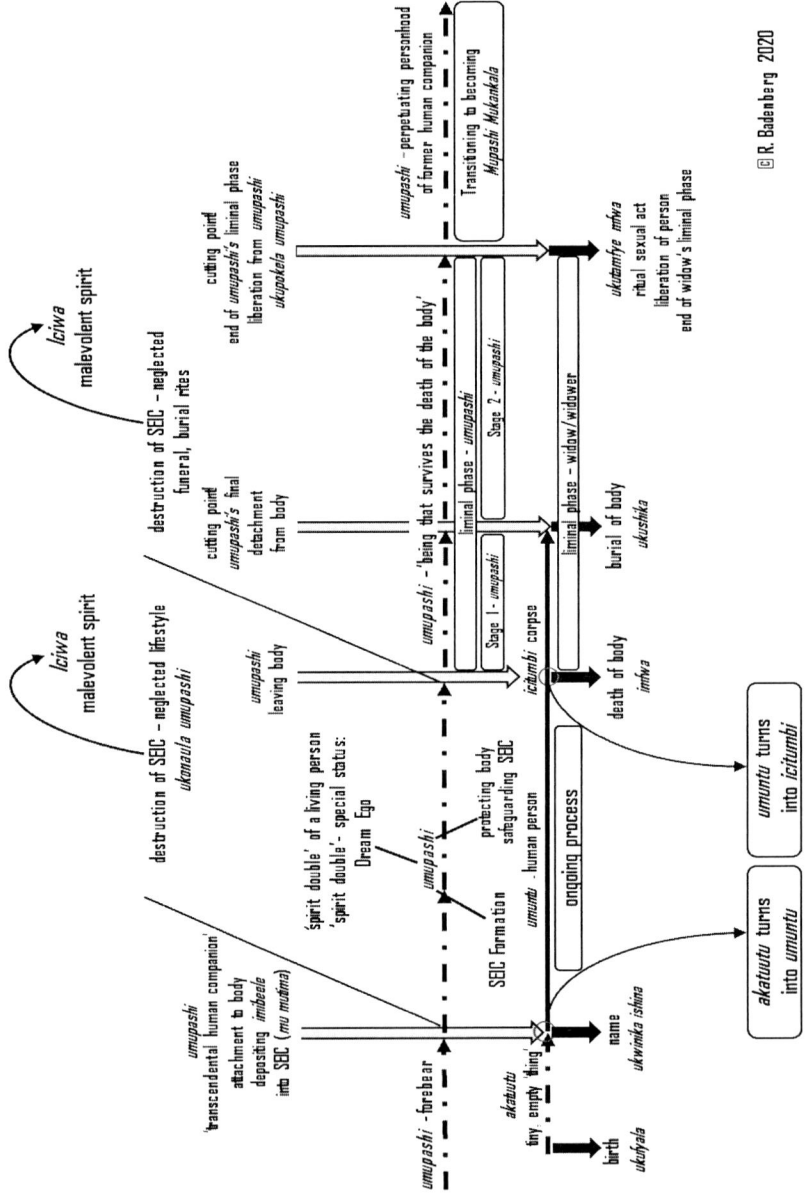

Figure 27: Umuntu-Umupashi 'Linear Life Companionship'

Umupashi 'Life-Cycle'

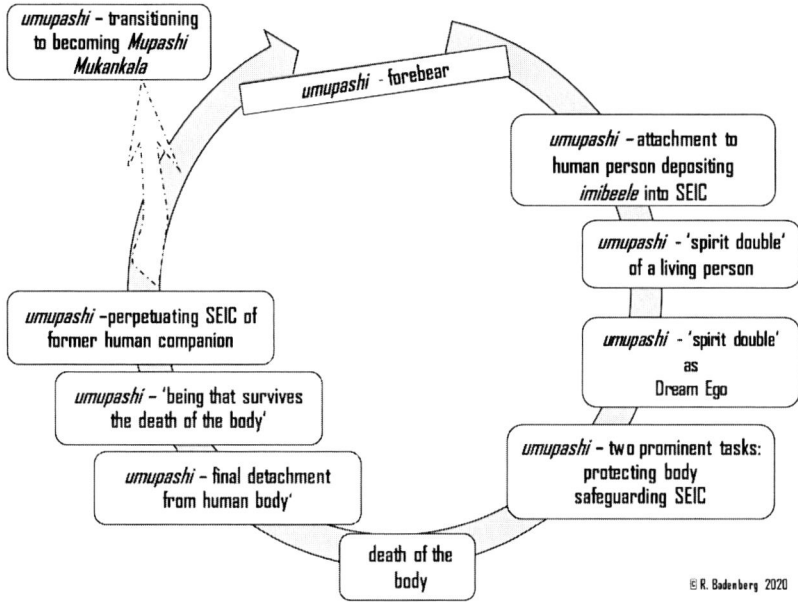

Figure 28: Umupashi 'Life-Cycle'

Conclusion

Succession and inheritance (*ubupyani*) for all human persons (except for those people who are technically non-human persons) is an axiom of the Bemba worldview. Its continued practice, albeit with noticeable non-coherence in contemporary Bemba society, shows that their roots are as deep as they are for the Chieftainship itself. Cleansing through ritualized sexual relations was already an essential, necessary element in the burial rites for Chiti the Great, the first Chitimukulu. With time the *ubupyani* system became more sophisticated, embracing all members of society.

The Bemba worldview is inhibited with a deep-seated striving for harmony and beliefs in how to obtain and maintain it. The cycle of life must be closed. Rituals transition a human person through the cycle of life. As Oduyoye observes "an individual's path through life is monitored, marked, and celebrated from even before birth to death, and thereafter the events in the life of a community echo this same cycle" (in Kaunda 2013:14).

The Bemba worldview is also instilled with a deep-seated desire for perpetuity. Rituals – from birth to death and beyond – never only benefit the living in various ways but more importantly, are of benefit to *umupashi* of a living person as well as to the time when he continues the *SEIC* of a human person as the being who survives the death of the body in particular, and the *imipashi* of the clan as a whole, as venerated ancestors. This is particularly true for the *imipashi* of chiefs, the royal spirits.

The number and the intensity of ritual observances demanded of the living, especially when death strikes a marriage and with it the families concerned, is in direct relation to the state of *umupashi*, and to be precise, to the inner state, the condition of his *SEIC*.

- rituals and tokens of respect please him, soothing *umupashi's* SEIC and preventing acts of revengeful actions on the living due to their disrespect and negligence
- rituals help and enact final separation from the body of his 'human companion'
- rituals sustain *umupashi* during the stages of the liminal phase
- rituals end his liminal phase – cutting all emotional ties to the surviving spouse
- rituals enable him to associate himself with another human being (either with a person alive, e.g. *impyani* or a future child born to the family)

- rituals guarantee his safe transition into the spirit world to eventually becoming a matrilineal ancestor, and to be more precise, hopefully a *Mupashi Mukankala*

Rituals trigger what I have called earlier the 'critical obligations' tied in with worldview structures. Also, no one ritual makes sense in isolation, but needs to be understood as part of a 'cycle', as Radcliffe-Brown argued in structural-functionalist fashion (in Kalusa and Vaughan 2013:68). Not only that. Goodenough asserts that customs and institutions are "not only largely interconnected and to be understood in terms of one another … but also that the understanding of some was dependent on the understanding of others" (2003:4).

Bemba rituals tie into the circle of life and understanding, for instance, the rationale of the *ukwinika ishina* (name-giving) ritual is dependent on the understanding that human identity is closely associated with *umupashi* as the spirit double of a named living person. Similarly, to understand death and burial rites requires understanding of *umupashi* as the spirit double whose "well-being" and "future" is at stake should ritual malpractice or even negligence occur.

Though one has relinquished biological life - *imfwa* (death) is certainly more than merely 'giving up the ghost'.

Endnotes: Chapter Six

[1] Andele, 2 June 1995. Interview with Mr. G. Chewe: "The death of Mr. C. Mwamba, the late Headman of Chafwa Village."

[2] This does not apply to mad people, lepers, wizards, and other people. The main criteria are the kind of *umupashi* one is associated with.

[3] The deeper meaning is to break the attachment of *umupashi* rightfully and appropriately to the late child and transfer the companionship of *umupashi* to the *impyani*.

[4] "…if the sound "i" in the word ukushikula is stressed the meaning of the word changes to mean "uncovering something that is buried" … ukushikula refers to the act of giving a token gift of money for the purpose of undoing a taboo or taboos" (Lumbwe 2009:326).

[5] The designation 'himself' does not ascribe gender to *umupashi* (see chapter five), but since there is no neuter in the Bemba language, a personal pronoun is required.

Tuli 'samfwe' – tumenena ukubola
We are like 'samfwe' (edible mushrooms) – we germinate only to rot:
Life is very short!
As the Philosopher said:
Life is neither a feast, nor a spectacle – but a predicament.

Postscript

Worldviews are creations of the mind. Their creation is, however, not purely rational, constructions of stringent reasoning and logical sequences but contain a great deal of psychological load, often conflicting in nature. Much has been written on, and about worldviews, but remarkably little on how they are actually developed or created. This much can be said: rational aspects are never alone sufficient to provide enough 'matter' from which to create a worldview. Burlington (2008) also rightly bemoans this situation. In his words:

> … it is the general lack of discussion about how worldviews are formed in the first place and, more specifically, the role of such decidedly non-rational factors as historical contingency and personal psychological motivations in their creation (:3).

Studying the life history of Emilio Chishimba Mulolani, a Bemba and founder of Zambia's Mutima Church, Burlington provides a detailed and thrilling account of Emilio's life, but more importantly, how he creates an extraordinary but "decidedly Christian-theistic" (:19) worldview. The big question is: how did he achieve this? In Emilio's case, one factor certainly was by not following the usual or accepted beliefs and opinions (:19) in relation to neither his cultural heritage nor his religious tradition, Catholic in his case. For in-depth details about his life, the circumstances and genesis of his worldview, and the impact this had on the founding of his Church, I refer to Burlington, *("I love Mary": Relating Private Motives to Public Meanings at The Genesis of Emilio's Mutima Church*, 2004).

Back to the question how worldviews are created. Emilio's life can furnish important factors for its creation and if one were to concentrate on mainly rational aspects of how he achieved it, and how in general worldviews are developed, in order to identify rational ingredients and to place them in contrast to other worldviews, Burlington (2008) opines that we ought to be on the alert for two problems:

First, to reduce worldviews "into timeless, a-historical and a-psychological constructs," will obscure "from our view the very dynamics that also make them so powerful"; powerful not only because they rationally order the world, "but that they do so in emotionally satisfying ways" (:19). It is precisely because of the emotional load, often of conflicting nature, which individuals bring to the arena, generating the very dynamics, which first serve the individual in bringing emotional reward and motivation to transcend self, and also communicating one's experience to others. Successful communication means tapping into the deep, central levels of one's own psyche as well as into the shared 'psyche' of a culture (:19 also Hinfelaar 1994:115); (perhaps the German *Volksseele* could be a close enough expression).

Second, rationalism, Burlington argues, "when it amounts to the comparison of the coherence of one worldview with another for purposes of evangelism" or any other *–ism* for that matter, "is something of an intellectualist and elitist orientation" (:20) to whatever cause one has in mind. Continuing, Burlington argues:

- "It assumes first that people are actually conscious of such an abstract structure in their own mental toolbox,
- and second, that they are capable of comparing abstract system to abstract system as systems for the purpose of coherence checking" (:20).
- "Third, rationalism assumes that people may be motivated to make comparisons between worldviews, perhaps by disappointment in the explanatory power of their current view. Some may even assume that comparison shopping for worldviews will almost automatically reveal the difference between good, better, and best. One must wonder what this reveals about the contingent and psycho-motivational roots of consumerist orientations in Western Christianity," and Western Culture in general!, "not to mention our reification and elevation of knowing as a category of human experience distinct from doing and being" (:20).

So, how then could we get a grip on Emilio Chishimba creating a worldview, in his case a Christian-theistic one? Contextualization has long since been a concept with which various disciplines have theorized and worked. Burlington, falling back on the missiologist Stephen B. Bevans (1992), suggests that what Chishimba did provides an example of what Bevans called the "transcendental model of contextualization. Whether this model is the best for theological development is open to question, but its processes best illustrate how worldviews are created" (Burlington 2008:11). In this model, Burlington, distilling Bevans' 'transcendental model of contextualization', states that "'self-transcending' (Bevans 1992:97) subjects examine their own 'affective and cognitive operations' (1992:97) to determine how these, too, unfold the numinous" (Burlington 2008:11).

> Chishimba himself remarked that, 'To become a Godlike group we had to enter the loneliness of the desert and fall back on our own resources' (quoted in Hinfelaar 1994:10). Perhaps, therefore, the missiological discussion of worldview [and that includes other disciplines too] will be advanced by a deeper study of those who, like Chishimba, spin a web of significance between things outsiders cannot think under the compulsion of things outsiders do not feel (Burlington 2008:11).

Worldviews change. For the most part it rarely happens rapidly and quickly, but they change. They change because culture changes. And culture changes because at times people are no longer pulled by the rationale, and more often so by the emotional force of certain cultural elements they exert on people. Some cultures are more open to progression, that is, its members feel less obliged to believe and do 'what-has-always-been-believed-and-done', hence more easily shift to new and differing views on issues of life, and in its wake come transformational processes of certain cultural elements, or taken to the extreme, their total abandonment, giving rise to societal and personal behavioural changes, too. And sometimes there are individuals with great powers of introspection who forge on the anvil of their own inner travail new personal meanings, so convincing and emotionally rewarding to others who then appropriate them for their own good. In all of it, in creating a worldview as well as changing worldview, man takes centre stage.

It is my hope that this monograph contributes toward unearthing salient features of the Bemba worldview and personhood. Of course, the eyes of the foreigner never see like the eyes of *Mubemba*. But perhaps there is some insight in what is presented here, as the eyes of the foreigner sees things which can easily, at times thoroughly, be camouflaged with total normality for cultural insiders, obstructing a fresh and conscientious look on cultural knowledge systems. Perhaps there is a chance for 'corporate eyes' to see that which cannot easily been seen – because so much of it is encased in language and ideas enveloped in minds on how the world and universe works – in an atmosphere of mutual respect and benefit.

Appendix 1: Bemba Main Chiefs & their Chiefdoms

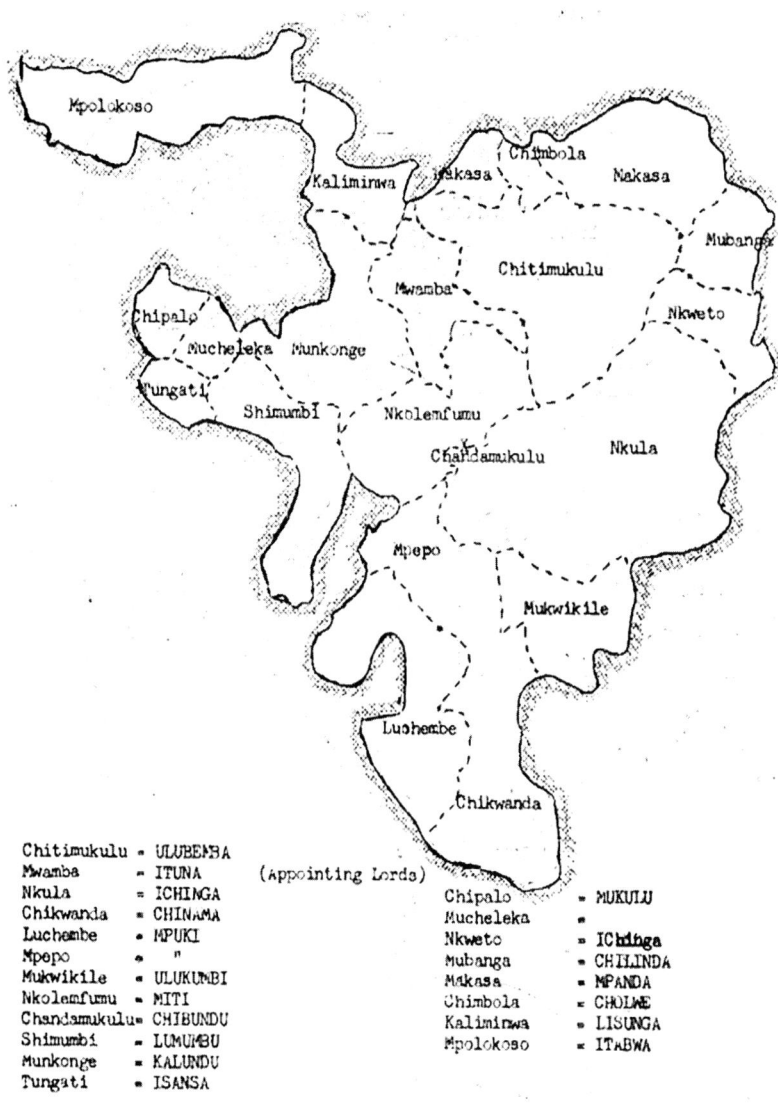

Source: Taken from Oger n.d.:10

Appendix 2: The Nine Noun Classes

The Nine Noun Classes showing the Prefixes, the Full Concords, the Modified Concords, and the Class Prepositions. The Prefixes have been hyphened in bold script to aid the eye.

CLASS	SINGULAR/PLURAL	NOMEN	ENGLISH	FULL CONCORD	MODIFIED CONCORD	CLASS PREPOSITION
1	Singular	*umu*-ntu	person	umu, û, uu	u	uwa
	Plural	*aba*-ntu	persons	aba	ba	aba
2	Singular	*umu*-pando	chair	û, uu	u	uwa
	Plural	*imi*-pando	chairs	î, ii	i	iya
3	Singular	*in*-koko	fowl	î, ii	i	iya
	Plural	*in*-koko	fowls	ishi	shi	isha
	Singular	*ulu*-kasu	hoe	ulu	lu	ulwa
	Plural	*in*-kasu	hoes	ishi	shi	isha
4	Singular	*ici*-ntu	thing	ici	ci	ica
	Plural	*ifi*-ntu	things	ifi	fi	ifya
5	Singular	*ili*-bwe	stone	ili	li	ilya
	Singular	*ulu*-kasa	foot	ulu	lu	ulwa
	Singular	*uku*-boko	arm	uku	ku	ukwa
	Singular	*ubu*-unga	meal, flour	ubu	bu	ubwa
	Plural	*ama*-bwe	stones	aya	ya	aya
	Plural	*ama*-kasa	feet	aya	ya	aya
	Plural	*ama*-boko	arms	aya	ya	aya
	Plural	*ama*-unga	meal, flour	aya	ya	aya
6	Singular	*aka*-nwa	mouth	aka	ka	aka
	Plural	*utu*-nwa	mouths	atu	tu	utwa
7	abstract Nouns	*ubu*-suma	goodness	abu	bu	ubwa
8	Infinitive	*uku*-bomba	to work	aku	ku	ukwa
9	Locative	*apa*-ntu	a place (nearby)	apa	pa	apâ
	Locative	*uku*-ntu	a place (vague)	aku	ku	ukwa
	Locative	*umu*-ntu	a place (in)	amu	mu	umwa

Source: derived from Geo W. Sims (1959).

Appendix 3: SEIC and Spirit Double – A little Excursion

The following list is a very crude attempt to pull together data I have collected from publications whose bibliographical details were – regrettably! – not taken down whenever they crossed my path. I never thought of using the information the way the material is presented here. Perhaps there are kind and informed readers out there who have much more to say and would be glad to collaborate. Welcome!

Africa
Alunda
wumi → life (all living things and creatures have it)
mwevulu → turns with the death of the body into *mukishi*
mukishi → being that perpetuates the personality after the death of the body

Luba
mutima → heart (organ)
→ SEIC
umvwe → *kufya umvwe mu lusengo* = to incarcerate the
umvwe (most probably the spirit double as dream ego) in a horn (of an animal)
umvwe wa kimano
umvwe wa bumi → turns with the death of the body into *mufu*
mufu → spirit of a dead person
ngeni → intellectual abilities, will-power
→ after the death of the body goes on to the abode of the dead
muya → breath

Kongo
ntima → heart (organ)
→ SEIC
mbunda → ?
moyo → spirit double (lives in the blood and in the heart)
mwela → spirit double (alternative term to *moyo*; possibly more connected with the breath)
Mfumu kutu → („Chief of the ear") can leave the body of a living

	person (no longer a common expression in Kikongo)
ukufwa ngambu	→ "dying through separation" = unconsciousness
	→ no relevance after death
nitu	→ body
Kaonde	
chimvule	→ shadow (spirit double?)
mukishi	→ being that perpetuates the personality after the death of the body
Bahuana	
bun	→ heart
doshi	→ spirit double
Bagala/Boloki	
elimo	→ spirit double (can leave the body during sleep → dream ego)
elilingi	→ spirit double (a dead person does not possess *elilingi*; a living person may lose it but can be restored by a specialist)
mongoli	→ disembodied soul (sends evil upon the living)
Baganda	
mwoyo	→ everyone has it
mulimu	→ being that perpetuates the personality after the death of the body
Bekwana	
moea	→ changes after death into *dimo*
dimo	→ spirit of the dead?
Bemba	
umutima	→ heart (organ)
	→ SEIC
mu mutima	→ in the heart (SEIC as chamber)
mu nda	→ immaterial spot in the belly
	→ "Innermost"
	→ collective psychic dispositions
umweo	→ breath, life (life force)
umupashi	→ benevolent spirit double
	→ dream ego
	→ upholds the functionality of the body
	→ being that perpetuates the personality after the death of the body
icibanda	→ malevolent spirit double

umubili	→ body
ubumi	→ life
icitumbi	→ corpse

Dschagga

nrima	→ intellectual, mental abilities
	→ ceases its function after the death of the body

Yao

ntima	→ heart (organ)
	→ SEIC
chiilu	→ body

Chewa/ Njanja

mtima	→ heart (organ)
	→ SEIC
moyo	→ life
thupi	→ body

Sena

mtima	→ heart (organ)
	→ SEIC
mumtima	→ in the heart
kuswipa mtima	→ worrying
mitimawo ili kutali na ine	→ their hearts are far from me
pansi pa mtima	→ down at the heart
moyo	→ life
kumoyo	
kutaya moyo	→ to throw, loose life
mzimu	→ "soul"
manungo	→ body

Shona

mweya	→ life-principle and its existence is manifest through breathing.
	→ life-principle' of man, incarnate in him and deveoping its personal & unique characteristics while he is alive
	→ turning into *madzimu* and taking its place in the spiritual hierarchy of the ancestors
mweya	→ surviving the death of the body
ngozi	→ avenging spirit
muviri or *nyama*	→ body
mutumbi or *chitunha*	→ corpse

shavi	→ spirits: inflicting the living with serious diseases (e.g. epilepsy, madness or other complexities)

Zulu

umoya	→ life, life force of a living person
Idhlozi/ itongo	→ being that perpetuates the personality after the death of the body

Lugbara

orindi	→ SEIC
endri-lendri	→ shadow/shade?
ori	→ being that perpetuates the personality after the death of the body
ma	→ body

Yoruba

okan	→ heart (organ)
	→ seat of the emotion and psychic energy
emi	→ the life-force which makes a person breathe;
	→ uncertain where it goes after departing from the body at death
obi	→ at death, the *obi* leaves the body but it does not survive.
ori	→ head
ori	→ guardian spirit of the person (maybe spirit double)
ojiji	→ self of a person
	(when the self leaves the body at death, the shadow ceases to exist)

Igbo

eke	→ the spirit of a deceased ancestor who reincarnates in a child
	→ the baby takes after the *eke* in appearance and/or character.
chi	→ an emanation of the Creator.
	→ it is a sort of spirit double or guardian genius associated with the person from the moment of conception.
	→ when a person dies, his *chi* goes back to God to give account of his work on earth.
	→ a man's abilities, faults or misfortunes are ascribed to his *chi*.
	→ when a person reincarnates, he is given a different

	chi by God, with a different kind of destiny in life.
	→ a person must achieve his *chi*'s destiny in life to be successful.
	→ everyone has his or her own cult where he or she propitiates the *chi*.
	→ however, a person who is yet to have a child only shares in the propitiation of his parents' *chi*.
	→ one establishes one's own cult after becoming a parent.
onyinyo	→ incarnates in the body and is assigned an ancestral guardian.
	→ being that perpetuates the personality after the death of the body and can in turn become an ancestral guardian

Near East
Ancient Israelites

leb	→ heart (organ)
	→ SEIC
hayim	→ life
nefesh	→ **two** components attached to each other
	- a bodily component (*nefesh habasar*) located in the blood (abbreviated as *hanefesh*)
	- a spiritual component bestowed by God - *ruach*
	→ part of the person, but not part of the body
	→ its presence upholds the functionality of the body
	→ survives the death of the body
	→ dream ego (could disengage from the body and wander about – 'dream-soul')
nefesh parachot	→ '*nefesh* to-fly' = dream ego that is trapped inside an empty pillow casing and turned into a '*nefesh* to-fly' ('bird-soul')
nefesh hajja	→ living being
	(Steiner 2015: *Disembodied Souls*)

North America
Navajo

tcǐ'ndi	→ the shade or "spirit" of the departed

Tlingit

du tuwu	→ a person's mind, thoughts, feelings, are "his in sides"
ka yu-ha-yee	→ "shadow"
qa ya-ha-yi	→ "human shadow, reflection, picture"
ka yu-ha-yee wha-goo	→ "man's shade" after the death of the body
qa yakwgwahe yagu	→ "ghost," or "reincarnated spirit"
	→ travels to a land of the dead, the place depending on the manner of death,
	→ may later be reincarnated in a living person
kasago	→ breath-life
	→ a vital central force through which the body functions during life and which, leaving the body, causes death;
	→ the only knowledge man has of this entity is the breath
	→ leaves the body during illness or fainting and which can be recovered by the shaman
Ka kin-ah yage or *Ka-ken-a yake* "	→ "up above spirit."
	→ this spirit tries to protect and guide its ward aright. But the spirit may desert its charge if offended, and it can be killed through great wrongdoing, which would likewise react upon its mortal charge.
	→ the only prayer made by the Tlingit is to this spirit.
	→ when in danger, the Tlingit would say,
	"Kluw-kut-hut thlar-tin uh khen-nah ya-gee"
	"Carefully me watch, my above spirit", or
	"Watch over me carefully, my Spirit Above."
qa da	→ body

Asia

Newar (Nepal)

nuga	→ heart
	→ memories, thoughts, and feelings are stored in
nuga	
	→ wilful actions come from *nuga*
	→ someone with no ability to commit himself or follow through on moral action as lacking "heart blood.

→ the self/heart was an abode of the sacred. The Newar spoke of a deity residing
in their hearts and dictating morally commendable actions."
(Parish 1991, 1994 in Holland et. al. 1998:19-20).

Gurung (Nepal)
sae → "the seat of will, memory, and emotion"
→ conceived as a kind of entity located in the chest"
(McHugh 1989:22 in Holland et. al. 1998:291).

Mixed caste Nepali speakers
man → where thoughts and feelings are stored and churn about.
→ located in the centre of the chest

Japan
tama → animating spirit residing in the body
→ can leave the body and wander elsewhere,
→ causing illness, unconsciousness, and death

Ibanags Northern Luzon
ikararua → companion of the body
makararuanan → in the case of shock it is said to leave the body while the body remains alive.
mangagaggakao → ritual inviting *ikararua* to return to the body implies this conviction.

Ilocanos Northern Luzon
al-alia or *ar-ria* → may come from *al-al* ("to pant, to breathe in a laboured manner")
→ the companion of the body (comes to the bedside of a dying person, stays in the area after death, and even appears to relatives in dreams or through other signs to ask for prayers and forgiveness).

al-alia → can mean "ghost, spectre, apparition, spirit."
→ *Ma-al-aliaen* is to be visited by an *al-alia*

karma or *karkarma* → "soul, vigour, energy, strength, power, ghost"
→ stays with the individual and leaves the body through the nose only when the person dies

aningaas	→ "a kind of ghost, specter" During the funeral period *aningaas*, visits those who failed when the deceased was still sick or dying.
kararua or *karuruwa*	→ a constant companion → when a person is frightened, his *kararua* or *karuruwa* strays from the body, resulting in sickness. → a medium or medicine man, through a ritual, invites the strayed *kararua* or *karuruwa* to return to the body.

Kankanai-speaking areas of Northern Luzon

ab-abiik	→ the spiritual self → also applies to a stone, mountain, tree, or a river as having its *ab-abiik*
awak	→ the physical self

Tagalog

kambal	→ spirit double or twin → "conceived as a gaseous substance" → later becomes the *malay* or "the tiny voice," → "the individual's capacity to think, to reason, to learn, and to have will power." → may travel around during the night. Its troublesome encounters, people say, are the cause of nightmares (*bangungut*) → turns into *kaluluwa* after death of the body
kaluluwa	→ spirit being of a deceased person

Ilocano-speaking town in Pangasinan

karurua or *kadua kadua*	→ spirit double or twin
ti biag	→ life partner
kakuyog	→ companion
gayyem	→ friend
kasibay	→ a companion by one's side
taribabay	→ guide

Hanunuo Mangyans (Mindoro)

karadwa or *kalag*	→ one opinion holds that a person has only one soul (*karadwa* tawo) → another opinion is that in addition to his one

karadwa, a person can have others in the form of animals (dogs, birds, mice, cats, etc.)
→ after death *karadwa* goes to "the place of the dead" (*karadwahan*), where "there is no disease, no starvation, no impact from the lowlanders, nor evil spirits" and no death."
→ can leave the body (e.g. when one is frightened) and the person will get sick.
→ through a ritual *karadwa* can be recalled to the body to restore health.
→ is afraid of evil spirits but can change itself into a swift animal and thereby outrun them
→ dream ego
When a person dreams, the *karadwa* strolls around. The matter of the dream is the subject of the strolling.

Cebuano Visayan

kalag → spirit of a deceased person
kaluha → double, twin, guardian
→ is the essence of his intellectual and moral powers and,
→ at death, becomes an *anito* or spirit.
anito → spirit of the dead
ginhawa → life, life force
→ stomach, pit of the stomach, breath, lungs, vital spirit, intestines (*ginhawaan*).
→ by extension *ginhawa* can also mean food (especially a cookie), appetite, disposition (good or bad), character, condition.
atay → liver – "seat of emotions."
The double is common to Philippine ethnic groups.
→ it is "generally located in the head" whereas "the *ginhawa* has its seat somewhere in the intestinal region, often in the liver or *atay*."
→ that the liver is the "seat of emotions." Hence we find expressions related to the liver such as:
→ *makapakitbi/makapakulo sa atay*
(lit, makes the liver curdle, makes the blood curdle),
→ *lapad* ang *atay* (lit., expanded liver, or to be flattered),

→ *makapadako sa atay* (lit., enlarges the liver, or make something go to one's head)
(F. Landa Jocano, *The Ilocanos*)

Benuaq - East-Kalimantan
senarikng	→ living person
juus	→ spirit double and dream ego
unuk	→ body
asakng	→ SEIC

Oceania
Chuuk
ngúún → the shadow of an object when the outer shape of the object is at least recognizable.
→ also, the mirror image of an object or a person is called *ngúún*.
→ conception that all things in this world, next to their material, physical existence, also exist in an immaterial, spiritual form. These two forms are so meticulously identical that one can easily be mistaken for the other.
→ the *ngúún* of a human person, however, outweighs the *ngúún* of the above mentioned contexts.

ngúnúyééch → benevolent spirit double
→ dream ego
→ upholds the functionality of the body
→ perpetuates the human's personality after the death of its body

ngúnúnngaw → malevolent 'spirit double'
inis → body
neenuuk, *neetip* and *tipey* → "place in the upper abdomen where emotional responses and intellectual processes are evident".
→ SEIC

Bibliography

Adeyemo, Tokunboh. 1983. "Towards an Evangelical African Theology." Evangel-ical Review of Theology 7, no. 1:147-154.African Elders 1949. *History of the Bena Ng'oma (ba-Cungu wa Mukulu)*. London: MacMillan & Co., Ltd.

Badenberg, Robert 2014. *The Concept of Man in Non-Western Cultures: A Guide for One's Own Research*. Handbook to Lothar Käser's Textbook *Animism – A Cognitive Approach*. Nürnberg: VTR Publications.

_____ 2008. 2nd ed. *Sickness and Healing: A Case Study on the Dialectic of Culture and Personality*. Edition afem - mission academics, Bd. 11. Nürnberg: VTR.

_____ 2002. 2nd ed. *The Body, Soul and Spirit Concept of the Bemba in Zambia: Fundamental Characteristics of Being Human of an African Ethnic Group*. Edition afem - mission academics, Bd. 9. Bonn: Verlag für Kultur und Wissenschaft.

Bandawe, Chiwoza 2010. *Practical uMunthu Psychology: An Indigenous Approach to Harmonious Living*. Balaka: Montfort Media Limited.

Barnes, H. 1922. "Survival after Death among the Ba-Bemba of North-Eastern Rhodesia." *MAN* 22:41-42.

Bateson, Gregory 1936. Naven: A Survey of the Problems suggested by a Composite Picture of the Culture of a New Guinea Tribe drawn from Three Points of View. Cambridge: University Press.

Bevans, Stephen B. 1992. *Models of Contextual Theology*. Maryknoll, NY: Orbis Books.

Bloch, Maurice 2015 (reprint). "Durkheimian anthropology and religion: Going in and out of each other's bodies." *HAU: Journal of Ethnographic Theory* 5 (3):285-299.

Bosch, David J. 1991. *Transforming Mission: Paradigm Shifts in Theology of Mission*. Maryknoll, NY: Orbis.

Brelsford, W. Vernon 1944. *The Succession of Bemba Chiefs: A Guide for District Officers*. Lusaka: Government Printers.

_____ 1944. *Aspects of Bemba Chieftainship*. Lusaka: Rhodes-Livingstone Institute Communications, No.2.

_____ 1942. "'*Shimwalule*': A Study of a Bemba Chief and Priest." *African Studies* vol. 1, no. 3 (September):207-223.

Burlington, Gary 2008. "God Makes a World of Difference: The Dialectic of Motivation and Meaning at the Creation of an African Theistic Worldview." *Missiology: An International Review,* Volume 36:4, October:435-445.

_____ 2004. '"I love Mary." Relating Private Motives to Public Meanings at the Genesis of Emilio's Mutima Church.' Doctoral Dissertation, Faculty of Intercultural Studies, Biola University.

_____ 1998. "Topography of a Zambian Storyland." *International Journal of Frontier Missions*, Vol. 15:2, Apr.-June:75-81.

Carey, Francis 1986. "Conscientization and In-Service Education of Zambian Primary School Teachers." Ph.D. thesis, Department of International and Comparative Education, Institute of Education, University of London.

Cash, Thomas F. 2012 (editor). *Encyclopedia of Body Image and Human Appearance*, Vol 1. San Diego: Academic Press.

Chileshe, Alexander Roy 2005. "Land Tenure and Rural Livelihoods in Zambia: Case Studies of Kamena and St. Joseph." Ph.D. dissertation, Faculty of Arts, University of the Western Cape (South Africa).

Clark, Mary 2002. *In Search of Human Nature*. London: Routledge.

Cook, Robert R. 1985. "Ghosts," *EAJET* vol. 4, no. 1:35-47.

Crawley, A. E. 1911. *Encyclopaedia of Religion and Ethics* (1911), s.v. "Doubles."

Cunnison, Ian G. 1969. *History of the Luapula*. Rhodes-Livingstone Paper No. 21, first published by the Rhodes-Livingstone Institute, Northern Rhodesia, 1951. London: Oxford University Press.

D'Andrade, G. Roy 1995. *The Development of Cognitive Anthropology*. Cambridge: Cambridge University Press.

Deigh, John 1999. "Moral Psychology". In *The MIT Encyclopedia of the Cognitive Sciences,* eds. Robert A. Wilson and Frank C. Keil, 561-562. Cambridge, Massachusetts and London: The MIT Press.

Dillon-Malone, Clive 1988. "*Mutumwa Nchimi* Healers and Wizardry Beliefs in Zambia." *Soc. Sci. Med.* vol. 26, no. 11:1159-1172.

Eckstein, Hans-Joachim 1983. *Der Begriff Syneidesis bei Paulus: Eine neu-testamentlich-exegetische Untersuchung zum ‚Gewissensbegriff'*. Wissenschaftliche Untersuchungen zum neuen Testament, 2. Reihe. Begründet von Joachim Jeremias und Otto Michel. Herausgegeben von Martin Hengel und Otfried Hofius. Tübingen: J.C.B Mohr (Paul Siebeck).

Elvi, Zetla K. 2009. "Soul". In *Encyclopedia of African Religion*, eds. Molefi Keti Asante and Ama Mazama, 627-629. Los Angeles, London, New Delhi, Singapore, Washington DC: SAGE Publications, Inc.

Etienne, Fr. Louis 1948. "A Study of the Babemba and Neighbouring Tribes." TMs (photocopy). Ilondola: The Language Centre.

Fischer, Anja 2010. "Unterhaltung in der Wüste: Verbale Interaktion und Soziabilität bei Imuhaê-NomadInnen." Ph.D. dissertation. Universität Wien.

Fowler, C. 2004. The Archaeology of Personhood. An anthropological approach. Routledge. London and New York.

Garrec, N. 1917. "Croyances et Coutumes Religieuses des Babemba." Rome: White Fathers.

Gehman, Richard J. 1990. *African Traditional Religion in Biblical Perspective.* Second Printing. Kijabe, Kenya: Kesho Publications.

Gleitman, Lila and Bloom, Paul 1999. "Language Acquisition". In *The MIT Encyclopedia of the Cognitive Sciences,* eds. Robert A. Wilson and Frank C. Keil, 434-438. Cambridge, Massachusetts and London: The MIT Press.

Goodenough, Ward H. 2003. "In Pursuit of Culture." *Annual Reviews Anthropology*. 32:1–12.

Gordon, David M. 2012. "Seeing Invisible Worlds." In *Invisible Agents: Spirits in a Central African History.* Athens: Ohio University Press.

Gouldsbury, Cullen and Herbert Sheane 1911. *The Great Plateau of Northern Rhodesia.* London: Edward Arnold.

Greenstein, Edward L. 2020. "The Heart as an Organ of Speech." In *Biblical Hebrew Semitic, Biblical, and Jewish Studies* in Honor of Richard C. Steiner, eds. Aaron J. Koller, Mordechai Z. Cohen and Adina Moshavi. Jerusalem and New York: Mosad Bialik and YU Press.

Groark, Kevin P. 2010. "Willful Souls: Dreaming and the Dialectics of Self-Experience Among the Tzotzil Maya of Highland Chiapas, Mexico." In *Toward an Anthropology of the Will*, eds. Keith M. Murphy and C. Jason Throop, 101-122; 199-215. Stanford, CA.: Stanford University Press.

Gruber, June. "Human Emotion: Shame and Guilt." YouTube Video, 04.06.2013, URL:https://www.youtube.com/watch?v=jKlMP-DJnE10, accessed on 29.01.2020.

Guthrie, Malcom 1962. "Some Aspects of the Pre-History of the Bantu Languages." *JAH* vol. 3, no. 2:273-282.

Heidemann, Frank 2009. "Körperbotschaften". Part of a TV series "Der lange Schatten von Kultur" (The long shadow of culture), BR alpha, Bayerischer Rundfunk. www.br-alpha.de

Hiebert Paul G. 1998, 2001. *Anthropological Insights for Missionaries*. Grand Rapids, MI: Baker Book House.

Hilgers, Micha 1996. *Scham: Gesichter eines Affekts*. Göttingen: V&R.

Hinfelaar, Hugo F. 1994. *Bemba Speaking Women of Zambia in a Century of Religious Change (1892-1992)*. Studies of Religion in Africa, eds., Adrian Hastings and Marc R. Spencer. Leiden: E. J. Brill.

Hoch E. n.d. *A Bemba Grammar with Exercises*. Ilondola, Zambia: Language Centre.

Hochegger, Herman 1965. "Die Vorstellungen von 'Seele' und Totengeist bei Afrikanischen Völkern." *Anthropos* 60:273-339.

Huntington, Richard and Peter Metcalf 1991. *Celebrations of death: The Anthropology of Mortuary Ritual*. Cambridge, New York: Cambridge University Press.

Hurrelmann, Klaus, 2006. 9.Aufl. *Einführung in die Sozialisationstheorie*. Weinheim, Basel. (Beltz Studium). Online in Internet: URL:http://www.content-select.com/index.php?id=bib_view&ean=9783407290960.

Ipenburg, At 1992. *"All Good Men:" The Development of Lubwa Mission, Chinsali, Zambia, 1905-1967*. Studies in the Intercultural History of Christianity, founded by Hans Jochen Margull, eds., Richard Friedli, Walter J. Hollenweger, Jan A. B. Jongeneel und Theo Sundermeier, Vol. 83. Frankfurt am Main: Peter Lang.

Jahoda, Gustav 2002. "Culture, biology and development across history." In *Between Culture and Biology: Perspectives on Ontogenetic Development*, eds. Heidi Keller, Ype H. Pootinga and Axel Schölmerich, 13-29. Cambridge, UK: Cambridge University Press.

Janowski, Bernd 2015. "Das Herz – ein Beziehungsorgan: Zum Personverständnis des Alten Testaments." In *Dimensionen der Leiblichkeit: Theologische Zugänge,* Hg. Bernd Janowski und Christoph

Schwöbel, Bd. 16, 1-45. Neukirchen-Vluyn: Neukirchener Verlagsgesellschaft mbH.

Kalusa, Walima T. and Vaughan, Megan 2013. *Death, Belief and Politics in Central African History*. Lusaka: The Lembani Trust.

Kambole, R. M. 1980. *Ukufunda Umwana Ukufikapo*. Lusaka: Zambia Educational Publishing House.

Kapolyo, Joe M. 2005. *The Human Condition: Christian Perspectives through African Eyes*. Leicester, UK: IVP.

_____ n.d. "The Conversion of Ubuntu – an African Vision of Human Nature." TMs, n.p.

Käser, Lothar, 2016. *A Chuukese Theory of Personhood – The Concepts Body, Mind, Soul and Spirit on the Islands of Chuuk (Micronesia): An Ethnolinguistic Study*. Nürnberg: VTR Publications.

_____ 2014a. *Animism: A Cognitive Approach. An Introduction to the Basic Notions Underlying the Concepts of the World and of Man Held by Ethnic Societies, for the Benefit of Those Working Overseas in Development Aid and in the Church*. Textbook to Robert Badenberg's Handbook *The Concept of Man in Non-Western Cultures*. Nürnberg: VTR Publications.

_____ 2014b. *Foreign Cultures: An Introduction to Ethnology for Development Aid Workers and Church Workers Abroad*. Nürnberg: VTR Publications.

_____ 1977. "Der Begriff Seele bei den Insulanern von Truk." Ph.D. dissertation, Geowissenschaftliche Fakultät, Albert-Ludwigs-Universität Freiburg i. Br.

Kasprus, Aloys SVD 1973. "The Tribes of the Middle Ramu and the Upper Keram Rivers (North-East New Guinea)". *Studia Instituti Anthropos*. St. Augustin bei Bonn: Verlag des Anthropos-Instituts, vol. 17:39-61.

Kaunda, Mutale Mulenga 2013. "Search for Life-giving Marriage: The Imbusa Initiation Rites as a Space for Constructing Well-being among Married Bemba Women of Zambia." M.Th. thesis, School of Religion, Philosophy and Classics in the College of Humanities, University of KwaZulu Natal (Pietermaritzburg Campus).

Ki-Zerbo, J. 1990. Ed. General History of Africa. Vol. I. "Methodology of African History." Abridged version. London: James Currey; Berkerley, CA: The University of California Press; Paris: UNESCO.

Klass, Morton 1995. *Ordered Universes: Approaches to the Anthropology of Religion.* Boulder, CO: Westview Press.

Kraft, Charles H. 1996. *Anthropology for Christian Witness.* Maryknoll, NY: Orbis Books.

Kroeber, A. L. and Kluckhohn, C. 1952. *Culture: a critical review of concepts and definitions.* Cambridge, MA: Peabody Museum.

Labrecque, Edouard 1934 (1982 edition). "Beliefs and Religious Practices of the Bemba and Neighbouring Tribes." TMs (photocopy). Translated by Patrick Boyd W.F. Edited by The Language Centre, Ilondola.

LeBacq, Frank (with E. Chisakuta, D. Mutale, M. Mubanga and W. Mulubwa) [1998]. "Community Based Health Promotion: An Opportunity within the Zambian Health Reforms for a New Cultural Approach to a Generic Community Based Health System in Kasama District, North-Central Health Region, Zambia." Kasama.

Lee, Dorothy 1959. *Freedom and Culture.* Harvard University: Prentice-Hall, Inc.

LeVine, R.A., Dixon, S., LeVine, S., Richman, A., Keefer, C., Leiderman, P.H. & Brazelton, T.B. 1994. *Child Care and Culture: Lessons from Africa.* New York: Cambridge University Press.

Lewis, Michael 1992. *Shame: The Exposed Self.* New York: Macmillan. GT:1993. Scham: Annäherung an ein Tabu. Übers. Rita Höner. Hamburg: Kabel.

Luthahoire, Sebastian K. 1974. *The Human Life Cycle Among the Bantu.* Arusha, Tanzania: Makumira Publication.

Lumbwe, Kapambwe 2009. *Ubwinga, a subset of Bemba Indigenous Knowledge Systems: a comparative study of pre-colonial and post-independence wedding ceremonies in Lusaka and Kitwe, Zambia.* Ph.D. Thesis, University of Cape Town.

_____ (2004). "The role of music in the traditional marriage ceremonies of the Bemba-speaking people of Northern Zambia." Unpublished M.Mus. thesis, University of Cape Town.

MacIntyre, Alasdair 1988. *Whose Justice? Which Rationality?* Notre Dame, Ind.: University of Notre Dame Press.

Makkreel, Rudolf A. 1999. "Dilthey, Wilhelm (1833–1911)", in The Cambridge Dictionary of Philosophy, second edition, ed. Robert Audi, 236-237. New York: Cambridge University Press.

Makopa Joel L. 1998. *Ukufunda Umwana Kufikapo,* "Providing Complete Traditional Education to a Young Person." Handwritten notes, Chinsali.

Mandunu, Joseph Kufulu 1992. *Das "Kindoki" im Licht der Sündenbocktheologie: Versuch einer Christlichen Bewältigung des Hexenglaubens in Schwarz-Afrika*, Studien zur Interkulturellen Geschichte des Christentums, begr. v. Hans Jochen Margull, Hg. Richard Friedli, Walter J. Hollenweger, Jan A. B. Jongeneel und Theo Sundermeier, Bd. 85, Frankfurt am Main: Peter Lang.

Matsumoto, Paul 1985. "The Missiological Implications of Shame in the Japanese World View." Th.M. thesis, Fuller Theological Seminary, School of World Missions.

Maxwell, Kevin B. 1983. *Bemba Myth and Ritual: The Impact of Literacy on an Oral Culture*. American University Studies, Series XI Anthropology / Sociology, vol. 2. New York: Peter Lang.

Mbiti, John S. 1997. "Dreams as a Point of Theological Dialogue Between Christianity and African Religion," *Missionalia* vol. 25, no. 4:511-522, 511.

McCollum, Chris 2002. "Early Precursors of Work-Family Tension: A Psychodynamic Study of Socialization." MARIAL Center, Emory University, Working Paper 10.

Meebelo, Henry S. 1971. *Reaction to Colonialism: A Prelude to the Politics of Independence in Northern Zambia 1893-1939*. Manchester: Manchester University Press.

Meiring, Arno 2007. "As below, so above: A perspective on African Theology." *HTS* 63(2):733-750.

Mesman, Judi, Basweti, Nobert & Joseph Misati 2018. "Sensitive infant caregiving among the rural Gusii in Kenya," in *Attachment & Human Development*, Routledge, Taylor & Francis Group (DOI:10.1080/14616734.2018.1454053).

Metuh-Ikenga, Emifie. 1991a. "The Concept of Man in African Traditional Religion: With Particular Reference to the Igbo of Nigeria." In *Readings in African Traditional Religion: Structure, Meaning, Relevance, Future*, ed. E. M. Uka. Bern: Peter Lang.

_____ 1991b. *African Religions in Western Conceptual Schemes: The Problem of Interpretation*. Studies in Igbo Religion. 2nd edition. Jos: IMICO Publishers.

Middleton, John 1973. "The Concept of the Person among the Lugbara of Uganda." In *La Notion de Personne en Afrique Noire*. Organisé dans le cardre des Colloques Internationaux du Center National de la Rechercher Scientifique, à Paris, du 11 an 17 Octobre 1971, par Madame G. Dieterlen, Directeur de Recherche au C.N.R.S. Paris: Editions L'Harmattan.

Moyo, P. H. 2007. "The African Worldview: A Help or Hindrance to African Christianity?" In *Word & Context*, Dr. H.M. van den Bosch and Dr. C.W. Retief, eds. *Journal of Justo Mwale Theological College*. Lusaka: Justo Mwale Theological College.

Müller, Klaus W. 2010. *Das Gewissen in Kultur und Religion – Lehrbuch Elenktik.* Nürnberg: VTR Publications.

Mushindo, Paul B. 1977. *A Short Story of the Bemba*. Lusaka.

Musonda, Damian Kanuma 1996. *The Meaning and Value of Life Among the Bisa and Christian Morality*. Roma: Pontificia Universitas Lateranensis, Academia Alfonsiana, Institutum Superius Theologiae Moralis.

Nangawe, Eli, et. al. 1998a. *Determinants of Action Against Malnutrition in Under Five Children Kasama District-Northern Province*. Applied Health Research, Series 2. Lusaka: ZPC Publications.

_____ et. al. 1997. "Applied Health Research, Malnutrition in Under Fives in Kasama District: Intervention Phase Analysis Report," GRZ M[inistry] o[f] H[ealth].

Naugle, David K. n.d. "Worldview: Definitions, History, and Importance of a Concept." TMs pdf. URL:https://www3.dbu.edu/naugle/pdf/Worldview_defhistconceptlect.pdf, accessed on 02.10.2020.

Newbigin, Lesslie J. E. 1989. "Religious Pluralism and the Uniqueness of Jesus Christ." *International Bulletin of Missionary Research* 13, 2 (April):50-52, 54.

Ng'andu, A. 1922. "Bemba cultural data," 2. Chinsali: The Language Centre.

Nuckolls, Charles W. 1996. *The Cultural Dialectics of Knowledge and Desire*. Madison, WI: The University of Wisconsin Press.

Obeyesekere, Gananath 1984 (paperback). *Medusa's Hair: An Essay on Personal Symbols and Religious Experience*. Chicago and London: The University of Chicago Press.

Oduyoye, Modupe 1983. „Man's Self and its Spiritual Double." In *Traditional Religion in West Africa,* ed. A. Ade Adegbola. Ibadan: Daystar Press.

Offe, Johanna 2010. *Verheiratet mit einem Toten: Witwen und die AIDS-Krise in Sambia.* Konstanz: Konstanz University Press.

Oger, Louis 1993. "Our Missionary Shadow: A Series of historical Flashes at the Occasion of the Centenary Celebrations of the Catholic Church in Zambia (1991) and Reflections on Second Evangelization 1992-1993." Paris.

_____ 1972b. "The Bemba of Zambia: Outlines of their Lifecycle and Beliefs." TMs (photocopy). Ilondola: The Ilondola Language Centre.

_____ n.d. "Bemba Topics – With Appropriate Vocabulary." Illondola: The Language Centre.

Ogunboye, A. O. Peter with Fuller, Lois 2000. "The Human Soul in Yoruba/Igbo tradition and the Bible." *Africa Journal of Evangelical Theology* 19.1:75-86.

Ojiwang, Benjamin n.d. "Death among the Acholi." Ed. Markus Piennisch. TMs (photocopy).

O'Shea, Michael 1986. *Missionaries and Miners.* Ndola, Zambia: The Missionaries of Africa, Mission Press.

Pau, Philip Cope Suan 2009. "For the Divine Name of the Christian God among the Chin Peoples: *Pathian* and the *Pau Cin Hau* Movement in Chin Hills Myanmar." *Korean Journal of Christian Studies* Vol. 63, April:229-244.

Pike, Kenneth L. 1967. „Etic and emic standpoints for the description of behavior." In *Language and Thought: An Enduring Problem in Psychology,* Donald C. Hildum, ed., 32-39. Princeton: D. Van Norstrand Company.

Potter-Efron, Ronald T. 1989. *Shame, Guilt and Alcoholism: Treatment Issues in Clinical Practice.* New York, London: Haworth Press.

Rasing, Tera 2001. *The Bush Burnt, The Stones Remain: Female initiation rites in urban Zambia.* Münster, Hamburg, London: LIT Verlag.

Richards, Audrey I. 1982 (reprint). *Chisungu: A Girl's Initiation Ceremony among the Bemba of Zambia.* Paperback. London and New York: Tavistock Publications Ltd.

_____ 1970 (reprint). *Mother-Right Among the Central Bantu*. Westport, CT: Negro Universities Press.

_____ 1968. 'Keeping the King Divine.' *Proceedings of the Royal Anthropological Institute of Great Britain and Ireland*, 23-35.

_____ 1951. "The Bemba of North-Eastern Rhodesia." In *Seven Tribes of British Central Africa*, eds. E. Colson and M. Gluckman, 164-193. London: Oxford University Press.

_____ 1940. *Bemba Marriage*. Lusaka: Rhodes-Livingstone Institute.

_____ 1939. *Land, Labour and Diet in Northern Rhodesia: An Economic Study of the Bemba Tribe*. London: Oxford University Press.

_____ 1936. "The Story of Bwembya of the Bemba Tribe, Northern Rhodesia." In *Ten Africans*, ed. Margery Perham. Faber and Faber Limited: London. TMs (photocopy). Ilondola: The Language Centre.

Richardson, Don 1974,1975, 2005. *Peace Child*. Regal Books.

Ritchie, J. F. 1968. *The African as Suckling and as Adult: A Psychological Study*. The Rhodes-Livingstone Papers No. 9, first published by the Rhodes-Livingstone Institute, Northern Rhodesia, 1943, second impression for the Institute for Social Research University of Zambia. Manchester: Manchester University Press.

Roberts, Andrew D. 1973. *A History of the Bemba: Political Growth and Change in North Eastern Zambia before 1900*. Madison: University of Wisconsin Press.

_____ 1970. "Chronology of the Bemba (N. E. Zambia)." *JAH* vol. XI, no. 2:221-240.

Roland, Alan 2002. "The Uses (and Misuses) Of Psychoanalysis in South Asian Studies: Mysticism and Child Development." Paper read at the South Asia Conference, University of Wisconsin, Madison, 11th October 2002. URL:http://alan-roland.sulekha.com/blog/post/2002/11/the-uses-and-misuses-of-pychoanalysis-in-south.html, accessed on 20.12.2010.

Schoffeleers, J. Matthew, ed. 1999 (reprint). "Introduction." In *Guardians of the Land: Essays on Central African Territorial Cults*, 1-46. Gweru: Mwambo Press.

Sims Geo. W. 1959. *An Elementary Grammar of Cibemba.* Fort Rosebery [today Mansa], Northern Rhodesia [today Zambia]: Mansa Mission, Christian Mission in Many.

Sing Khaw Khai 1995. *Zo People and Their Culture: A Historical, Cultural Study and Critical Analysis of Zo and Its Ethnic Tribes*. New Lamka, Manipur: Khampu Hatzaw.

Sire, James S. 2004. *Naming the Elephant: Worldview as a Category*. Downers Grove, IL: Intervarsity Press.

_____ 1997. The Universe Next Door: A Basic Worldview Catalog. Downers Grove, IL: Intervarsity Press.

Snelson, Peter 1990 (2nd ed.). *Educational Development in Northern Rhodesia 1883-1945*. Lusaka: Kenneth Kaunda Foundation.

Sosala, Henry Kanyanta 2016. "The illusive role of the Chitimukulu as the chief executive of the Bemba people and tribe." Article published in LT (Lusaka Times) on May 20, 2016. https://www.lusakatimes.com/2016/05/20/illusive-role-chitimukulu-chief-executive-bemba-people-tribe/

Steiner, C. Richard 2015. *Disembodied Souls. The Nefesh in Israel and Kindred Spirits in the Ancient Near East, with an Appendix on the Katumuwa Inscription*. Ancient Near East Monographs. Number 11. Atlanta: Society of Biblical Literature.

Tanguy, Francois 1996 (reprint). *Imilandu ya Babemba*. Lusaka: Zambia Educational Publishing House.

_____ 1983 (1954). "The Bemba of Zambia: Beliefs, Manners, Customs." Ilondola: The Language Centre, Edited by The Language Centre. (TMs photocopy). The Society of Missionaries of Africa. Ilondola.

Thomas, Helen and Jamilah Ahmed 2004. Eds. *Cultural Bodies: Ethnography and Theory*. Oxford: Blackwell Publishing Ltd.

Toren, Christina 2002. "Childhood". In *Encyclopedia of Social and Cultural Anthropology*, eds. Alan Barnard and Jonathan Spencer, 139-142. London & New York: Routledge.

Turner, Terence S. 2012 (reprint). "The social skin." *HAU* Journal of Ethnographic Theory 2 (2):486–504.

Ulin, Robert C. 2001. 2nd ed. *Understanding Cultures: Perspectives in Anthropology and Social Theory*. Malden, MA and Oxford UK: Blackwell Publishers.

Van Binsbergen, Wim M. J. 1999 (reprint). "Explorations in the History and Sociology of Territorial Cults in Zambia." In *Guardians of the Land: Essays on Central African Territorial Cults,* ed. J. M. Schoffeleers, 47-88. Gweru: Mwambo Press.

Van Tilburg Clark, Walter 1940. *The Ox-Bow Incident*. New York: Random House.

Venz, Oliver 2012. „Die autochthone Religion der Benuaq von Ost-Kalimantan – Eine ethnolinguistische Untersuchung." Ph.D. dissertation. Philosophische Fakultät der Albert-Ludwigs-Universität Freiburg i. Br.

Warren-Rothlin, Andy L. 2005. "Body Idioms and The Psalms." In *Interpreting the Psalms*, ed. David Firth and Philip S. Johnston, 195-212. Downers Grove, IL: InterVarsity.

Wendland, Ernst 2000. *Preaching that Grabs the Heart: A Rhetorical-Stylistic Study of the Chichewa Revival Sermons of Shadrack Wame*. A Kachere Monograph. Blantyre: Christian Literature Association in Malawi (CLAIM).

_____ n.d. "Dimensions of Dynamism: The Vital Influence of Traditional Socio-Religious Context upon Christian Communication in Central Africa."

Werden, Rita 2013. "Schamkultur und Schuldkultur: Revision einer Theorie." Ph.D. dissertation, Philosophische Fakultät der Albert-Ludwigs-Universität Freiburg i. Br.

Werner, Douglas 1999 (reprint). "*Miao* Spirit Shrines in The Religious History of The Southern Lake Tanganyika Region: The Case of *Kapembwa*." In *Guardians of the Land: Essays on Central African Territorial Cults*, ed. J. M. Schoffeleers, 89-130. Gweru: Mwambo Press.

_____ 1971. "Some Developments in Bemba Religious History," *JRA* vol. 4, no. 1:1-24.

Whitely, Wilfred 1950. "Bemba and Related Peoples of Northern Rhodesia." In *Ethnographic Survey of Africa*, ed. Daryll Forde, 1-54. London: International African Institute.

White Fathers 1991 (revised edition). *The White Fathers Bemba-English Dictionary*. Ndola, Zambia: The Society of the Missionaries for Africa (White Fathers).

Wiher, Hannes. 2003. *Shame and Guilt: A Key to Cross-Cultural Ministry*. Edition *iwg*, mission academics scripts vol. 10. Bonn: Verlag für Kultur und Wissenschaft.

Willis, Roy 2002. "Body". In *Encyclopedia of Social and Cultural Anthropology*, eds. Alan Barnard and Jonathan Spencer, 114-115. London & New York: Routledge.

Willoughby, W.C. 1970 (reprint). *The Soul of the Bantu: A Sympathetic Study of the Magico-Religious Practices and Beliefs of the Bantu Tribes of Africa*. Westport, CT: Negro Universities Press.

Wilson, Monica 1959. *Divine Kings and the 'Breath of Men'*. Cambridge: Cambridge University Press.

Wunderli, Samuel 1990. "The Significance of Shame and Guilt-oriented Consciences for Cross-Cultural Ministry." MA Thesis, Columbia Biblical Seminary and Graduate School of Missions, Columbia, South Carolina.

Name Index

Abel, Robert 215
Adeyemo, Tokunboh 3
African Elders 8
Ahmed, Jamilah 33
Apostle Paul 162
Badenberg, Robert 3, 5, 13, 36, 38, 52, 59, 66, 80, 156, 169, 170, 188, 193, 203, 205
Bandawe, Chiwoza 19
Barnes, H. 182
Barth, Karl 166
Bateson, Gregory 156
Bevans, Stephen B. 259
Bloch, Maurice 208
Bloom, Paul 141, 142
Boas, Franz 181
Bosch, David 148
Brelsford, Vernon W. 7
Burlington, Gary 1, 58, 231, 257, 258
Burton, R. 7
Carey, Francis 7, 8, 183
Cash, Thomas F. 33
Chileshe, Alexander R. 13, 244
Clark, Mary 1, 4
Cook, Robert 217
Coxhead, J.C.C. 16
Crawley, A.E. 191

Cunnison, Ian 17
D'Andrade, Roy 63
Deigh, John 144, 145, 148
Dillon-Malone, Clive 206, 216
Durkheim, Emile 217
Eckstein, Hans-Joachim 162, 164, 165
Elvi, Zetla K. 191
Etienne, Louis 7
Father Pinto 16
Fischer, Anja 181
Fonda, Henry 165
Fowler, C. 4
Fuller, Lois 191, 192
Gamitto 7, 16
Garrec, N. 7
Gehman, Richard 217
Gleitman, Lila 141, 142
Goodenough, Ward 148, 255
Gordon, David 193
Gouldsbury, Cullen 7
Greenstein, Edward L. 74, 179
Groark, Kevin 208, 209
Gruber, June 155, 157
Guthrie, Malcom 7
Heidemann, Frank 33, 35
Hiebert, Paul G. 1, 2, 141, 249
Hilgers, Micha 159

Hinfelaar, Hugo 8, 9, 12, 17, 53, 56, 58, 183, 250, 258, 259
Hirschberg, Walter 181
Hoch, Ernst 30, 183, 185, 214
Hochegger, Herman 182
Hume, David 146
Huntington, Richard............... 244
Hurrelmann, Klaus 149
Ipenburg, At 7, 17, 183
Jahoda, Gustav 148
Janowski, Bernd 74, 119
Kalusa, Walima 11, 192, 226, 229, 230, 232, 248, 250, 255
Kambole, R. 51, 53, 63
Kant, Immanuel............... 145, 148
Kanyanta Sosala, Henry 14
Kapolyo, Joe .19, 20, 148, 220, 238
Käser, Lothar 6, 74, 141, 143, 148, 160, 161, 165, 181, 187, 188, 200, 210
Kasprus, Aloys 180
Kaunda, Mutale Mulenga 254
Ki-Zerbo, J................................. 9
Klass, Morton 250
Kluckhohn, C. 161
Kraft, Charles H. 2, 141
Kroeber, A. L. 161
Labrecque, Edouard 7, 167, 172, 220, 221, 223, 232, 236, 243, 246
Lacerda 7, 16
Leach, Edmund 229
LeBacq, Frank 215
Lee, Dorothy 57

LeVine, R. A. 153
Lewis, Michael 158
Lumbwe, Kapambwe 220, 221, 222, 234, 246, 247, 249, 256
Lutahoire, Sebastian K. 167
MacIntyre, Alasdair 148
Makkreel, Rudolf A. 1
Makopa, Joel 63
Mandunu, J. K. 208
Matsumoto, Paul 156
Maxwell, Kevin 7, 10, 11, 16, 20, 31, 54, 61, 182, 183, 243, 248
Mbiti, John............... 209, 217, 238
McCollum, Chris 150, 151, 152
Meebelo, Henry 8
Meiring, Arno 20
Mesman, Judi 152, 154
Metcalf, Peter 244
Metuh-Ikenga, Emifie 191, 214
Middleton, John...................... 192
Mill 146
Moyo, P. H. 3
Müller, Klaus W. 162
Mulolani, Chishimba Emilio.. 58, 231, 257, 259
Mushindo, Paul 8, 227
Musonda, Damian Kanuma... 63, 217
Nangawe, Eli........................... 216
Naugle, David K. 2
Newbigin, Lesslie 148
Ng'andu, A............................... 7
Nuckolls, Charles 156, 161

O'Shea, Michael 10
Obeyesekere, Gananath 217
Oduyoye 254
Offe, Johanna 241, 242, 243, 244, 245, 247
Oger, Louis 7, 8, 20, 21, 27, 28, 30, 31, 61, 182, 184, 207, 261
Ogunboye, A.O. Peter ... 191, 192
Ojiwang, Benjamin 220
Ong, Walter 16
Pau, Philip Cope Suan 193
Pike, Kenneth 181
Potter-Efron, Ronald T. 157
Radcliffe-Brown, Alfred 255
Rasing, Tera 53, 54
Richards, Audrey I. 7, 11, 13, 31, 54, 55, 182, 186, 226, 229, 230, 232, 233, 238, 248
Richardson, Don 179
Ricoeur, Paul 93
Ritchie, J.F. 215
Roberts, Andrew 7, 8, 231
Roland, Alan 154
Schoffeleers, J. Matthew 214
Sheane, Herbert 7
Sims, Geo W. 179, 183, 262
Sing Khaw Khai 193
Sire, James W. 1
Snelson, Peter 7, 8

Steiner, Richard C. 195, 214
Tanguy, Francois 7, 8, 13, 52, 168, 172, 182, 219, 220, 228
Thomas, Helen 33
Toren, Christina 141, 148
Turner, Terrence S. 33
Ulin, Robert C. 93
Van Binsbergen, Wim 11
Van Tilburg Clark, Walter ... 165, 166
Vaughan, Megan 11, 192, 226, 229, 230, 232, 248, 250, 255
Venz, Oliver 5, 194, 210
Vitebsky 226
Warren-Rothlin, Andy L. 35, 62, 93
Wendland, Ernst 16, 180
Werden, Rita 150
Werner, Douglas .. 7, 16, 182, 183
White Fathers 63, 214, 215, 216
Whitely, Wilfred 7, 16
Wiher, Hannes 148, 158, 159, 162, 165
Willis, Roy 62
Willoughby, W.C. 247
Wilson, Godfrey 192, 193, 248, 250
Wunderli, Samuel 149, 154, 156, 159

289

Forschungen zu Sprachen und Kulturen Afrikas / Researches on African Languages and Cultures / Recherches sur les Langues et les Cultures Africaines
begründet von Prof. em. Dr. Rüdiger Schott (†)

Thunar Jentsch
Die steinernen Wächter der Dogon
Unbekannte Steinskulpturen aus Mali
Anstoß zur Entdeckung eines unbekannten Kults der Dogon in Mali gab eine in den 1950er- und 1960er-Jahren zusammengetragene Privatsammlung mit mehr als 500 steinernen Objekten. Der Kult mit Fokus auf kunstvoll skulptierten Steinen kam Anfang des 20. Jahrhunderts zum Erliegen. Formenreichtum und stilistischer Ausdruck der anthropomorph oder zoomorph geformten Steine beeindrucken und erinnern an archäologische Funde aus Guinea oder Sierra Leone. Der Autor stellt die Sammlung vor, beleuchtet Hintergründe und Ausrichtung des Kults und belegt, dass Stein in Afrika häufiger zur Herstellung sakraler Objekte verwendet wurde als bislang angenommen.
Bd. 16, 2019, 464 S., 69,90 €, gb., ISBN 978-3-643-14241-2

Hans Scheutz
Die vergessene Kultur
Terrakotten aus Nordghana
Dieses Buch gewährt einen neuen aufschlussreichen Einblick in eine bisher noch weitgehend unerschlossene Kultur Afrikas der Komaland anhand zahlreicher Abbildungen.
Die Terrakotta-Objekte des Komalandes wurden erst um 1980 in Nordghana entdeckt und haben sowohl Wissenschaftler als auch Kunstexperten überrascht und eine intensive Beschäftigung mit dieser Kultur notwendig gemacht. Da es keine zeitgenössischen, schriftlichen Quellen über die Komaland-Terrakotten gibt, wurden sie mit denen untergegangener und noch lebender Kulturen (Akan, Djenné, Bulsa, Lobi, Gan) verglichen und nach neustem Stand der archäologischen Forschung wissenschaftlich aufgearbeitet.
Bd. 15, 2016, 248 S., 39,90 €, gb., ISBN 978-3-643-50780-8

Lena Mengers
Afrikanische Feste – Geschichte, Erscheinungsformen, Veränderungen
Festwesen der Akan im südlichen Ghana und bei einer *twi*-sprachigen Migrantengemeinde in Münster (Westfalen)
Die ethnologische Studie erfasst Tendenzen von Kontinuität und Wandel im afrikanischen Festwesen, auch im Zuge der Migration aus dem südlichen Ghana nach Deutschland. Mit einer kontextuell ausgerichteten historischen Untersuchung macht die Autorin deutlich, wie eng religiöse Vorstellungen und Rituale mit sozialen und wirtschaftlichen Beziehungen, mit Fragen der Repräsentation, auch mit ästhetischen und emotionalen Bereichen verflochten sind. Ein Überblick über die Forschungsgeschichte und ein Beitrag zur Definition des Begriffes „Fest" führen in die Arbeit ein.
Bd. 14, 2012, 360 S., 49,90 €, br., ISBN 978-3-643-11952-0

Franz Kröger; Ben Baluri Saibu
First Notes on Koma Culture
Life in a Remote Area of Northern Ghana
Although the Koma are known throughout the world as a result of the so-called Komaland-terracottas, excavated in the 1980s, no extensive ethnographic publication about their culture has appeared yet.
The present book comprises some of the results of Franz Kröger's surveys during six field research trips between 1984 and 2008. It is also based on the profound knowledge of the co-author, Ben Baluri Saibu, a lawyer from the Koma village of Yikpabongo.
The main focus of the book is the social, political and economic structure of the Koma, as well as their material culture, and, above all, their traditional religion and the extraordinarily dynamic history. A Konni-English word list with approximately 2400 entries might be interesting for linguists specialised in the West African Gur languages.
vol. 13, 2010, 568 pp., 54,90 €, br., ISBN 978-3-643-10543-1

LIT Verlag Berlin – Münster – Wien – Zürich – London
Auslieferung Deutschland / Österreich / Schweiz: siehe Impressumsseite

Domitien Ndihokubwayo
Nachbarschaft in Burundi
Eine Untersuchung mit Auswertung von Eigennamen, Begriffen und Sprichwörtern im Kirundi
Bd. 12, 2009, 312 S., 24,90 €, br., ISBN 978-3-8258-1657-5

Rüdiger Schott
Bulsa Sunsuelima
Erotic Folktales of the Bulsa in Northern Ghana
Bd. 11, 2006, 312 S., 29,90 €, br., ISBN 3-8258-9335-9

Franz Kröger
Materielle Kultur und traditionelles Handwerk bei den Bulsa (Nordghana)
Bd. 10, 2001, 1148 S., 61,90 €, br., ISBN 3-8258-5512-0

Jan Jansen
The Griot's Craft
An Essay on Oral Tradition and Diplomacy
vol. 8, 2000, 120 pp., 15,90 €, br., ISBN 3-8258-4352-1

Ulrike Blanc
Musik und Tod bei den Bulsa (Nordghana)
Bd. 6, 2000, 312 S., 25,90 €, br., ISBN 3-8258-4437-4

Ronald P. Schaefer; Francis O. Egbokhare (eds.)
Oral Tradition Narratives of the Emai People
vol. 5 (2 vols.), 1999, 1288 pp., 97,90 €, br., ISBN 3-8258-4030-1

Rüdiger Schott
Bulsa Sunsuelima – Folktales of the Bulsa in Northern Ghana
Series S: Folktales of the Supernatural
Vol. 1: Tales of the Sky-God (Wen, Naawen), Part II–III
vol. 4, 1996, 566 pp., 40,90 €, br., ISBN 3-8258-2499-3; 76,90 €, gb., ISBN 3-8258-2500-0

Ulrike Blanc
Lieder in Erzählungen der Bulsa (Nordghana)
Eine musikethnologische Untersuchung.
Songs in Folktales of the Bulsa (North Ghana). A study in the ethnology of music
Bd. 3, 1993, 160 S., 24,90 €, br., ISBN 3-89473-969-x

Rüdiger Schott
Bulsa Sunsuelima – Folktales of the Bulsa in Northern Ghana
Series S: Folktales of the Supernatural
Vol. 1: Tales of the Sky-God (Wen, Naawen) Part I
vol. 2, 1993, 420 pp., 40,90 €, br., ISBN 3-89473-616-x; 76,90 €, gb., ISBN 3-89473-971-1

Franz Kröger
Buli-English Dictionary
With an Introductory Grammar and an Index English – Buli
vol. 1, 1992, 584 pp., 40,90 €, br., ISBN 3-88660-821-2; 76,90 €, gb., ISBN 3-88660-820-4

LIT Verlag Berlin – Münster – Wien – Zürich – London
Auslieferung Deutschland / Österreich / Schweiz: siehe Impressumsseite